MANAGEMENT OF TEMPOROMANDIBULAR JOINT PROBLEMS

A practical manual of diagnosis and treatment

THE POSTGRADUATE DENTAL LECTURE SERIES

MANAGEMENT OF TEMPOROMANDIBULAR JOINT PROBLEMS

A practical manual of diagnosis and treatment

ARTHUR S. FREESE, D.D.S.

Postgraduate Instructor, First District, Dental Society of New York, New York, N. Y.; Member, American Prosthodontic Society; Member, American Equilibration Society; Assistant Attending Dentist (Prosthetics), New York Polyclinic Hospital and Postgraduate Medical School, New York, N. Y.; Lecturer and Clinician

PAUL SCHEMAN, B.S., D.D.S.

Director of the Department of Dentistry, The Hillside Hospital, Glen Oaks, N. Y.; Chief of Oral Surgery, New York Polyclinic Hospital and Postgraduate Medical School, New York, N. Y.; Chief of Oral Surgery, Jewish Memorial Hospital, New York, N. Y.; Associate Visiting Oral Surgeon, Queens Hospital Center, Jamaica, Long Island, N. Y.; Senior Research Scientist and Chief Stomatologist, Waldemar Medical Research Foundation; Diplomate, American Board of Oral Surgery; Diplomate, New York State Board of Oral Surgery; Fellow, Long Island Academy of Odontology

With 127 illustrations

THE C. V. MOSBY COMPANY ST. LOUIS 1962

Printed in the United States of America
Library of Congress Catalog Card Number 62-13025
Distributed in Great Britain by Henry Kimpton, London

This volume is sincerely dedicated
to Ruth and Blanche whose
love, help, and forbearance alone
made it possible.

PREFACE

A few short years ago it would have been difficult to write a manual on the temporomandibular joint problem which would have been of value to the general practitioner. Too little was then known of both theory and practice. Since then, much has been written that has begun to illuminate the etiology and treatment of the diseases and dysfunctions of this complex articulation. We hope that this manual will supply the practitioner with the necessary knowledge and technique to manage most of the problems in this area that he is likely to encounter in his daily practice.

Some of the material presented, although entirely new, has withstood the test of clinical practice to date. We believe that the theoretical concepts of Carl-Herman Hjortsjö of Lund, Sweden, on the biomechanics of the temporomandibular joint offer the most rational explanation for many of the puzzling aberrations of joint function. The pioneering work of Janet Travell in the field of musculoskeletal pathophysiology has contributed significantly to the rationale of treatment of the painful aspects of temporomandibular joint disease.

The chapters have been divided between the two authors. Paul Scheman wrote the chapters on anatomy, embryology, physiology, pathology, and treatment of anterior dislocations. He developed and used his specialized technique for dissections on fresh autopsy specimens in order to resemble accurately the actual situations seen in surgery on the living patient. The result has been his unique illustrations demonstrating the true functional anatomy of the joint. He has also published here for the first time new findings on the role of calcification of some of the accessory ligaments in the pain syndromes of this area together with a new anatomical explanation for the origin of temporomandibular joint clicking and its treatment. Arthur Freese has contributed the chapters on the myofascial trigger mechanism, diagnosis and treatment of the occlusal problem, occlusal rehabilitation, and roentgenography. He has also contributed his original findings on Costen's syndrome. The remaining chapters are the result of the authors' working together.

We should like to acknowledge the invaluable contribution of Mr. Julius Weber, medical photographer and photomicrographist. Mr. Gary Cooper is responsible for the excellent drawings. We are grateful to the Waldemar Medical Research Foundation, to Dr. Norman Molomut, its scientific director, and to Dr. Molomut's staff for their help and encouragement; to Carl-Herman Hjortsjö of Lund, Sweden; and to the New York Polyclinic Hospital and Postgraduate Medical School for the use of its anatomy laboratory. We are also grateful to the librarians and technicians too numerous to mention who gave their help unselfishly.

In particular, we are indebted to our wives, Ruth Freese and Blanche Scheman, for their cooperation, forbearance, and faith.

Arthur S. Freese
Paul Scheman

CONTENTS

MANAGEMENT OF TEMPOROMANDIBULAR JOINT PROBLEMS

A practical manual of diagnosis and treatment

CHAPTER 1

INTRODUCTION

Few texts devoted to a single articulation or joint can be found in medical or dental literature, and in the past few years members of the dental profession have contributed most of those that exist. Among such works are those of Sarnat and contributors (namely, Brodie, Sicher, Thompson, Weinmann, and Zimmerman), Laszlo Schwartz, Bell, and Shore on the temporomandibular joint. Among the best of the anatomical and physiological treatises is that of Carl-Herman Hjortsjö of Sweden. Many other investigators have worked with great dedication on the temporomandibular articulation mainly because it represents a recurrent and persistent problem in clinical practice that has not as yet readily yielded to the known techniques and practices of dental and medical disciplines.

In this book we propose to elaborate on yet another dimension in the study of this structure based upon consideration of the total patient and upon newer anatomical and physiological observations.

In mandibular function there are three points of ultimate stress. One lies in the teeth and their supporting structures, a second lies in the joint itself, and the third lies in the neuromuscular apparatus. Dentistry has been concerned mainly with the first of these.

THE TEMPOROMANDIBULAR ARTICULATION

During recent years the temporomandibular articulation has commanded a great deal of interest. The reason lies in the fact that as part of the functioning mouth it is perhaps the only joint in the body that is intimately connected with the totality of human experience and expression from infancy throughout life.

Before the advent of anesthesia, biting upon a bullet during the surgery required on battlefields was once a method of helping the soldier bear extremes of agony. The image of the Churchillian jaw has become a standard of tenacity and courage. Uses of the lower jaw as the only movable part of the face, apart from the muscles of expression, have imparted to it many functions quite unrelated to the main one of mastication. The history of art, particularly poetry and drama, bears witness to use of the jaws and mouth as the most direct means for expression of human emotion, so much so that we are confronted with a truism.

THE NONMASTICATORY USE OF THE JAWS

Many of the problems related to the temporomandibular articulation and to the mouth and its dentition would not exist or would be of far lesser severity if the use of these structures were limited to the act of masticating food. Unfortunately as organs of expression a whole host of abnormal and even perverse functions takes place and are in the main responsible for the greater degree of damage that is observed. Grinding and clenching (bruxism) are obvious causes of oral stress that may result in breakdown of structure or in its pathological alteration. Less familiar causes are tongue habits, disturbances in the mechanism of swallowing, aerophagia (air swallowing) which produces excessively hard tooth contact, obstruction of the upper respiratory passages, overrefinement of food (that is, absence of grit or abrasives), abnormal muscular movements related to oral gratification, tension of the head and neck musculature related to anxiety states, and many others. The complexities are such that each patient must be examined carefully from the point of view of the total person and his habits as they appear to bear on the symptoms that he presents. For example, many instances of unilateral pain in the area of the temporomandibular joint in young persons are due to the habit of leaning the jaw against the hand during long periods of reading or studying. As simple an act as pipe smoking may have etiological significance. As shall be pointed out later, only a comprehensive and detailed history will reveal the vital and often determining information.

THE ROLE OF THE EMOTIONS IN TEMPOROMANDIBULAR JOINT PROBLEMS

No consideration of the temporomandibular articulation is complete unless the dynamics of human psychology are included. Some authors have held that certain joint disturbances are wholly due to psychological causes, the implication being that spontaneous regression of joint disease would occur when the disturbing psychological factors were removed, whereas others have held a converse view. Both of these views, however, represent oversimplification of the problem.

Although an emotional disturbance is undoubtedly an important factor in aggravating the symptoms of joint disease and may even play a role in initiating it, the two disease processes, once begun, exist side by side. It is possible to cure either one without necessarily effecting a cure of the other. One must be cautious when dealing with symptoms that serve some deep-seated neurotic need. Removing such an emotional crutch may precipitate a serious psychiatric disorder. Many patients cured of neuroses have learned to live with temporomandibular joint disturbances.

Case A. R. A 44-year-old woman complained of severe clicking in her temporomandibular joints. She had many neurotic complaints, some of which were related to the eating situation. She believed that she was disgusting when she ate, that she made too much noise. Consequently, she ate little in company and was silent and morose at the dining table. She was extremely conscious of superfluous hair and in general considered herself an ugly person. Her inability to function socially led her to seek psychotherapy. At the same time she sought dental treatment in her search for greater attractiveness. Her dentist noted the clicking joints and made a diagnosis of "subluxation." An oral surgeon treated her for the disorder with injections of a sclerosing solution. The joint sounds disappeared, but the patient went into a severe depression, requiring psychiatric hospitalization.

Case J. S. A similar case is that of a patient who had his uvula shortened to overcome a habit of noisily clearing his throat, supposedly related to the irritation caused by the excessive length of this structure. He has a serious emotional disturbance since he can no longer use his long uvula as an excuse for exercising an irritating habit which subserved a deep neurotic need.

Case C. M. A young physician who was receiving psychotherapy discontinued dental treatment for joint dysfunction when he discovered that preoccupation with dental care was part of his emotional disease. He now considers the joint dysfunction of minor importance.

ORIENTATION OF THE THERAPIST

In a field as new as this one in which cause and effect have not yet been scientifically established, there is a tendency for the therapist to overvalue his early successes and to generalize from them. As a result, more is promised than can be produced by the therapeutic plan. It is important to include the therapist in the equation of treatment. The novelty of a new field offers many temptations. Among them is the desire to cure a host of obscure symptoms that have resisted usual and accepted treatment methods. There is no escape from the rigid requirements of causality. Much study must intervene before cause and effect are firmly established. Exaggeration of the importance of the disease is to be avoided. Many patients are not seriously handicapped by noisy temporomandibular joints, and most individuals with clicking joints are not even aware of their presence. Function is not impeded. It would be a significant mistake to make such patients aware of their abnormality. In the ordinary sense of the word this would constitute iatrogenic disease, that is, physician-caused disease.

SUMMARY

This book is concerned only with the diagnosis and treatment of those abnormalities of the temporomandibular articulation that result in disturbances of function, that interfere with the patient's ability to enjoy life, and that do not subserve some psychotic or neurotic need.

REFERENCES

1. Abraham, Karl: Manifestations of the female castration complex; contributions to the theory of the anal character; the influence of oral eroticism on character formation, Selected papers, London, 1927, Hogarth Press.
2. Alvarez, W. C.: Lessons to be learned from the results of tonsillectomies in adult life, J.A.M.A. **80**:1513, 1923.
3. Bennett, A. E.: Faulty management of psychiatric syndromes simulating organic disease, J.A.M.A. **130**:1203, 1946.
4. Bleuler, E.: Textbook of psychiatry (translated by A. A. Brill), New York, 1951, Dover Publishers.
5. Cobb, S.: Emotions and clinical medicine, New York, 1950, Norton Press.
6. Freud, S.: The loss of reality in neurosis and psychosis, Collected papers, London, 1924, Hogarth Press, vol. 2, pp. 277-282.
7. Freud, S.: Basic writings, New York, 1938, Modern Library.
8. Freud, S.: General introduction to psychoanalysis, New York, 1943, Garden City Publishing Co.
9. Miller, N. F.: Hysterectomy: therapeutic necessity or surgical racket? Am. J. Obst. & Gynec. **51**:804, 1946.
10. Sadler, W. S.: Mental mischief and emotional conflicts: psychiatry and psychology in plain English, St. Louis, 1947, The C. V. Mosby Co.

CHAPTER 2

TEMPOROMANDIBULAR JOINT SOUNDS

DISTURBANCES OF THE ARTICULATION OF THE MANDIBLE

Disturbances of the articulation of the mandible may be divided into two types: those that result in limitation of joint movement and those that result in excessive joint movement. The feature common to both types (except in complete ankylosis, either fibrous or bony) is disharmony in movement of the heads of the mandible when the mouth is opened. The disturbance may be either asymptomatic (the patient having made adequate muscular and ligamentous adjustments) or symptomatic. This discussion concerns disturbances in which any or all of the following conditions may prevail:

1. Pain and tenderness in the joint and region of the joint and referred pains and sensory disturbances in the muscles of mastication and muscles of the head and neck
2. Various degrees of noises or clicking with jerking or bouncing of the lower jaw at various degrees of opening, with or without pain or discomfort
3. Repeated dislocations of the head of the mandible subsequently maintained anterior to the articular eminence by muscular spasm

Early diagnosis and treatment of disturbances of the mandibular articulation may perhaps prevent the chronic intractable joint disease that is so resistant to treatment. It is for this reason that a method for making an accurate and early diagnosis of functional or organic joint dysfunction is so important.

TYPES OF JOINT SOUNDS

Many sounds may be heard when the mandibular joint is auscultated, and with electrical amplification normal joints are noisy. Although it is difficult to explain the origin of all of the sounds that may be heard during movement of the joints, the following are commonest in the normal temporomandibular joint:

1. Crackling sounds much like those made by crumpling cellophane. These are brittle and flamelike and most often are produced by the presence of dry ceruminous material in the external ear canal.
2. Roaring or rumbling sounds, usually due to the effect of muscular contraction upon the stethoscope diaphragm. These contractions can be felt by placing one's fingers against the masseter muscle and contracting them vigorously by repeatedly clenching the jaws.
3. Rasping or grating sounds. These are usually heard in men and are caused by movement of the bristly hairs of the beard against the diaphragm of the stethoscope.
4. Temporal artery pulse. This sound is sometimes heard with higher amplifications.

These sounds that are heard over the normal joint may also be heard over the malfunctioning joint. However, the sounds whose diagnostic significance will be considered here are clicking or snapping sounds of varying amplitude that can be heard clearly above the background noise, sometimes without a stethoscope. To understand more clearly the origin of these latter sounds, a review of the anatomy of the temporomandibular articulation is essential. The anatomy and embryology of the temporomandibular joint as they relate specifically to joint mechanics will be discussed in detail in Chapter 3.

ANATOMY OF THE TEMPOROMANDIBULAR ARTICULATION

The bony component. The surfaces that articulate in the mandibular joint are complex in shape and present a different

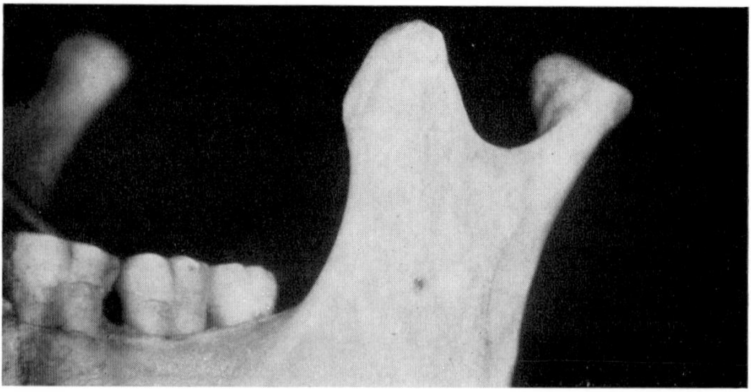

Fig. 1. The mandible is turned toward the viewer to demonstrate the triangular shape of its head. Note that the base of the triangular head is curved to fit the concavity of the glenoid fossa as well as the concavity in the center of the articular tubercle.

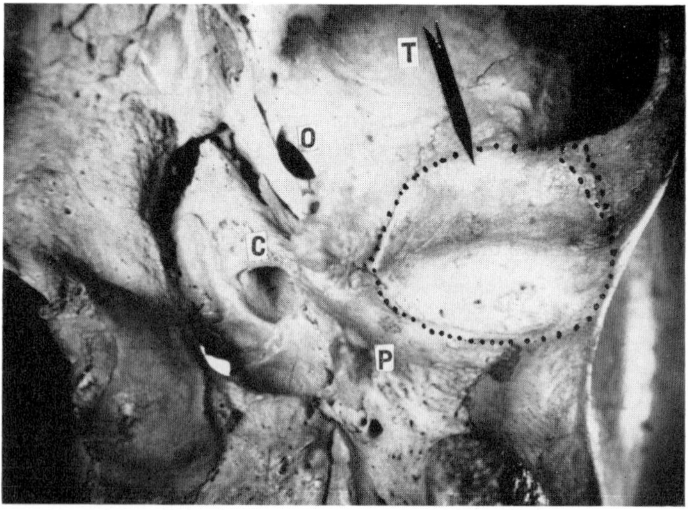

Fig. 2. Inferior surface of the skull; top of photograph is anterior. Dark area in the corner of the lower left is the foramen magnum. Arrow points to the concavity in the articular eminence which accommodates the head of the forward moving mandible, **T. P,** Petrous portion of the temporal bone; **C,** carotid canal; **O,** foramen ovale. Dotted lines indicate attachment of the articular capsule. Double lines are the area of attachment of stronger fibers, the temporomandibular ligament.

contour in the various planes. The usual diagrammatic representation of the joint presents a misleading simplicity. The head of the mandible cannot be visualized properly if it is shown as a bluntly pointed projection. Actually it is a thick triangle (Fig. 1) with a curved base designed to fit the concave path from the glenoid fossa and over the articular eminence. Both the base and the altitude of this triangle, which represent the head and neck of the articular condyle, are tilted laterally, that is, with the sagittal corner pointing slightly posteriorly (dorsally) and inferiorly (caudally). Whereas the posterior surface is fairly flat, the anterior surface has an eminence at about its midpoint that fits into a corresponding depression in the articular eminence which is itself a three-dimensional structure almost exactly duplicating the shape of the head of the mandible (Fig. 2).

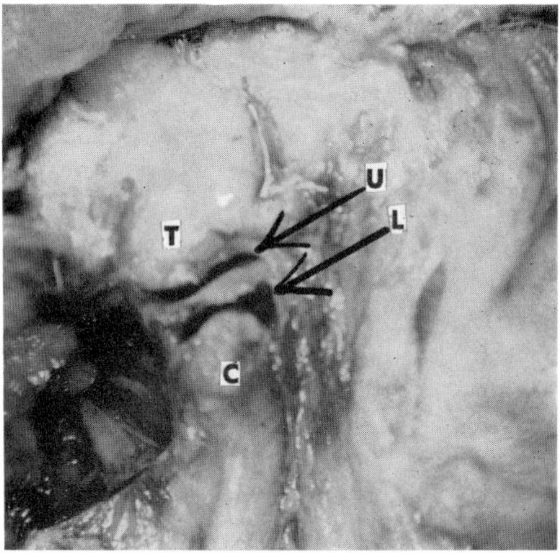

Fig. 3. Dissection of the joint in a fresh autopsy specimen to show upper synovial cavity, **U**; lower synovial cavity, **L**; articular tubercle, **T**; and head of the mandible (condyle, **C**). Note relationship of the condyle and the articular tubercle to the disk. These are the articulating surfaces. This is an accentuated grinding joint with an interposed disk.

The glenoid fossa in the inferior surface of the temporal bone is shaped to provide a close but unrestricted space for rotation of the head of the mandible on the balancing side while allowing for an easy path of anterior and lateral movement of the head of the mandible of the opposite side, that is, on the working side. It is obviously not a stress-bearing structure, as can be deduced from its translucent thinness. The exact correspondence of shape between the head of the mandible and the glenoid fossa is even more remarkable if we consider (as will be described later) that between these two surfaces is interposed an articular disk that divides the joint space into the upper and lower synovial cavities (Figs. 3 and 4) and that this disk provides the true articulating surface for both the head of the mandible and the articular tubercle and

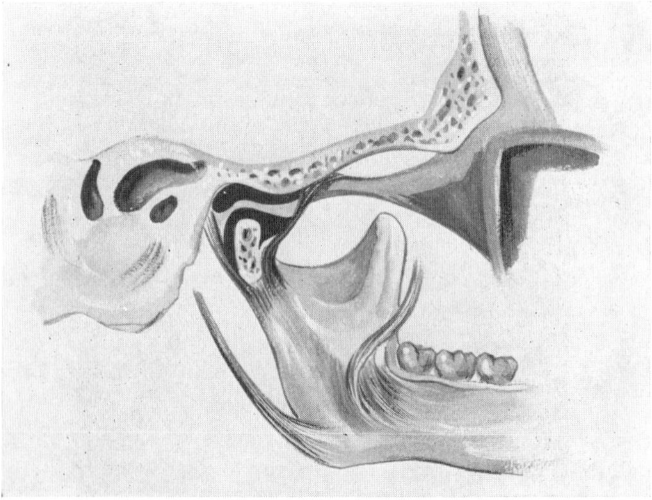

Fig. 4. Diagrammatic representation of the upper and lower synovial cavities of the temporomandibular joint. Sagittal view. Compare with dissection in Fig. 3. Note that lower synovial cavity is larger. (After Jackson, C. M., editor: Morris' human anatomy, Philadelphia, 1933, P. Blakiston's Son & Co.)

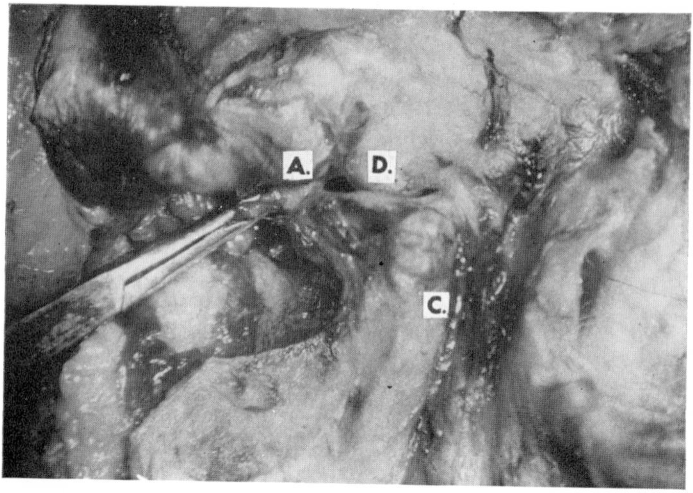

Fig. 5. Hemostat pulling on the attachment of the superior belly of the external pterygoid muscle, **A.** The disk is seen at **D.** The head of the mandible, **C,** does not move. This is a fresh autopsy specimen.

can itself be moved independently (Fig. 5). These facts require a fundamental re-examination of the mechanics of this joint.

The soft tissue component. The articular capsule is a loose sack attached above to the posterior end of the zygomatic process, to the anterior margin of the articular process, to the medial edge of the mandibular fossa, and to the posterior edge of the mandibular fossa in front of the petrotympanic fissure. These attachments are indicated in Fig. 2 by dotted lines.

The articular disk is a plate of fibrocartilage with the approximate shape of a distorted erythrocyte, that is, the edges are thickened (Figs. 6 and 7). If a disk such as the peak of a jockey's cap were stretched, it would be approximately the shape of the articular disk (Fig. 8). The disk is considerably thinner in its center and may even be perforated, providing a communication between the upper and lower synovial cavities

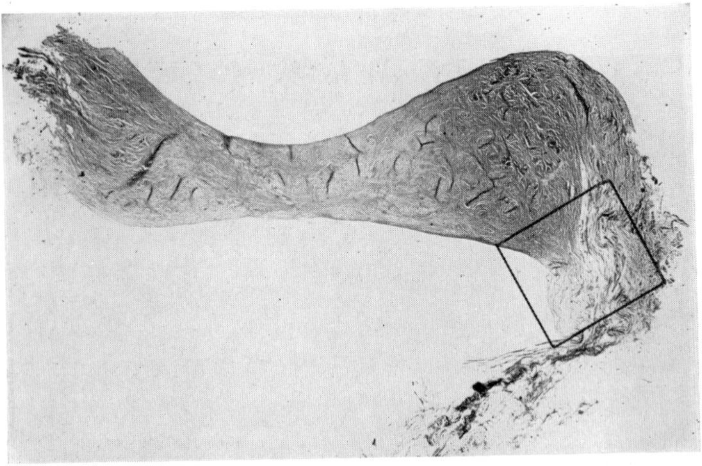

Fig. 6. Photomicrograph of an articular disk. The leading or anterior edge is on the left. Note the jockey's cap shape and the loose arrangement of the fibrous tissue at the posterior edge which permits forward movement. Area indicated in square is reproduced in higher power in Fig. 7.

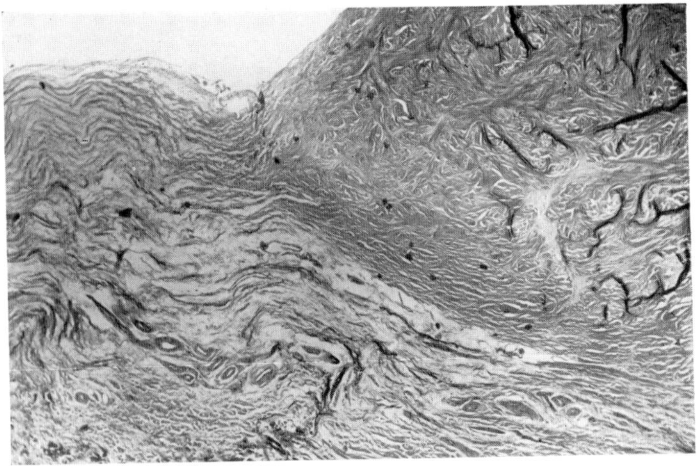

Fig. 7. Higher power view of Fig. 6. Note wavy fibrous tissue at left in photomicrograph. This arrangement permits forward movement of the articular disk. Compare it with the straight dense arrangement of the fibrous tissue on the anterior edge of the disk in Fig. 6.

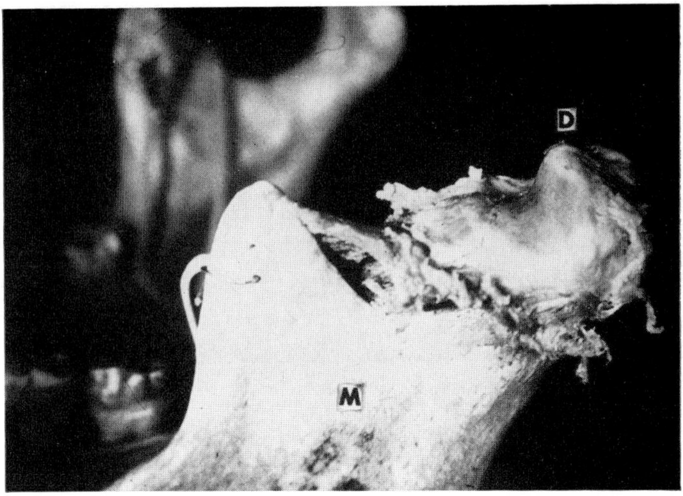

Fig. 8. Articular disk, **D,** is fitted over the head of mandible, **M.** Note the jockey's cap shape and the concave articular surface on the disk for the articular tubercle.

that are formed by virtue of the fact that the articular disk is attached to the capsule at its periphery while its whole anterior surface is intermingled with the tendon and slips of muscle fibers from the upper belly (or fasciculus) of the external pterygoid muscle (Fig. 7). Again it is important to note this relationship and also to note that the reason the upper belly of the external pterygoid muscle is flattened in a horizontal plane is because of the nature of its attachment to the anterior border of the articular disk. When the disk is dissected in toto, the superior belly of the external pterygoid muscle comes away with it (Fig. 9).

Other ligaments contribute to the formation of the mandibular articulation, but they will only be mentioned here for although they have a stabilizing function, they do not play an important role in the dynamics of the functioning joint. They are the temporomandibular ligament, which forms the

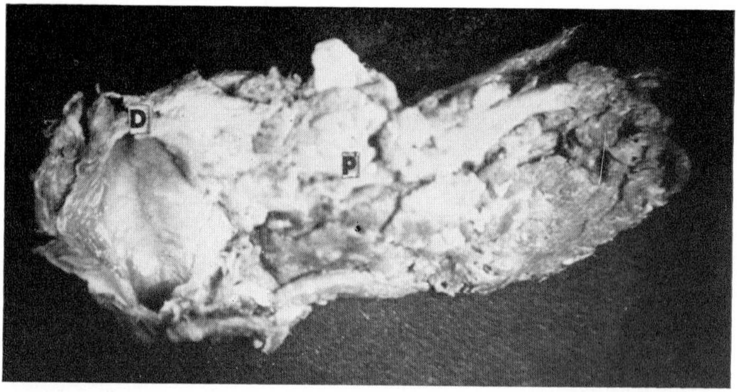

Fig. 9. Articular disk, **D,** with attached superior belly of external pterygoid muscle, **P,** viewed from the inferior (caudal) surface.

lateral anterior wall of the articular capsule; the sphenomandibular ligament, which extends from the lingula of the medial surface of the ramus of the mandible to the base of the sphenoid bone; and the stylomandibular ligament, whose connection is from the posterior border of the ramus near the angle to the styloid process. Most important, however, in connection with pain that is often referred to the region of the temporomandibular joint is the stylohyoid ligament. Although not part of the articulation, this ligament is sometimes calcified and, when it is, may be responsible for confusing symptoms. This is considered in Chapter 6.

The musculature. The muscles that act upon the temporomandibular joint are of the greatest importance. Those that elevate the mandible are the temporals, the masseters, and the internal pterygoids. Those that depress the mandible are the mylohyoid, the digastric, the geniohyoid, the strap muscles that fix the hyoid from below so that the geniohyoid can exert its action, and the mass of the mandible itself which produces a depressor effect. The muscles that retrude the mandible are the posterior fibers of the temporals and some of the deep fibers of the masseters. Those that protrude the mandible are the external pterygoids. These latter muscles will be described in detail since it is when the mandible is protruded that sounds occur that may be indicative of functional or organic disease of the mandibular articulation.

External pterygoid muscle. The external pterygoid is a double muscle consisting of two fasciculi. Each is rather thick and forms a triangle whose apex points toward the joint although the main mass of each bundle is not in the same plane. The superior fasciculus or belly is flattened in a horizontal plane, whereas the inferior belly is flattened in a vertical plane (Figs. 10 and 11).

The two bellies are separated by a space and indeed are enclosed in separate fascial envelops except at their origins. The inferior belly, the larger belly, arises by short tendinous processes from the lateral aspect of the lateral plate of the pterygoid bone, from the pyramidal portion of the palatal bone, and from the adjacent maxillary tuberosity. All these

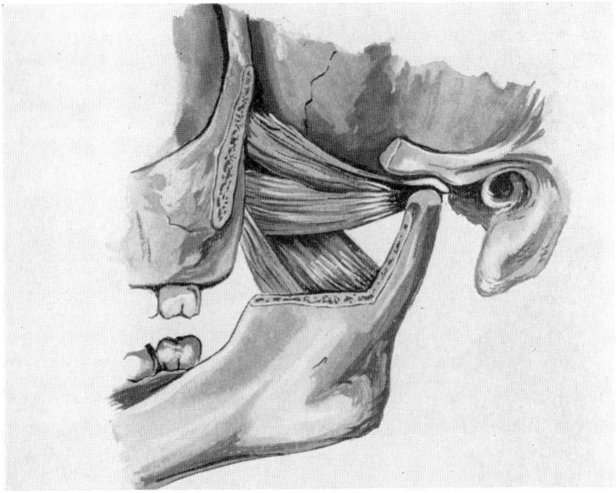

Fig. 10. Upper muscles are the two bellies of the external pterygoid. Superior belly is attached to the articular disk. Lower group of muscles are the internal pterygoids; note how they enclose the inferior belly of the external pterygoid. (After Jackson, C. M., editor: Morris' human anatomy, Philadelphia, 1933, P. Blakiston's Son & Co.)

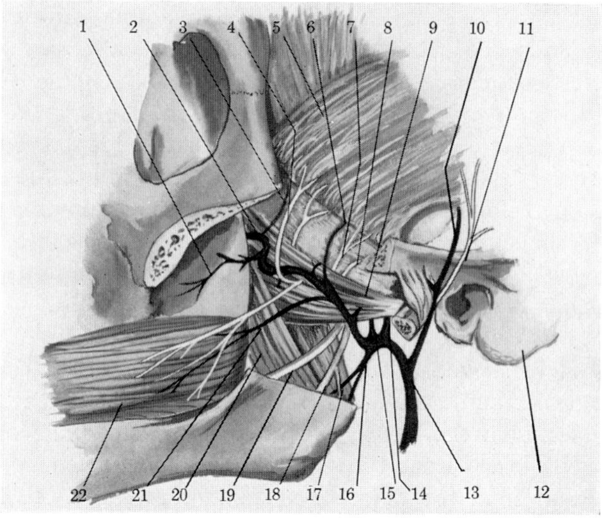

Fig. 11. Nerve and blood supply to the masticatory muscles. **1,** Posterior superior alveolar artery; **2,** internal maxillary artery; **3,** anterior deep temporal artery; **4,** anterior deep temporal nerve; **5,** temporal muscle; **6,** posterior deep temporal artery; **7,** posterior deep temporal nerve; **8,** nerve to masseter muscle; **9,** two bellies of the external pterygoid muscle; **10,** superficial temporal artery; **11,** auriculotemporal nerve; **12,** mastoid process; **13,** external carotid artery; **14** and **15,** accessory meningeal arteries; **16,** inferior alveolar artery; **17,** mylohyoid artery and nerve; **18,** inferior alveolar nerve; **19,** lingual nerve; **20,** internal pterygoid muscle; **21,** buccinator nerve and artery; **22,** buccinator muscle. (After Cunningham, D. J.: A manual of practical anatomy, New York, 1937, Oxford University Press.)

fibers converge toward their insertion in a depression on the flattened surface of the neck of the condyle. The superior belly, the smaller of the two, arises from the infratemporal pterygoid crest and from the adjoining surface of the greater wing of the sphenoid bone. Its fibers, arranged in a flattened fan, converge toward the articular capsule and attach by a tendinous process accompanied by some slips of muscle and insert into the capsular ligament, the articular disk itself, and the front of the neck of the condyle in its upper third.

The nerve supply of the external pterygoid muscle is from the masticator nerve, the origin of which is in the motor root of the trigeminal nerve. It approaches the upper border of the muscle from its medial side and first sends a branch into the upper belly and then a branch into the lower belly. This represents strong evidence that these two bellies are functionally separate muscles.

The anatomical relations of the external pterygoid muscle are equally important. It is partly covered by the maxillary fasciculus (anterior belly) of the internal pterygoid muscle (Fig. 11) and by the masseter and temporal muscles. Medially is the chief belly of the internal pterygoid muscle. The masseteric, posterior, and middle temporal nerves, the buccinator nerves, and the internal maxillary artery often pass between the two bellies, emphasizing the fact that these two fasciculi of the external pterygoid muscle can be regarded as anatomically separate structures rather than as divisions of the same muscle (Fig. 11). In man and anthropoid apes this may represent an evolutionary development from the single muscle mass, as exemplified by the adductor mandibulae of the selachians.

Other anatomical relations that may have some bearing on the involved nature of some of the observed symptoms of temporomandibular joint dysfunction are the auriculotemporal, the lingual, and the inferior alveolar nerves that pass across the deep surface of the external pterygoid muscle (Fig. 11). Recently Pinto described a ligament attached both to the posteromedial aspect of the articular disk and to one of the ear ossicles, the malleus, lateral to the chorda tympani nerve. The discovery of this ligament, absent from standard anatomy texts, opens up the possibility that an anatomical and physiological explanation for the complexities of temporomandibular joint dysfunction may yet be found.

These relations may be involved in the myofascial trigger mechanisms discussed in subsequent chapters, particularly in Chapter 7.

THEORETICAL CONSIDERATIONS OF MANDIBULAR JOINT MECHANICS

Theoretically, it is possible anatomically for the two bellies of the external pterygoid muscle to act separately. Indeed it would appear from the complexity of the movement that the

---

Fig. 12. The normal positions of the mandibular condyle and the articular disk are shown in black and in the open (white line) relationships to the articular fossa and the articular eminence. Disk pulled forward by the external pterygoid muscle maintains the same relative position to the head of the condyle, which is being moved by the same muscle. There is no sound.

Fig. 13. The disk moves forward first and the head of the condyle rides over the thickened trailing edge of the disk, producing a clicking sound at the beginning of mandibular opening. When the muscles relax and the jaw moves back, the head of the condyle is then anterior to the edge of the disk; hence there is no sound upon closing.

Fig. 14. The disk does not move forward, and the head of the condyle rides over the thickened leading edge of the disk. There is a sound upon opening and another when the condyle returns to the closed position. This happens most frequently in rotation.

Fig. 15. The disk moves forward first. The first sound is heard when the head of the condyle rides over the thickened trailing edge of the disk. If the disk returns with the head of the condyle, there will be no sound upon closing. If the disk remains in a forward position, there will be a sound upon closing as the head of the condyle rides over the anterior margin of the thickened trailing edge of the disk. If masseter and temporal muscles are engaged in forcible contraction, this closure will be accompanied by jolting of the mandible which can be felt as well as heard.

Fig. 16. The various consequences of a loose capsular ligament and joint capsule. The disk moves a considerable distance forward, as does the head of the condyle. The first sound is heard when the condyle rides over the thickened trailing edge, and a second sound is heard when it rides over the thickened leading edge. If the disk returns promptly, there will be a single sound upon closing. If the disk lags behind, there will be a single sound as the head of the condyle rides over the leading edge. In extreme cases the head of the condyle will also ride over the trailing edge of the disk, and there will be another sound upon closing.

mandibular joint is capable of performing that such insertion of the two heads of the external pterygoid muscle would be required. If this is so, it would follow that disharmony in the contraction of the two heads of the muscle would result in a disturbance in which the articular disk would not necessarily

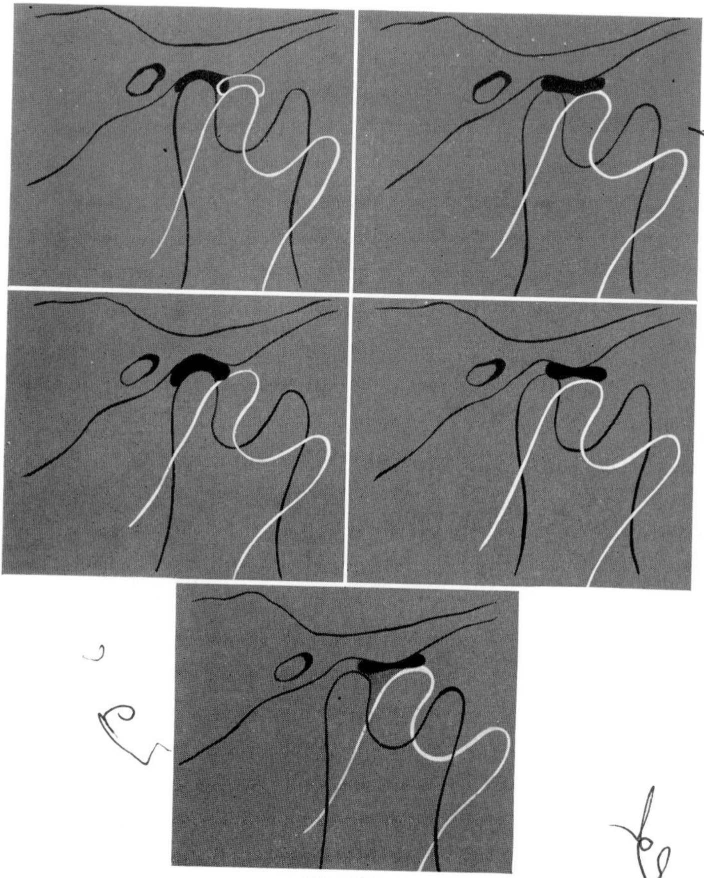

Fig. 12

Fig. 13

Fig. 14

Fig. 15

Fig. 16

Figs. 12-16. For legends see opposite page.

be in normal relation to the moving condylar head. It is our purpose to examine a possible explanation of the sounds made in abnormal temporomandibular joint function and to offer an explanation that is consistent with clinical observation and with anatomical facts.

A RATIONALE FOR SOUNDS HEARD DURING ABNORMAL MANDIBULAR MOVEMENT

Figs. 12 to 16 represent a sagittal plane that extends from the midpoint of the head of the mandible to the pterygopalatine fossa and that is roughly parallel to the lateral pterygoid plate. In this sense it represents the existing inclination of the articular head and fossa which together are turned inwardly, toward the midsagittal plane about 30 degrees. The movements are therefore to be visualized as taking place over the midpoint of the articular eminence roughly parallel with the midsagittal plane.

In normal excursion of the mandible, the articular disk moves forward with the head of the mandible; hence its thinnest portion (Fig. 6) is in constant relationship to the center of the head of the mandible (Fig. 12). The disk and the head of the mandible are moved harmoniously by the two heads of the external pterygoid muscle; hence there is no tripping or interference in smooth mandibular lateral movement and therefore the movement is not accompanied by any sounds except those mentioned previously, which are not interarticular. In Figs. 17 and 18 the insertion of the inferior belly of the external pterygoid muscle and in Fig. 7 the loose folded arrangement of the posterior fibrous attachment of the disk which makes such movements possible can be seen.

In patients with temporomandibular joint dysfunction two clinical observations are important: (1) the mandible upon opening deviates to one side, and if a marker such as a toothpick is placed between the maxillary and mandibular incisors, this deviation may be easily observed (Fig. 19); (2) such abnormal movement is often accompanied by sounds of which,

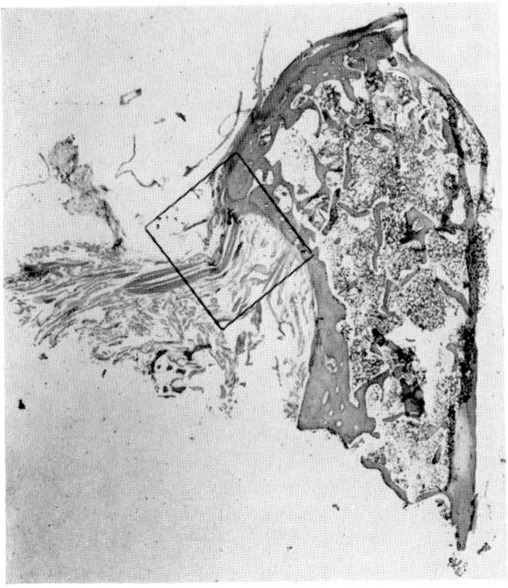

Fig. 17. Photomicrograph of the head of the mandible. The square encloses the insertion of the inferior belly of the external pterygoid muscle. Note the large marrow spaces, some of which are red marrow. The articular condyle is responsive to metabolic changes and to stress.

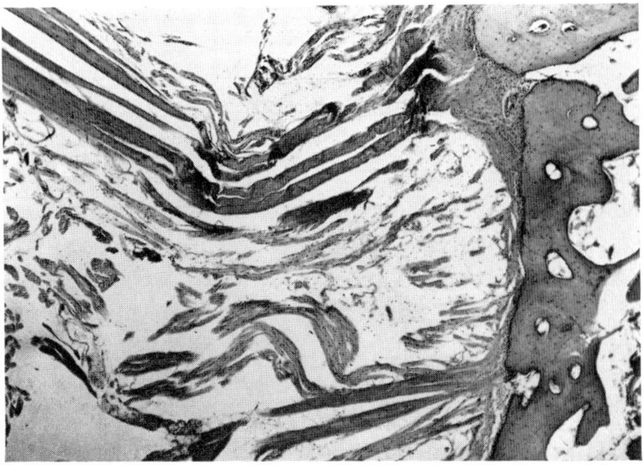

Fig. 18. Higher power of area indicated by square in Fig. 17. Note muscle insertion.

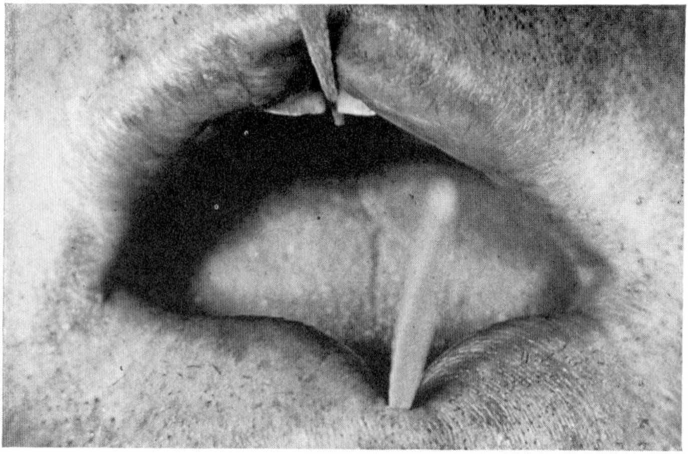

Fig. 19. Toothpick markers clearly indicate deviation of mandible on opening. This patient had painful and noisy mandibular joint dysfunction.

clinically, there are four variations: (a) a single sound at the beginning of mandibular opening, (b) a single sound toward the end of mandibular opening and at the beginning of closing, (c) a single sound at the middle of opening and possibly another sound at the beginning of closing, and (d) a sound at the midpoint of opening, a second sound at the end of opening, and possibly a third sound at the beginning of closing. Although these variations are by no means all of the types of sounds that may be heard in patients with mandibular dysfunction, they represent the main types. All of these variations have one thing in common—disharmony in the muscular action of the superior and inferior fasciculi of the external pterygoid muscle.

Single sound at the beginning of mandibular opening

In this instance the articular disk moves forward first, and the head of the mandible rides over the thickened trailing edge of the disk (Fig. 13), thus producing a clicking sound of low intensity and force. When the muscles relax, permitting the mandible to move backward, the head of the mandible, being anterior to the edge of the disk, moves back into the fossa without producing a sound.

Single sound toward the end of mandibular opening and at the beginning of closing

This variation of mandibular sound is heard when the articular disk does not move forward when the head of the mandible is pulled forward by the inferior belly of the external pterygoid muscle. As shown in Fig. 14, the head of the mandible rides over the thickened leading edge of the disk. Since this can occur only toward the end of opening, the sound is heard then rather than at the beginning of opening.

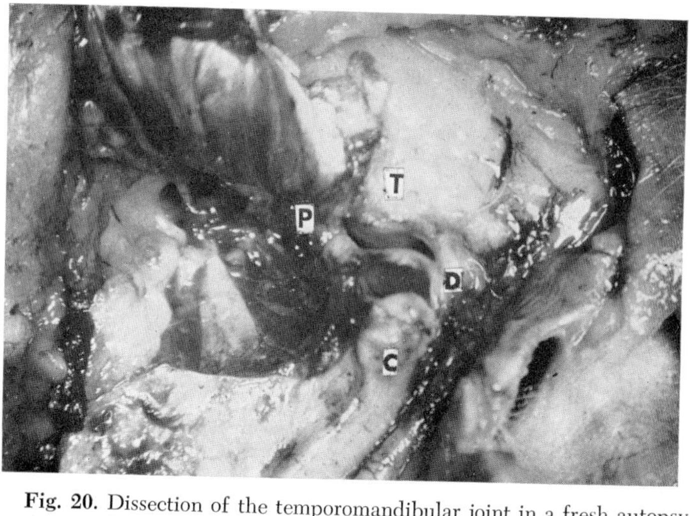

Fig. 20. Dissection of the temporomandibular joint in a fresh autopsy specimen. The mandible is pulled down so that its head (capitulum, **C**) distracts the joint cavities and reveals the articular disk, **D.** The articular tubercle (tuberculum, **T**) is clearly seen as an articulating surface. The superior belly of the external pterygoid muscle, **P**, is exposed so that traction may be applied to it. The coronoid process had been cut off to expose the infratemporal fossa.

The head of the mandible is then anterior to the thickened leading edge, hence a sound is heard at the beginning of closure. If the midline is marked, it will be seen that this variation occurs most frequently when the mandible appears to be rotating about one or the other condyle. Actually this is a rotation about a tuberculum-capitulum axis; this is explained in Chapter 3 in the discussion on the mechanics of the temporomandibular articulation. Nevertheless, it should be noted that in these instances the deviation to one side (that is, away from the midline) is most marked.

Single sound at the middle of opening and another sound possibly at the end of closing

In this variation the articular disk moves forward first. The first sound is heard approximately at the middle of opening

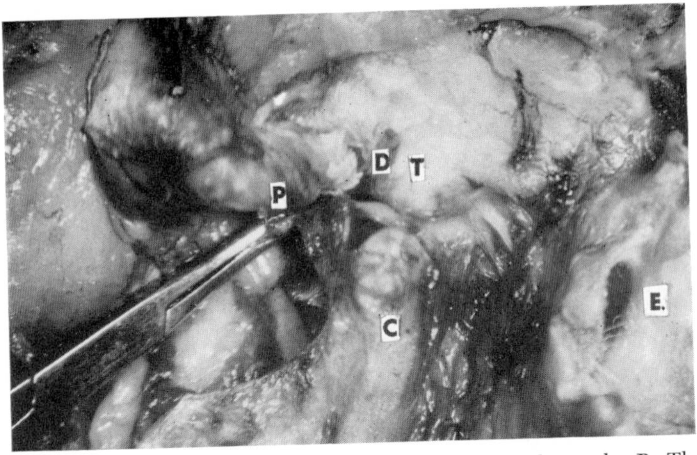

Fig. 21. Traction applied to the external pterygoid muscle, **P.** The head of the mandible (capitulum, **C**) moves forward until it lies under the articular tubercle (tuberculum, **T**). Continued traction on the superior belly of the external pterygoid muscle moves the disk, **D,** ahead of the condyle. See Fig. 5 in which the superior belly of the external pterygoid muscle moves only the disk. The external ear opening, **E,** is indicated here for orientation of the photographs.

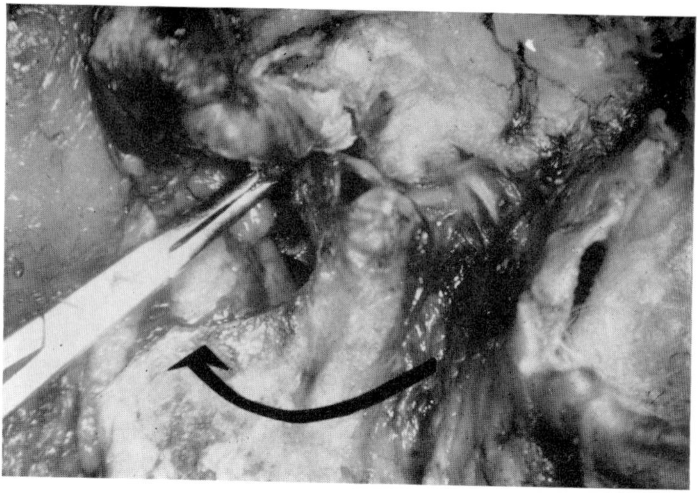

Fig. 22. As in Fig. 21 the hemostat is applying traction to the superior belly of the external pterygoid muscle. Photograph is unlabeled so as not to obscure anatomical detail. Black arrow indicates direction of continued rotation of the head of the mandible around the tuberculum axis, labeled **T,** in Fig. 21. This is possible in this edentulous specimen. However, it is at this point that protrusive or lateral movement produces a sound. A sound can also be produced when the mandible is returned.

when the head of the mandible rides over the thickened trailing edge of the disk (Fig. 15). If the disk returns with the head of the mandible, there will be no sound upon closing; however, if the disk remains in a forward position, there will be a second sound at the beginning of closing as the head of the mandible rides over the anterior margin of the thickened trailing edge of the disk. Some patients with this condition may voluntarily demonstrate a more forcible sound accompanied by a jolting closure of the mandible if at the same time the masseter and temporal muscles contract. This situation can be produced experimentally in a fresh autopsy specimen by first pulling the articular disk forward, by applying traction upon the superior belly of the external pterygoid muscle, and then by manually moving the mandible forward in an imitation of a protrusive or a lateral and protrusive motion. The sound that is produced and the physical sensation of a jolt is indistinguishable from the same condition in a living patient (Figs. 20 to 22). In some patients this will occur voluntarily, as we observed in one hysterical patient. It is difficult to determine whether this type of closing of the mandible is the result of perverse habituation or is an actual abnormality of function.

Sound at the midpoint of opening, a second sound at the end of opening, and a third sound possibly at the beginning of closing

Fig. 16 illustrates this variation of sound, which is usually present in patients with loose articulation. In the past, the condition was labeled subluxation. Patients with this condition were often treated with injections of sodium psylliate or sodium morrhuate into the synovial spaces to produce sclerosis of the joint capsule and thus limit the extent of movement. In these patients there may also be simultaneous sounds on both sides unlike those previously described. There may also be little or no deviation from the midline as invariably occurs in patients exhibiting the other variations of sound.

In such a loose joint the articular disk moves forward for a considerable distance, as does the head of the mandible. The first sound is heard when the condyle rides over the thickened trailing edge of the disk, and a second sound is heard when it rides over the thickened leading edge. If the disk returns promptly, there will be a single sound as the head of the mandible rides over the leading edge. In extreme cases the head of the mandible will ride over the trailing edge of the disk, and there will be a fourth sound at the end of closing.

SOUNDS IN THE NORMAL JOINT

Not all articular dysfunctions are based on trauma, infection, or occlusal abnormalities. Habit and perversion of function for many reasons may play a role, and we observed a patient in whom such a symptom was a feature of conversion hysteria. With practice it is possible to produce some of the sounds in the normal patient by bizarre manipulation of the mandible in opening and closing. Usually this can be accomplished by first exaggerating lateral movement before forcibly closing or opening the lower jaw. Interestingly enough, when the lower jaw is supported by a rigid surface such as a table top and the jaw is opened by tilting the head back, there are no sounds. We may therefore say that irregularities in the surface of the condyle or the articular fossa play no role in production of sound. As a matter of fact, when there are gross irregularities in the usually smooth surface of the head of the mandible these irregularities are faithfully reproduced by the contacting surface of the articular disk, which would not be the case if these surfaces moved in relation to each other (Fig. 23). This specimen had widely disseminated osteoarthritis, and

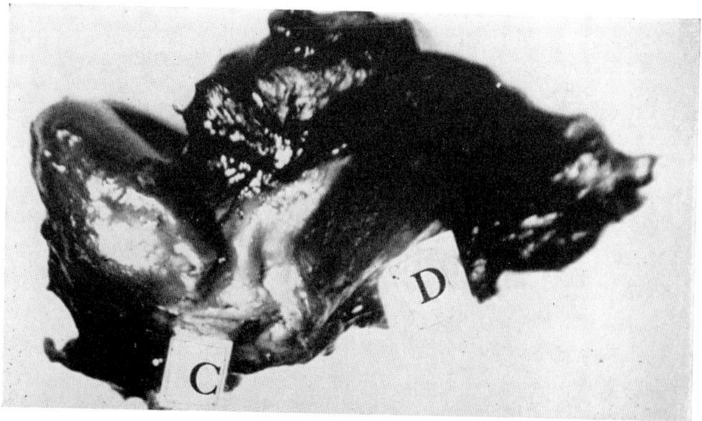

Fig. 23. Above and to the left of **C** is the mandibular condyle. Irregularities in the light area are due to osteoarthritis. The light area above and to the left of **D** is the articular disk which has been freed from the posterior border of the condyle and laid open so that its condylar surface is exposed. Note depressions in the surface of the disk which exactly correspond to the elevations in the condyle.

the temporomandibular joint was also involved. The patient died from causes unrelated to this disease. To my knowledge there was never any evidence of joint sounds.

Finally, in patients whose mandibular movements are accompanied by sounds, a firm grip on the mandible to guide its movement so that deviation from the midline during slow opening is rendered difficult results in no sound and often there is no pain when this is the presenting symptom. It is obvious that to understand the temporomandibular joint and its malfunction a thorough examination of its mechanics is needed. For this reason a separate chapter has been devoted to this study (see Chapter 3).

TREATMENT

From the foregoing discussion it may be concluded that the pathogenesis of mandibular dysfunction, from whatever cause, leads eventually to a derangement in the function of the external pterygoid muscles. These muscles, by reason of their anatomical and functional nature, are capable of moving two elements of the mandibular articulation disharmoniously, resulting in symptoms of functional joint disease. In view of this, treatment consists of retraining these muscles.

Methods of retraining the muscles of mastication

In the training of voluntary muscles, of which the muscles of mastication are a special example, we use a conscious purpose, the kinesthetic sense, and the reference points of the eyes as guides. The function of the muscles of mastication and, for our purposes, of the pterygoid muscles (though voluntary) is perfected in a way that is not responsive to either kinesthetic sense or visual points of reference and, since training begins in infancy, have almost instinctual beginnings. The process by which we learn to eat and chew is imitative and quickly becomes a matter of such strong habituation that for the most part the complex muscular movements are almost involuntary in nature. This of course poses a difficulty in any attempt at retraining. However, it does point to a training method that uses both the kinesthetic and visual senses. The motivation, of course, is the patient's desire and need to be rid of disease, discomfort, or pain.

Although it is difficult for most patients to move the mandible into various positions upon command, they can be assisted in this by the therapist. For many years the problem of recording a centric relationship has called forth a host of methods, all of them based upon pre-existing motor patterns such as swallowing and head positions, or upon a specific point recorded along the locus of paths described during free lateral movement. Some methods are frankly sessions in muscle training by which the patient is taught an unstrained mandibular position.

For our purposes the insight provided by these methods is important, even if the specific techniques are not particularly so. The method proposed here consists of inserting a marker,

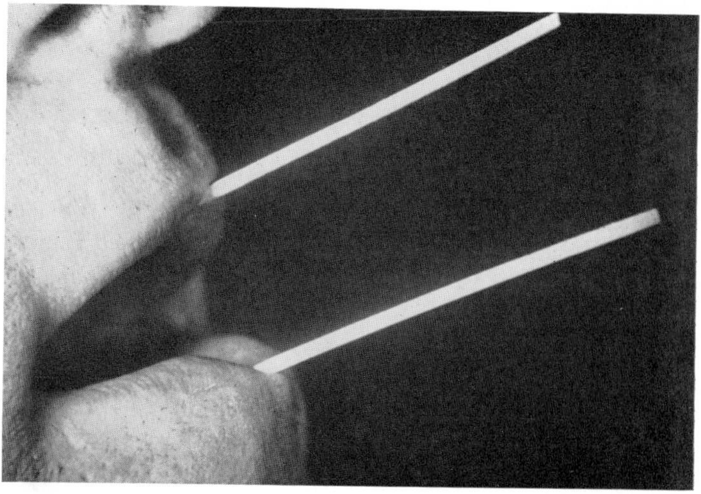

Fig. 24. Anatomical midlines of the mandible and maxilla are aligned by the patient while he looks at the alignment of the toothpick markers in a mirror.

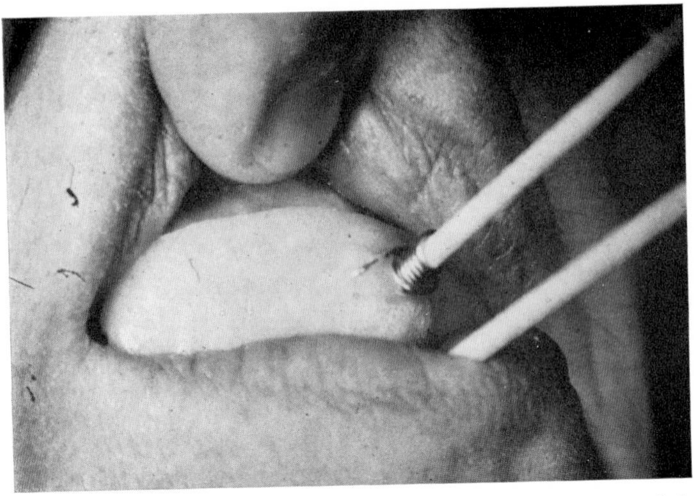

Fig. 25. When the existing condition does not permit the use of the central incisors to mark the anatomical midline, a prosthetic device may be inserted to establish a maxillo-mandibular midline.

such as a toothpick, between the upper central and the lower central incisors (Fig. 24) if they are not off center or of inserting a carrying device for these markers so that in the closed position they coincide, thus marking the anatomical center of the mandible and the maxilla (Fig. 25). The patient, using a mirror, is then taught to open his mouth slowly so that at all times the two markers are in the same sagittal plane. The patient is told not to exceed any degree of opening at which the lower jaw begins to deviate. With practice a normal opening without deviation will be achieved and if done slowly enough will eliminate any sounds. As the patient develops skill, he will be able to open his mouth more rapidly without deviation or sounds. The end result of retraining the muscles, particularly the external pterygoid muscles, is disappearance of the associated symptoms or joint dysfunction.

Since in many patients dysfunction of the mandibular joint has a strong emotional component, the simplicity of the method often is not impressive. Many patients feel that because of the magnitude or the seriousness of their complaint a more impressive or serious treatment is required. Consequently it is important to explain the rationale of the treatment in terms of muscle retraining. The remarkable results in physical medicine, in which simple exercise methods have effected rehabilitation of patients with seemingly hopeless musculoskeletal disabilities, may be used as an example of muscle retraining. It is important actually to guide the mandible as it opens so that it does not deviate. In this way it can be demonstrated to the patient that opening without the accompanying discomfort or noises is possible. Such a demonstration is almost indispensable in the management of these patients. It is important to mention here that an attitude of assurance and confidence on the part of the therapist is of equal value.

The chronicity of the condition and the usual history of multidirected and repeated therapy of limited or transitory value often imbue the patient with greater than normal skepticism. The ultimate objective of the method outlined here is to place the patient's problem in a different light. The patient must become aware of the fact that mandibular dysfunction, except in patients with osteoarthritis or frank injury to the joint, is not the result of organic disease and therefore does not require surgical or medical modalities. The treatment is therefore ultimately one of self-help, in much the same way as home care is an indispensable feature of so much of dental therapy. Definitive treatment, which would prevent recurrence, would of course consist of thorough diagnosis and correction of occlusal disharmonies and defects and the elimination of bad habits in oral function. These aspects of the problem are discussed in detail in subsequent chapters.

SUMMARY

Early diagnosis of dysfunction of the temporomandibular articulation is essential to successful treatment. Early diagnosis is facilitated by auscultation of the joint to detect typical sounds of joint dysfunction. The basic problem of mandibular joint dysfunction may be understood through study of the anatomy of the joint, its muscles, and the mechanics of their function. In the normally functioning mandibular joint there is harmony in the function of the two parts of the external pterygoid muscle so that the articular disk and the head of the mandible move together. In a malfunctioning temporomandibular joint, sounds may result from lack of coordination in the movement of the articular disk and the head of the mandible by the two fasciculi of the external pterygoid muscle.

The basis of initial or emergent therapy in the light of this concept consists of retraining the muscles to contract and function in a coordinated manner. The definitive treatment consists of correction of occlusal disharmonies and abnormal habits of mandibular movements.

REFERENCES

1. Becker, Walter H.: Report of ten years' experience in the treatment of subluxation and luxation of the temporomandibular joint by the injection of a sclerosing agent and immobilization of the mandible, Oral Surg., Oral Med. & Oral Path. **7**:732, 1954.
2. Bellinger, D. H.: Internal derangements of the temporomandibular joint, J. Oral Surg. **10**:47, 1952.
3. Blackwood, H. J. J.: Intra-articular fibrous ankylosis of the temporomandibular joint (excellent post-mortem sections of the temporomandibular joint), Oral Surg., Oral Med. & Oral Path. **10**:634, 1957.
4. Block, Louis J.: The prosthodontist and the temporomandibular joint, J.A.D.A. **46**:671, 1953.
5. Borland, Loren R.: Psychological considerations in the diagnosis and treatment of facial and oral pain: some applications of communication theory, J.A.D.A. **53**:539, 1956.
6. Burman, M., and Sinberg, S. E.: Condylar movements in the study of internal derangements of the temporomandibular joints, J. Bone & Joint Surg. **28**:351, 1946.
7. Costen, J. B. A.: Syndrome of ear and sinus symptoms dependent upon disturbed function of temporomandibular joint, Ann. Otol., Rhin., & Laryng. **43**:1, 1934.

8. Cunningham, D. J.: A manual of practical anatomy, ed. 9, New York, 1937, Oxford University Press.
9. Gerry, R. G.: Clinical problems of the temporomandibular articulation, J.A.D.A. **34**:261, 1947.
10. Granger, E. R.: Occlusion in temporomandibular joint pain, J.A.D.A. **56**:659, 1958.
11. Granger, Ernest R.: Functional relations of the stomatognathic system, J.A.D.A. **48**:638, 1954.
12. Jackson, C. M. (editor): Morris' human anatomy, ed. 9, Philadelphia, 1933, P. Blakiston's Sons & Co.
13. Lindblom, Gösta: The value of bite analysis, J.A.D.A. **48**:657, 1954.
14. Lindblom, Gösta: Disorders of the temporomandibular joint, J.A.D.A. **49**:30, 1954.
15. Lindblom, Gösta: Technique for roentgen-photographic registration of the different condyle positions in the temporomandibular joint, D. Cosmos **78**:1227, 1936.
16. Markowitz, H. A., and Gerry, R. G.: Temporomandibular joint disease, Oral Surg., Oral Med. & Oral Path. **2**:1309, 1949; **3**:75, 1950.
17. Perry, Harold T., Jr.: Muscular changes associated with temporomandibular joint dysfunction, J.A.D.A. **54**:644, 1957.
18. Pinto, O. F.: A new structure related to the temporomandibular joint and middle ear, J. Pros. Dent. **12**:1, 1962.
19. Roydhouse, Richard H.: The temporomandibular joint: function, dysfunction and dental treatment, J.A.D.A. **56**:34, 1958.
20. Roydhouse, Richard H.: The temporomandibular joint (study of the upward force of the condyles on the cranium), J.A.D.A. **50**:166, 1955.
21. Scheman, Paul: A preliminary report on the role of the dentist in a mental hospital, J. Hillside Hosp. **5**:488, 1956.
22. Schreiber, Harold R.: An anatomic and physiological approach to treatment of the temporomandibular joint disturbances, J.A.D.A. **48**:261, 1954.
23. Schuyler, C. H.: The effect of abnormalities of occlusion upon the temporomandibular joint and associated structures, New York, 1940, Procedures Dental Centenary, p. 303.
24. Schwartz, L. Laszlo: Pain associated with the temporomandibular joint, J.A.D.A. **51**:394, 1955.
25. Schwartz, L. Laszlo, and Cobin, Harold P.: Symptoms associated with the temporomandibular joint, Oral Surg., Oral Med. & Oral Path. **10**:339, 1957.
26. Sherrington, C. S.: Integrative action of the nervous system, New Haven, 1906, Yale University Press.

27. Sicher, H.: Oral anatomy, St. Louis, 1960, The C. V. Mosby Co.
28. Sicher, H.: Structural and functional basis for disorders of the temporomandibular articulation, J. Oral Surg. **13**:275, 1955.
29. Sicher, H.: Positions and movements of the mandible, J.A.D.A. **48**:620, 1954.
30. Thoma, Kurt H.: Oral surgery, ed. 2, St. Louis, 1952, The C. V. Mosby Co., vol. 2.
31. Thompson, J. R.: Concepts regarding function of the stomatognathic system, J.A.D.A. **48**:626, 1954.
32. Vaughn, H. C.: Temporomandibular joint pain. A new diagnostic approach, J. Pros. Den. **4**:694, 1954.
33. Wilkinson, S. H.: Hysterical trismus and other neuroses of the jaw, Brit. D. J. **41**:318, 1920.

CHAPTER 3

DYNAMICS OF ANATOMY AND EMBRYOLOGY AND MECHANICS OF THE TEMPOROMANDIBULAR ARTICULATION

ANATOMY

The condyloid process. The condyloid process consists of a capitulum and a narrow stemlike portion, the neck (Fig. 1).

The capitulum. The capitulum is a bulbous, oval structure with its long axis placed transversely in relation to the ramus of the mandible. Its roughened lateral face is inclined more anteriorly than its smoother medial face. Its superior surface is convex cranially and fits into the lower concavity of the articular disk with which it articulates.

The articular tubercle (tuberculum). The mandibular fossa and the articular tubercle are parts of the squamous portion of the temporal bone (Fig. 2). The other two portions, tympanic and petrous, provide related and adjacent structures but do not contribute to any of the future joint structures.

The articular tubercle or tuberculum lies at the inferior part of the base of the zygomatic process. It is convex caudally and articulates with the concave superior surface of the biconcave articular disk. The mandibular fossa, which is separated from the external auditory meatus by the petrotympanic fissure, is not an articulating surface. Its roof is extremely thin and in some dried specimens is actually translucent.

EMBRYOLOGY

The mandible. The mandible is often erroneously thought of as an enchondral bone. This is only partly true. Actually it is primarily a membraneous bone that forms around the cartilage of the first branchial arch. This cartilaginous bar, extending in a long loop from the area of the middle ear to the sympyhsis of the mandible, disappears almost entirely in the course of development. In the adult its remnants may persist as the genial tubercles of the mandible. It also functions as the antecedent of the sphenomandibular ligament and the malleus and incus.

The mandible of an 8 to 10 cm. fetus is already recognizable. With the exception of the condyloid process and its lack of fusion in the midline, it bears all its essential landmarks, including the dental anlage on its superior margin. At this stage Meckel's cartilage is a slender bar passing through the center of the body of the mandible roughly approximating the inferior alveolar canal in later life.

The styloid process. The styloid process develops from part of the hyoid arch which also forms a part of the stapes and part of the body and lesser cornua of the hyoid bone. Calcified or long styloid process is a cause of pain (see Chapter 4).

The coronoid and condyloid processes. The coronoid and condyloid processes are not part of Meckel's cartilage but are formed as cartilaginous extensions of the mandibular bone. The ossification of the mandible begins as early as the thirty-ninth day, and by four months the essential structures are present. At 4 months the capitulum of the condyloid process is at the same level as the alveolar crest of the body of the mandible. This is the measure of the extent to which the condyloid process contributes to the later development of the mandible. In the adult it may be as much as 1.5 to 4 cm. above the occlusal plane of the teeth.

MECHANICS OF THE TEMPOROMANDIBULAR ARTICULATION ACCORDING TO THE PRINCIPLES OF CARL-HERMAN HJORTSJÖ

General principles of joint function. The function of joints is to facilitate and to mediate movement of the skeleton. The function of the temporomandibular joint is to permit not only movement of the mandible but also the masticatory strokes demanded by the dentition and the movements required by speech, respiration, and deglutition. Joints have various degrees of freedom of motion. This depends on the ability of a joint to rotate around a central axis and upon its ability to change its position in space. The first type of movement is known as angular movement and the second as linear movement. When we move bodily, the first type of movement occurs when we turn ourselves around in place, and the second type occurs when we walk along a path. The mandibular joint is capable of both types of movement because of its unique arrangement.

The concept of the biaxial nutcracker. Fig. 26 represents schematically a simple hinge joint compared with the same arrangement if a disk were interposed. The simple nutcracker is capable only of rotation around the single axis. The biaxial nutcracker can rotate around each one of its pins, but in

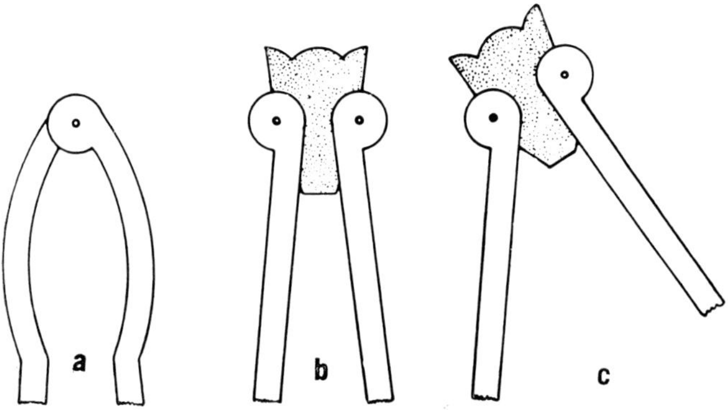

Fig. 26. Schematic drawings of uniaxial, **a**, and biaxial, **b** and **c**, nutcrackers. The uniaxial nutcracker with its single axis is capable only of hinge motion; the "joint heads" are capable only of rotation around the axis. The biaxial nutcracker has two axes; each limb is capable of a simple hinge motion, but, in addition, one of the joint heads is capable of changing its position in space, **c**. This is analogous to a joint with two joint heads and a biconcave disk (see Fig. 27).

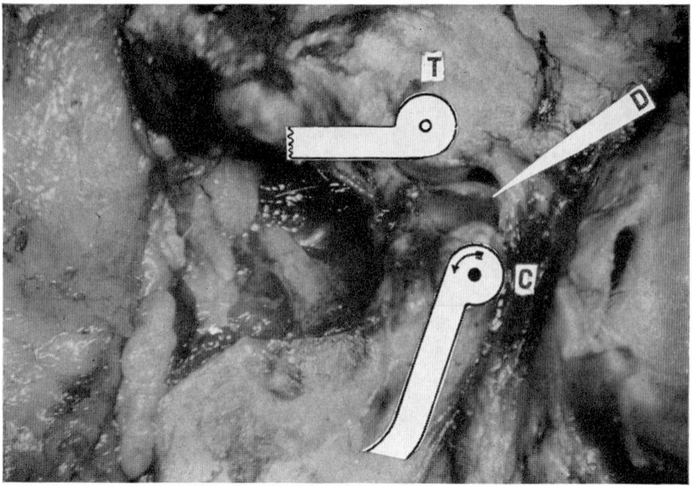

Fig. 27. Superimposed upon a dissection of a temporomandibular joint are schematic drawings of a biaxial nutcracker showing tuberculum axis, **T,** capitulum axis, **C,** and interposed biconcave disk, **D.** The head of the mandible, **C,** is free to rotate around its own axis as well as to move bodily in space as it rotates around the articular tubercle.

addition, as the drawing on the right (*c*) shows, it can move in space. This translation in space, linear motion, makes the temporomandibular joint unique.

The articular disk forms the anatomical basis on which the temporomandibular joint assumes the form of two joint heads. The superior joint head is formed by the articular tubercle and the concave superior surface of the disk, while the inferior joint head is formed by the head of the mandible and the concave inferior surface of the articular disk (Fig. 27).

Raising and lowering the mandible. The mandible can rotate around a transverse axis passing through the center of its head. When the mandible rotates forward, it is lowered, that is, the jaws are opened. When the mandible rotates backward, it is raised, that is, the jaws are closed. This axis of rotation is known as the capitulum axis.

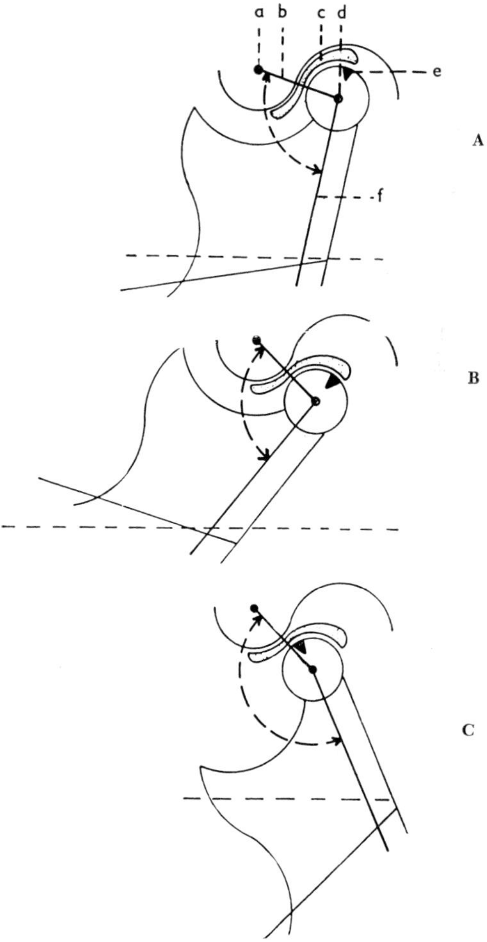

Fig. 28. Schematic drawing showing from above down the stages involved in lowering the mandible in actual function. **A,** The mandible in centric occlusion: **a,** tuberculum center; **b,** center line joining the tuberculum center to the capitulum center, **d; c,** the disk; **e,** upper pole of the head of the mandible (condyle); **f,** ramus line drawn from the center of the capitulum (capitulum axis) and dropped parallel to the posterior border of the ramus; the angle between this line and the one joining the capitulum–tuberculum centers measures the degrees of opening. **B,** Only tuberculum rotation with forward rotation of the disk has taken place. **C,** Capitulum rotation forward has also taken place.

The mandible can also rotate around the articular tubercle. This is a transverse axis passing through the center of the tubercle, the tuberculum axis. When the head of the mandible rotates forward around the tuberculum axis it is accompanied normally by a forward rotation of the disk. Similarly when it rotates backward it is accompanied by a backward rotation of the disk.

An exact analysis of the components of the motion involved in lowering the mandible can be found in the work of Hjortsjö and co-workers.[2,3] In practice, however, lowering of the mandible consists of (1) a forward rotation of the head of the mandible (capitulum) in combination with (2) a forward rotation of the head of the mandible around the tuberculum axis and (3) a forward rotation of the disk (Fig. 28).

When the mandible is raised, all of these movements take place in reverse. The need for coordinated contraction of the superior belly of the external pterygoid muscle (inserted into the disk) and the inferior belly of the external pterygoid muscle (inserted into the head of the mandible) is here apparent.

Protrusive and retrusive movements of the mandible. The mechanics involved in protrusive and retrusive mandibular movements are the same as those involved in raising and lowering except that the tuberculum axis involved is a transverse axis that passes through the centers of the articular tubercles of both sides. These movements are normally made with the teeth in contact. Obviously a dentition that is in occlusal harmony will facilitate these movements (Fig. 29).

Lateral movements of the mandible. The mechanics involved in lateral movements of the mandible are the most complex. Bertil Sonneson, basing his work upon the studies of Hjortsjö and co-workers, conducted a tomographic investigation of the temporomandibular joint during lateral movement in the living person. He confirmed the theoretical concepts of his colleagues.

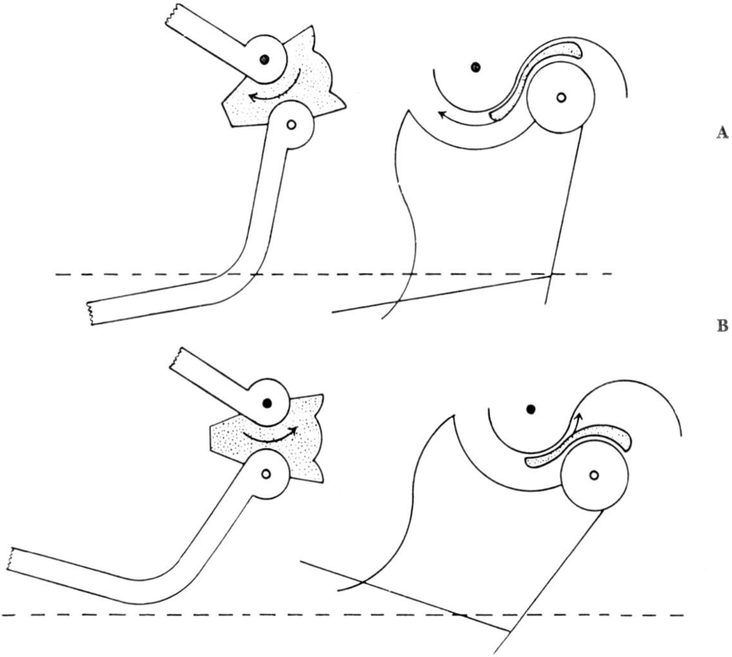

Fig. 29. A, Tuberculum rotation with forward motion of the disk. **B,** Tuberculum rotation with backward rotation of the disk.

In order to understand lateral movement of the mandible, it is first important to realize that in normal chewing the magnitude of motion is not great. In addition, one must realize that for all of its seeming complexity only one other axis of rotation is added, namely a capitulum-tuberculum axis. Specifically this is an axis that passes transversely but obliquely through the center of the articular tubercle of one side to the center of the head of the mandible of the opposite side. During rotation about this axis, which occurs during lateral movement, the head of the mandible on the working side remains in the glenoid fossa. On the balancing side the head of the mandible rotates around the tuberculum-capitulum axis. In some cases the head of the mandible on

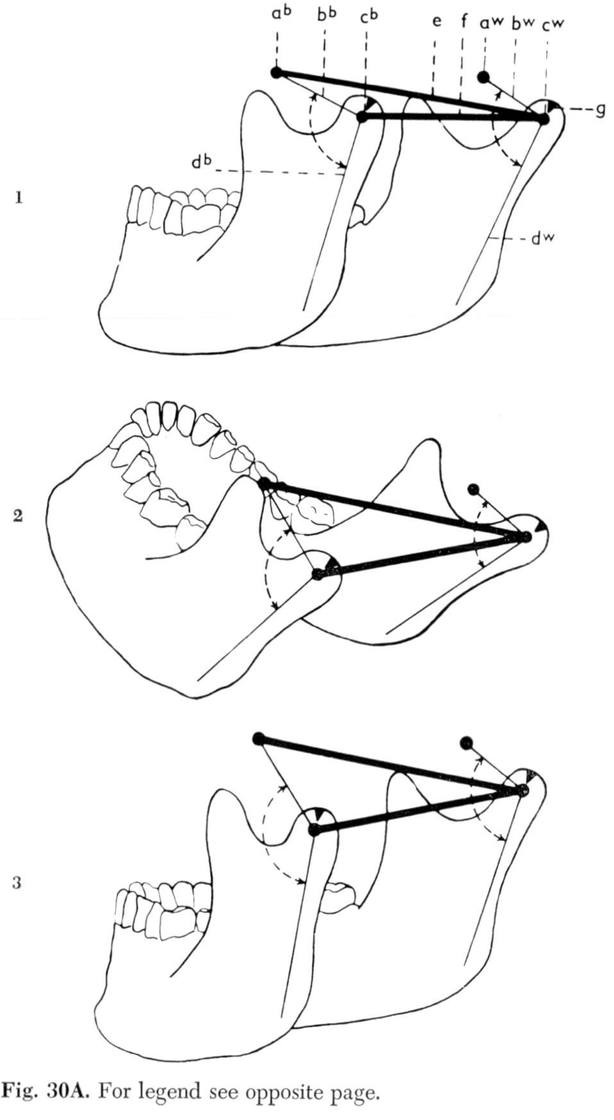

Fig. 30A. For legend see opposite page.

the balancing side will move forward. This motion does not affect the general concept since what is added is normal tuberculum rotation as in protrusive movement (Fig. 30, *A*).

Lateral shift of the mandible. There is evidence that in lateral excursions of the mandible the head of the mandible shifts laterally in what has come to be known as Bennett movement. This motion accompanying the other movements of the mandible gives the articulation the character of a screw joint. The significance of this movement is not clearly understood and, although it is not extensive, occasionally persons have been observed in whom it may be responsible for a type of joint sound that could be due to tripping of the sagittal margin of the condyle over the sagittal edge of the articular disk (Fig. 31).

The role of the occlusion. The occlusion is discussed in greater detail in subsequent chapters. For the present consider the relations of the dentition as part of a biomechanical system. It is apparent, since the mandible develops more rapidly than the dentition which it will bear, that the mandible has an organizing influence on the arrangement of the

---

Fig. 30A. Schematic drawing by Hjortsjö showing the mechanics involved in lateral movement of the mandible. **1,** Mandible in centric relation: $\mathbf{a}^b$, Center of the articular tubercle on the balancing side (tuberculum center); $\mathbf{b}^b$, a line joining the center of the articular tubercle with the center of the condyle on the balancing side; $\mathbf{c}^b$, center of the condyle on the balancing side; $\mathbf{d}^b$, ramus line drawn from the tuberculum center and parallel to the posterior margin of the condyle and the angle of the mandible, used to measure degree of tuberculum rotation; $\mathbf{a}^w$, $\mathbf{b}^w$, $\mathbf{c}^w$, $\mathbf{d}^w$, same as $\mathbf{a}^b$, $\mathbf{b}^b$, $\mathbf{c}^b$, and $\mathbf{d}^b$ on the working side; **e,** tuberculum (articular tubercle) capitulum (head of mandible) axis; **f,** capitulum axis (passing from center of left condylar head to center of right condylar head); **g,** blunt arrow indicating upper pole of head of mandible and following its movement. **2,** Only balancing tuberculum rotation has taken place on the balancing side. **3,** Bilateral rotation of head of mandible (capitulum rotation) has taken place. This process can occur without any capitulum rotation on the working side. In short hard strokes this is usually the case.

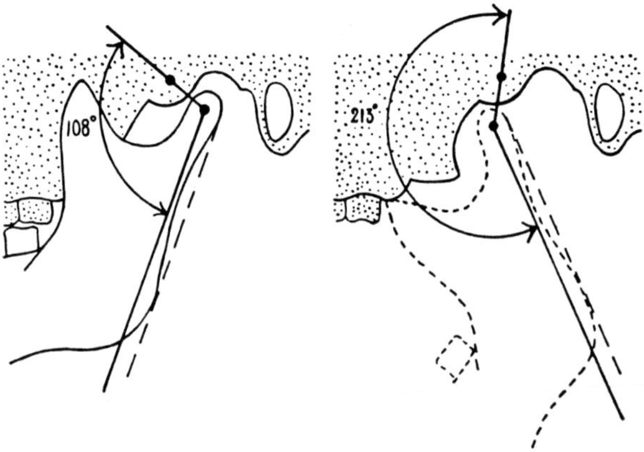

Fig. 30B. Schematic drawing of a method suggested by Hjortsjö for measuring the degree of rotation of the head of the mandible around the articular tubercle. Lines used to measure the angle in question are (1) a line joining the centers of the articular tubercle (tuberculum) with the center of the head of the mandible (capitulum), (2) line drawn parallel to a tangent to the posterior border of the head of the mandible and the angle of the mandible but through the center of the capitulum. Before movement, the angle is 108° (drawing on the left) and after forward rotation of the head of the mandible, 213° (drawing on the right). This method is applicable to measurement on cephalometrically accurate radiographs.

teeth and on the way in which they will eventually meet or occlude. It is common experience in orthodontics to find that gross malocclusion, for example in prognathism, is determined primarily by the growth pattern of the mandible and not by the number, size, or shape of the teeth.[6] This is generally true of those other deformities that are based essentially on disparities in growth of the mandible in relation to the maxilla, although many other factors such as habit, musculature, respiratory patterns, and deglutition play essential roles.

As a biomechanical system it is important to recognize that the mandibular growth imperative influences the intermaxillary relationships of the teeth and that the teeth in disharmonious arrangement will cause not gross deformity of the jaws and the joint relatively but rather minor changes. If malocclusion persists, the result will be disease at the main end points of stress, that is, in the periodontium and ultimately in the temporomandibular articulation in its broadest sense—bone, connective tissue, nerve, vascular supply, and muscles.

A B

C D

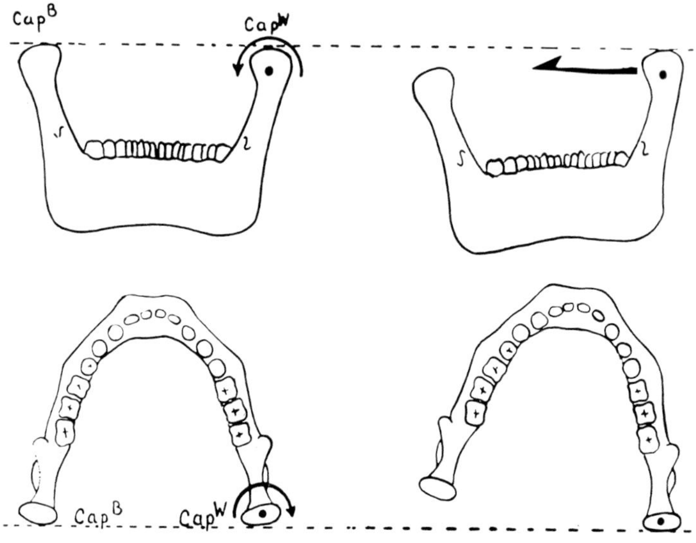

Fig. 31. A more conventional concept of the movements of the mandible in lateral excursion requiring two additional axes of rotation. **A,** An anteroposterior (ventral-dorsal) axis passing through the capitulum of the working side, **Cap**^{W}, and, **C,** a superior-inferior (cephalic-caudal) axis passing inferiorly through the center of the superior surface of the head of the mandible. **B,** The capitulum on the balancing side, **Cap**^{B}, undergoes tuberculum rotation while on the working side, **Cap**^{W}, the condyle remains in the glenoid fossa and rotates around the anteroposterior axis. The arrow in **B** indicates direction of lateral shift (screw joint, Bennett movement). **D,** View from above, the head of the mandible on the balancing side, **Cap**^{B}, undergoes tuberculum rotation forward while on the working side it remains in the fossa and rotates around a superior-inferior (cephalic-caudal) axis.

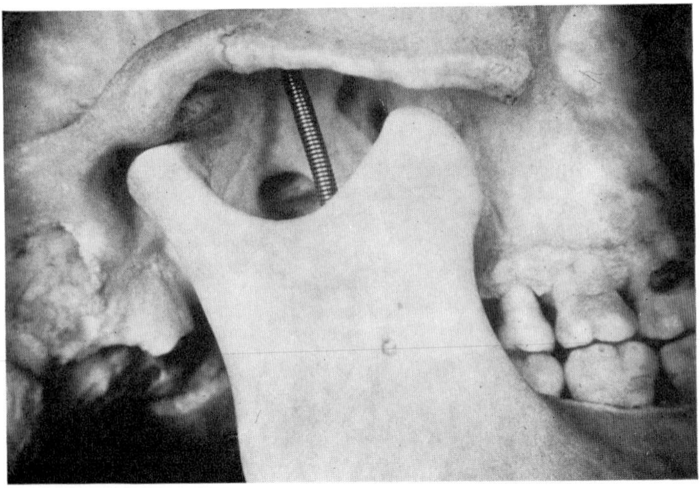

Fig. 32. Head of mandible in an anterior relation to the glenoid fossa. Note normal occlusion of the teeth, presence in an uncrowded state of the third molars, and excellent level of the alveolar bone. There is no evidence of bony disease and no irregularities of this joint.

One may say that the normal joint is not one in which the relationship of the head of the mandible to the glenoid fossa meets an arbitrary standard of position, since it is possible for this position to be anterior to the accepted one without producing joint disease, provided that the occlusion is a good and functioning one (Fig. 32). The normal joint is the final outcome of harmonious development of a functioning system whatever the adjustments and accommodations of size, shape, or position, whereas the abnormal joint is a failure in such an accommodation. This is perhaps the reason that joint dysfunction appears earlier in the adolescent female (whose structural maturity comes earlier) than in the adolescent male and why as an over-all observation it appears to be a disease of maturity and advanced age (for fuller discussion of this highly important clinical situation see Chapter 9).

A recent study by Gösta Lindblom is potentially of tremendous import, but its final evaluation must await further investigation. It included 318 patients and 2,000 roentgenograms were taken. Lindblom's conclusions were that in patients with normal and abnormal bites there was no significant correlation between the bite and either the anatomical features or the temporomandibular joint or the incidence of arthroses.

REFERENCES

1. Fomon, Samuel J. (editor): Growth and development of dental and skeletal tissue—clinical and biological aspects, Report of the Seventeenth Pediatric Research Conference, March 28-30, 1955, Boston, Mass., pp. 53-67. (Participants involved in this section: Sherwood L. Washburn, Ram S. Nanda, Robert E. Moyers, Coenraad F. A. Moorees, Josef Warkany, Frederick M. Deuschle, Theodore H. Ingalls, and A. Baird Hastings.)
2. Hjortsjö, Carl-Herman: Views on the general principles of joints and movements, Acta orthop. scand. **29**:134, 1959.
3. Hjortzjö, Carl-Herman: The mechanics of the temporomandibular joint, Department of Anatomy, University of Lund, Sweden, 1959, Archives of Scientific Films, No. 1.
4. Hjortsjö, Carl-Herman: A new apparatus for demonstrating the mechanics of the temporomandibular joint, Odontologisk revy **8**: 443, 1957.
5. Hjortsjö, Carl-Herman: Studies on the mechanics of the temporomandibular joint, Lund, 1951-1954, Lunds Universitets Arsskrift **51**: 2, 1954.
6. Lindblom, Gösta: Anatomy and function of the temporomandibular joint: clinical bite rehabilitation and roentgenographic findings in patients with arthrosis, Acta odont. scand. **17** (supp. 28):1, 1960.
7. Sonneson, Bertil: The temporomandibular joint during lateral movement of the mandible, a tomographical investigation on the living person, Odontologisk revy **7**:369, 1956.

CHAPTER 4

PATHOLOGY OF THE TEMPOROMANDIBULAR ARTICULATION

The temporomandibular joint, which is so often the site of functional disorders, is rarely involved in serious intrinsic disease.[22, 23] With the advent of antibiotics and chemotherapy in the treatment of infectious diseases even osteomyelitis with its crippling deformity of the mandible has become a rarity.[24] Congenital deformities due to agenesis, ankylosis, and untreated condylar fractures occurring during a period of significant growth are the only remaining disorders that result in severe underdevelopment of the mandible.[23] Other congenital conditions to be described in this chapter do not seriously affect form or function and are often discovered fortuitously in a radiograph. It can be said that intrinsic disease of the temporomandibular articulation is not the clinician's main area of concern. Temporomandibular joints with normal configurations and normal adnexa *do* present a problem, but the disease is mainly functional. Nevertheless, it is important for the practitioner to familiarize himself with the range of disease that can affect this joint if only to deepen his understanding of the total problem. This background of knowledge will enable him to provide the reassurance that his patients require, since most patients who complain of joint pain or disability are convinced that they are suffering from a serious disorder. In a sense then, this chapter is concerned more with the problems of the clinician than with the problems of the patient.

GENERAL CONSIDERATIONS

Many structures in addition to the bone ends need to be considered in joint disease. The overlying skin, the joint capsule, the ligaments, synovial membrane, cartilage (in this case fibrocartilage), and the periarticular tissues immediately adjacent to the joint can be involved in disease that affects the function of the joint. The synovial cavities, which are not really cavities in health but are potentially so, are also separate areas for consideration. Normally the surfaces that line the synovial cavities are smooth and shiny, and the total fluid which is evenly spread over their surfaces would scarcely make a few drops.[5] In disease, effusion into these potential spaces will, because of actual lack of room, cause considerable pain and impairment of function in the joint. In addition, the muscles that actuate the joint may be the seat of problems referred to it. Generally speaking, mature joints are resistant to serious invasive disease such as neoplasia and acute infections but are more likely to be the seats of trouble for the "wear and tear" diseases and functional disturbances, which are more the result of muscular malfunction than the result of changes in the joint itself. It may be said that the chief insults to joint physiology lie in the dynamics of disturbed muscle function. The joint is primarily a passive structure that of itself would not be involved often in disease if it were always moved and used properly. The combination of the unique upright position of man and his employment of joints to express the strains and conflicts of life are as much to blame for the great amount of functional joint disease as anything else. When a man says he "feels something in his bones," he is referring to his most fundamental emotions whether they be pleasure or dread. These expressions belong, however, to maturity and suggest that functional diseases of joints are diseases of maturity. Modern urban man does not use his muscles and joints anywhere near their capacity. The habitué of exercise (for instance, the dancer or manual laborer) may develop the necessary joint flexibility as well as a set of conditioned reflexes for joint function that help to keep them free of functional disease.[20] Most of us who live a comparatively sedentary life suffer from disuse or, worse, from perversions of use unrelated to purposeful movement. The key to joint form as well as bone form is muscle function.

THE RELATIONSHIP OF FORM AND FUNCTION TO THE MASTICATORY APPARATUS

Since muscle function is the key to joint form and bone form, it would seem important to examine the relationship of form and function in the determination of the character of the masticatory apparatus.

As stated by the anthropologist Sherwood L. Washburn, "An interest in human evolution and in the varieties and forms of the human face during growth includes interest in the interrelations between bones, teeth and muscle of the facial system. . . . Muscles can make bone; muscles can decrease bone. Muscles can twist the face in one direction or another."*

Experimental work in comparative anatomy suggests that parts of the human mandible may vary independently of one another. The coronoid process varies with the degree of function of the temporal muscle. If the temporal muscle of a rat is sectioned early in life, the coronoid process fails to develop. The angle of the mandible grows in response to the function of the masseter muscle and the internal pterygoid muscle. The tooth-bearing portion of the mandible does not develop if the teeth do not erupt or if they are congenitally missing. This concept suggests division of the mandible into four independent segments: (1) the angle of the jaw; (2) the coronoid process; (3) the alveolar bone; and (4) the core of the mandible which consists of the head of the mandible (articular condyle), the ramus of the mandible, and the main part of the body of the mandible minus the alveolar bone. It is this

*Washburn, Sherwood L.: Growth and development of dental and skeletal tissue—clinical and biological aspects, Report of Seventeenth Ross Pediatric Research Conference, Boston, Mass., March 28-30, 1955.

last or basal part of the mandible that is responsive, in experiments on growth and development, to changes caused by hormones such as androgens and corticosteroids. (Fig. 33.)

One of the consequences of this concept is that in the study of the function of the masticatory apparatus, the zygomatic arch (which bears the origin of the masseter muscle), and the pterygoid plates of the sphenoid bone (which bear the origin of the pterygoid muscle) in addition to other related structures, must be considered as part of the masticatory apparatus although they are usually considered part of the face and the base of the skull. It is entirely possible that some instances of deep-seated pain are due to spasm at these insertions. Fortunately treatment of these muscles at the site

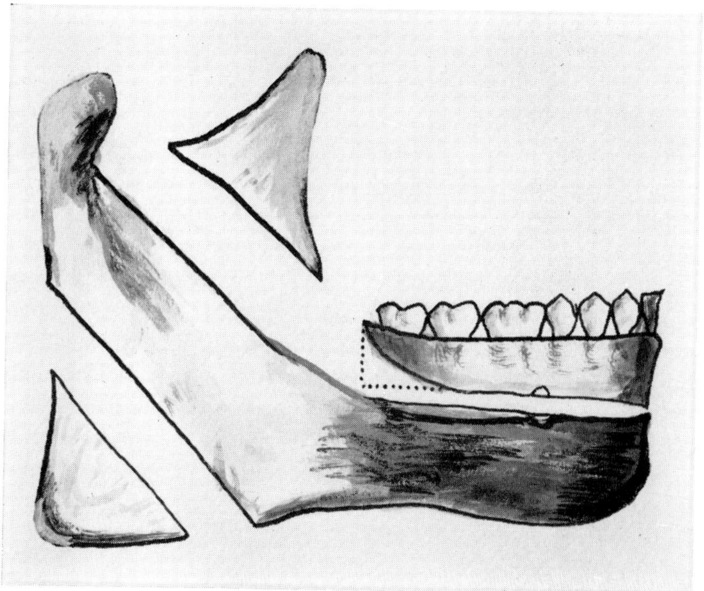

Fig. 33. Areas of the mandible that have independent developmental potential. Beginning at lower left (clockwise): angle of the mandible; main body of the mandible; coronoid process; tooth-bearing or alveolar portion of the mandible.

of their more accessible areas serves to relieve the symptoms. (See Chapter 7.)

Another consequence of this concept is of great importance in the management of severely resorbed mandibles. One of the more recent methods of treating these patients, who require complete mandibular restorations, has been by the use of metallic supraosseous implants bearing abutments upon which a modified type of partial denture is constructed. We have observed that the mental foramen of such a patient is often located upon the superior surface of the mandible and that dehiscences of the inferior alveolar canal are encountered. This is consistent with the view that the portion of the mandible that bears the teeth is an independent functional entity that disappears in time when the teeth are no longer present. (Fig. 33.)

DEVELOPMENTAL DISEASES

Congenital agenesis

Congenital malformations of the mandible and the temporomandibular articulation are rare especially when compared with the frequency, for example, of cleft palate. In infants, hypoplasia (marked underdevelopment) of the mandible is a condition of some importance because it produces respiratory difficulty.[4] The stridor that results is due to the lack of skeletal support of the tongue which therefore partially occludes the pharyngeal space. This condition can be relieved temporarily by pulling the tongue forward and by placing the infant in a prone (face downward) position. The temporomandibular joint in such a patient is normal though hypoplastic, that is, smaller.

Double condyle

This condition, which results in the replication of the head of the mandible usually in the anteroposterior aspect, occurs rarely. It causes no symptoms and therefore is not discovered except through radiography.

Hypoplastic deformities

Hypoplastic deformities are usually the result of hormonal disturbances. While they affect the total size of the mandible (increasing or decreasing it) or the development of the dentition, they do not affect the articulation. The temporomandibular joint may become involved later as the result of functional disturbances resulting from a disparity in size between the mandible and maxilla or from absence of dentition or severe disturbances in the arrangement of the dentition. In this sense, the temporomandibular joint is not usually a primary site of the disease. If the dentition and occlusion are functionally good, even a hypoplastic condylar head will function well. (Fig. 32.)

Gorlin, Chaudry, and Kelln reported a case of Pierre Robin syndrome consisting of underdevelopment of the mandible, cleft palate, and glossoptosis (tendency to swallow the tongue) in an infant.[4] They also report a case of lipochondrodystrophy (Hurler-Pfaundler syndrome, gargoylism), which results from deposition of abnormal substances, that is, a complex polysaccharide and a water soluble glycolipid, within the central nervous system. These patients show no signs characteristic of the syndrome at birth, but by the end of the first year they may have dwarfism, a large head and prominent forehead, saddle nose, lumbar kyphosis, hypoplasia of the second lumbar vertebra, hirsutism, umbilical hernia, enlarged liver and spleen, noisy mouth breathing, corneal clouding, mental retardation, congenital heart disorders, and limitation of joint movement *especially of the temporomandibular joint.*

Hyperplastic deformities

These rare conditions are due to overdevelopment of the joint. They are usually unilateral and therefore may result in disorders of movement. Few cases have been reported. However, Thoma reported an interesting case—a 37-year-old man in whom the condition may have existed from birth. At the time of treatment, partial condylectomy, there was considerable unilateral enlargement of the left head of the mandible with pain and inability to chew. Surgery did not completely eliminate the deformity, but the patient was free of pain and was able to chew.[21]

INFLAMMATORY DISEASES

Exostosis

Most exostosis of the head of the mandible is a reactive process marked by bony proliferation in response to a low-grade infection or some idiopathic inflammation which does not result in necrosis.[21] The ultimate result of continuation of such a process is either severe limitation in movement of the joint or finally ankylosis with or without fusion across the articular space.

Acute suppurative arthritis

The chief organisms that have been found in infections of the joint are staphylococci, streptococci, tubercle bacilli (rare), and gonococci.[23] Occasionally infections have resulted from abscesses of the overlying skin. During World War II some cases of joint infection resulted from wound contamination even though the initial wound did not penetrate the joint. Before the advent of antibiotics and potent chemotherapeutic agents, tenderness and inflammation of the temporomandibular articulation was often encountered in gonorrheal infections. Tenderness over the temporomandibular joint and the sternoclavicular joints was considered pathognomonic of gonorrheal disease.

Arthritis

Since more people are living longer, the problem of arthritis is becoming a matter of greater concern to the clinician. While the underlying pathogenesis of this group of diseases is as yet unknown, an examination of their general characteristics will aid the clinician in his diagnostic and therapeutic task.

The following classification of joint disease is recommended by the American Rheumatism Association and has been accepted by all hospitals as evidenced by its appearance in the *Standard nomenclature of diseases and operations.*

"1. Arthritis due to specific infections—specify organism when known
"2. Arthritis due to rheumatic fever
"3. Arthritis, rheumatoid—specify as multiple or of spine
"4. Degenerative joint disease, multiple due to unknown cause; osteoarthritis
"5. Arthritis due to direct trauma*
"6. Arthritis due to gout
"7. Neurogenic arthropathy†
"8. New growths of joints
"9. Hydrarthrosis, intermittent
"10. Periarticular fibrosites
"11. Diseases with which arthritis, arthropathy, or arthralgia are frequently associated (diagnose disease, list joint manifestation as symptom).‡"

Rheumatoid arthritis

Rheumatoid arthritis is a chronic proliferative arthritis which causes inflammatory changes in the joint and in the structures associated with it. It is a systemic disease, and its lesions may involve any part of the body. The inflammatory disease of joints however predominates and, if this condition persists, changes from fibrosis to bony ankylosis can occur in the joint. It is a chronic disease which may go into remission for no apparent reason but which recurs, so that the joint changes and the disability tend to be additive until the disease "burns itself out" in from 10 to 20 years.

---

*It is our opinion that this classification should be limited to actual direct physical trauma. For indirect trauma due to extra-articular causes, malocclusion, etc., category 11 is preferable.

†Myofascial trigger mechanisms may be included under this heading.

‡See No. 5 in classification.

Etiology. The exact etiology of rheumatoid arthritis is unknown; however, there is some evidence that it is related to a disturbance in the adrenal cortical hormones. Elevation of the serum titer of agglutinins against the beta-hemolytic streptococcus, which occurs with notable frequency in many patients after the first year of the disease, has led some to believe that this is the causative agent. Doubt has been cast upon this belief because there is evidence that this is a nonspecific response to abnormal serum proteins. Dentists have been concerned with following the latest medical opinion on the etiology of rheumatoid arthritis since the belief that a local infection caused the disease led to the extraction of many teeth that perhaps were innocent in this regard. Many endodontic procedures and periodontal treatment methods have been approached with caution and often set aside in favor of tooth extraction as a result of this view. Fortunately, later and more careful examination of the progress of patients who had "foci of infection" removed has led to the present view that the course of the disease was not altered. Most investigators and clinicians have abandoned this idea.

There seems to be some empirical evidence that psychogenic factors influence the course of rheumatoid arthritis; however, it is believed that the effect is not direct but may be related to the more complex mechanisms involved in the stress reaction.

The lesions in patients with rheumatoid arthritis have much in common with those of the other "collagen diseases" such as disseminated lupus erythematosis, scleroderma, periarteritis nodosa, rheumatic fever, and dermatomyositis. The chief finding is increased amounts of hyaluronic acid, one of the protein mucopolysaccharides found in connective tissue.[5] In this disease the hyaluronic acid exists in an incompletely polymerized form that renders the synovial fluid less viscous than normal. Since hyaluronidase, the "spreading factor," which is responsible for depolymerizing hyaluronate is not found in the fluid of joints or the periarticular tissues, it is believed that the deficiency in complete polymerization of hyaluronate is due to lack of its proper synthesis by connective tissue cells.

Other opinions relate to the possibility that rheumatoid arthritis is an example of an autoimmune mechanism, that is, a reaction between an antigen (abnormal protein) and an antibody (autoantibody).[17] The reaction is believed to be responsible for the local changes that occur in the fibrous tissue. There is much experimental evidence to support this view.

Cortisone (17-hydroxy-11-dehydrocorticosterone) has a dramatic effect upon rheumatoid arthritis. The doses used exceed those required to treat true adrenal insufficiency as it occurs in Addison's disease, which would indicate that cortisone has a direct pharmacological effect rather than correcting a deficiency.[5]

Pathology. The early local changes closely resemble chronic inflammation with infiltration of lymphocytes into the synovial tissues followed by edema and hyperemia. Later there is proliferation from the synovial surfaces with resultant destruction of cartilage, resorption of bone, and ankylosis. The proliferating synovial membrane is densely infiltrated with lymphocytes and capillaries and thus developes into a kind of chronic granulation tissue, "pannus." This pannus invades the joint spaces so that often the articular disk is eroded from both sides. It is this effect plus the resorption of bone that is responsible for the final reparative bridge that results in bony ankylosis. In less severe varieties of the disease the pannus may be responsible for a fibrous ankylosis,[19] however in the temporomandibular joint, which is one of those frequently involved, the resultant lack of mandibular function as distinguished from the effects of bony ankylosis is purely academic.

Relation of symptoms to pathology. Thickening of the capsule and the interarticular disk may be responsible for early pain and joint noises because of both the space-occupying nature of the proliferation of tissue and the result of muscle spasm. Changes in the occlusion of the teeth may result from dislocation of the joint due to capsular thickening, disk invasion, or bony resorption. It is important, therefore, to make continual examinations of the occlusal relationships in such patients and to initiate those adjustments that seem indicated. Failure to do so will tend to aggravate the inflammatory reaction by adding a traumatic factor.

Epidemiology. The incidence of rheumatoid arthritis is highest in women between the ages of 30 and 40, although it can occur in infants and may occur in the ninth decade of life. There seems to be a familial tendency. Of interest to the dentist is the fact that attacks of rheumatoid arthritis may be precipitated by surgical procedures. *Surgery for such patients should be approached with caution and if required should be done in easy stages.*

Clinical course. Rheumatoid arthritis has a slow and often insidious start. The patient will give a history of fatigue, anorexia, and weight loss. Usually when the dentist sees the patient he has been receiving treatment from a physician for some time and has often been considered psychoneurotic since the early joint pains may be slight and the muscle spasms may be vague and fleeting. Unfortunately, many patients do not consult their physician during the early stages of the disease and so will be seen after joint symptoms have advanced to the stage of swelling and acute pain. Such patients presenting the chief complaint of temporomandibular pain and swelling who give a long and sometimes vague history of mild fever, weight loss, lassitude, or some of the other symptoms mentioned should be referred promptly for a thorough physical examination. It is of value to elicit a history of pain in other joints. Joints most frequently involved are the knees, interphalangeal joints of the hands, the wrists, hips, sternoclavicular joints, temporomandibular, ankles, and joints of the feet. The spine may also be involved, and the patient may complain of pain when seated in the dental chair especially if the headrest or backrest is improperly adjusted.

Rheumatoid arthritis is not usually a disease of unremitting progression. There are many remissions and many relapses. In the early stages joint movement is painful, and later there may be muscle atrophy. This is more characteristic of the extremities. In the jaws the massive muscles and the complex arrangement by which muscle groups can take over the impaired function of involved muscles tends to mask the atrophy that does occur. Many patients adjust their diet over a period of years in order to accommodate to this decreased level of muscle function. The deformities of flexion that occur because flexor muscles are stronger than extensors do not occur in the jaws since normally the weak extensors do not play a great role in jaw function. However, protrusive movement may be impaired because of the close association of the external pterygoid muscles with the joint space and, as was mentioned before, may be the cause of changes in occlusal relationships. In the early phases when muscle spasm is a greater feature of the disease, false protrusive relations may develop. In the later stages, marked more commonly by muscle atrophy, retrusive relations may occur as the external pterygoid muscles weaken.

Treatment. It would be a grave error to attempt to treat rheumatoid arthritis as a local disease of the temporomandibular joint. If there is any suspicion that a painful temporomandibular joint may be the result of rheumatoid arthritis, the patient should be referred promptly to a physician since this is a systemic disease. However, after the patient is under the care of a physician the dentist will play an important role in the dental management of the case for many years.

The dentist may be involved in the earliest phase of treatment in the event that the mandibular joint is involved early. This is actually a frequent occurrence since many patients who have this as a first symptom may consult their dentist first.

It is generally considered a mistake to treat rheumatoid arthritis by systemic medication while ignoring the involved joint.[5] The principles of therapy for the joint are rest, carefully graded exercise, and heat or cold, or contrasting applications. Therapy for rheumatoid arthritis in the jaw will involve removing occlusal interference, making the proper adjustment for vertical opening, and altering the diet. While rest will help relieve the pain of a "hot joint," excessive immobilization will result in a stiff and even more painful joint during subsequent function. Injection of local anesthetics around the temporomandibular joint will often produce dramatic relief of pain. During this period of freedom from pain exercise has its chief value since the vicious cycle of pain, followed by muscle spasm, followed by pain is interrupted. The chief value of exercise is prevention of muscle atrophy which results from disuse.

While physiotherapy and regulation of the diet are primary in the treatment of rheumatoid arthritis, there are specific measures that the physician may elect to use. The two chief drugs that have been used are gold sodium thiosulfate and cortisone. Of the two, cortisone shows the greater promise, although no present treatment has shown uniformly beneficial results.

Prognosis. Patients who have asymmetric joint involvement or disease in a few joints have a better prognosis than those who have generalized joint involvement. Unfortunately, patients with symptoms in both temporomandibular joints usually have the disease in many joints. Other factors that indicate a more favorable prognosis are disease of less than 12 months' duration before treatment, absence of weight loss, age under 40, males, mild joint symptoms, and stable temperament. About 5 per cent of patients with rheumatoid arthritis will never be free of the disease, although they have many remissions of long duration. While rheumatoid arthritis is not generally considered a direct cause of death, it does contribute to mortality because it opens the way to other sepsis, causes debilitation, and may result in degenerative disease of vital organs, principally in the deposition of amyloid.

Variants of rheumatoid arthritis

There are several recognized variants of rheumatoid arthritis. Still's disease is the term given to rheumatoid arthritis of children. When pigmentation of the skin and leukopenia are outstanding features it is called Felty's disease, and psoriatic arthritis when it is accompanied by psoriasis, but the variant of rheumatoid arthritis that is of most importance to the dentist is rheumatoid spondylitis or Marie-Strümpell disease.[21] Thoma reported several cases that resulted in ankylosis of the temporomandibular joints. The distinguishing features of this variety of rheumatoid arthritis are that it occurs chiefly in men and results in stiffening of the spine, diminished chest expansion, low-grade fever, and tenderness over the spine and chest. The temporomandibular joints are not infrequently involved. In this disease the object of treatment, after local pain and muscle spasm are controlled by means of physiotherapy and local anesthetics, is prevention of fusion. The dentist has a great responsibility in rheumatoid spondylitis, and he must use ingenuity in devising exercises that involve all of the mandibular excursions as well as a carefully planned program of massage in the office and in the home. Chewing-gum exercises and careful and complete chewing of food followed by local application of heat should be encouraged. The physician will advise deep-breathing exercises and attention to good posture to ensure maximum expansion of the chest and if fusion of the spine is to occur, to attempt to have it occur in a position of good posture. The dentist can advise regular opening and closing of the jaws during deep breathing and proper closure and opening of the jaws as well as good swallowing habits to assist in the achievement of good posture, since proper balance of the jaws affects the posture of the head and the neck.

Again it is necessary to caution that rheumatoid spondylitis is a systemic disease and that treatment must be pursued with this fact in mind. Local joint therapy is important, but general medical therapy is primary.

This disease tends to burn itself out in from one to two decades. After that time surgical correction of fused joints may be attempted and in the case of the temporomandibular joint is most essential. Excision of the fused juncture with the interposition of plastic substances or layers of soft tissue will produce good results, although if the fusion occurred early in life a serious cosmetic defect due to an underdeveloped mandible may also have to be corrected. At any rate the treatment of these patients requires the cooperative effort of many professional disciplines including all of the members of the usual rehabilitative team.

Degenerative joint disease (osteoarthritis)

Degenerative joint disease or osteoarthritis, as the first of its names indicates, is a disease of "wear and tear" and has its effects upon the joint itself. It is not a systemic disease and therefore when it occurs in the temporomandibular articulation the etiological factors must be sought in some disturbance in joint relation or in some disorder or perversion of function. Of course, the underlying factor may be normal aging of the tissues of the joint, but this does not necessarily have to result in disease, that is, discomfort or disability in function. Many patients who show joint changes do not have symptoms and therefore have no complaints referable to the joint.

Etiology. In the normal aging process the chief change in joints, and the temporomandibular joint is no exception, is loss of elasticity of the structures. In addition, continued trauma will cause surface changes on the head of the mandible and the associated disk surfaces resulting in bony elevations on the bone and pits and folds on the adjacent disk surface (Fig. 23). A similar process of spurring and surface defect will occur on the surface of the articular tubercle and its adjacent disk surface. Erosions of the disk may occur and may perhaps explain the appearance in dissection rooms of a certain number of specimens with perforated articular disks. Another reason for these changes is perhaps the decreasing vascularity of the parts that occurs with aging. Cartilage, fibrocartilage, and bone subjected to continued traumas do not repair quickly. As a result the degenerative change tends to be progressive. The slower this process is, the less marked will be the symptoms. Indeed, in many instances the disease progresses so slowly that the normal decrease in muscle vigor and activity neatly matches the degenerative change, creating a successful balance between structure and function with a resultant absence of handicap or symptoms.

Clinical course. Degenerative joint disease as just described produces symptoms in less than 5 per cent of patients. The percentage is higher if the temporomandibular joint is affected because the changes that it is subject to as the result of the loss of teeth, vertical dimension, and sudden shifts in neuromuscular equilibrium that result produce symptoms in a larger proportion of patients. Also, many emotional and psychological factors that accompany aging and the process of aging influence the level of complaint. Fortunately, in other joints degenerative joint disease does not cause invalidism, but in the temporomandibular joint it may become the basis for prolonged complaint related to the wearing of dentures or other restorations of the dentition, partial or complete. It is important to be sure that the patient has degenerative joint disease and not rheumatoid arthritis. The patient with degenerative joint disease may arise in the morning feeling stiffness and some discomfort which will gradually lessen with function only to return if function is excessive during the day. The patient with rheumatoid arthritis has pain at rest and also during function. The chief clinical finding in degenerative joint disease is thickening or enlargement of the joint without marked local tenderness. Effusions into the joint space are rare, but noise of a grating character may be heard. Clicking is not an outstanding feature but may be related to muscle imbalance or dysfunction and often predates the degenerative change by many years. Radiating pain occurs because of pressure and myofascial trigger mechanisms due to malfunction, poorly compensated function, or gross malocclusion of the natural dentition, or of dentures following restorative procedures. In brief, degenerative changes in the temporomandibular joint do not permit it to adjust as readily to changes in maxillomandibular relations as does a younger or more normal joint.

Diagnosis. The chief diagnostic modality is the radiograph which will show the irregularities of the articular surfaces commonly referred to as "spurring." In addition there may be significant alteration in the position of the articulating surfaces as well as a decrease in joint spaces. No specific clinical finding or alteration in systemic homeostasis is characteristic of degenerative joint disease. Gross destruction of joint surfaces should be viewed with suspicion, and in these cases tumors, especially metastatic carcinoma or infiltrations of multiple myeloma, must be ruled out.

Treatment. Reassurance is of primary importance in the management of patients with degenerative joint disease. Sometimes an explanation of the nature of the disease with a concomitant promise that much can be done to provide comfort will go a long way toward relieving anxiety and making the patient more amenable to the difficulties that the period of adjustment to prosthesis will incur.

Relief of trauma is the next essential step in therapy. This can be accomplished only by the most thoroughgoing investigation of mandibular function in all of its complex ramifications. It may be said that nowhere in dentistry is attention to every aspect of occlusion and masticatory function as important as in treating these patients. Exercise is important, but fatigue should be avoided.

Local heat and massage of not only the joint but also the musculature, particularly the masseters and the temporals, are helpful. Infiltration of local anesthetic is rarely required. Relief of muscle spasm that may originate outside the joint is far more important. There is no specific medication, but salicylates have beneficial results in patients with this disease if used in sufficient doses. Ten grains (0.65 Gm.) of acetylsalicylic acid administered three times daily will help relieve the soreness that may be a feature of the disease in some patients. In any event, unlike rheumatoid arthritis for which systemic medication is the main emphasis of therapy and the physician the chief therapist, for degenerative disease of the temporomandibular joint, physical means are the mainstays of therapy and the dentist is the prime therapist in its management.

Prognosis. Degenerative joint disease is rarely a crippling disease, but the degree of comfort and function that the patient may expect is directly proportional to the energy, intelligence, and zeal of his dentist in seeking out and correcting any traumatogenic factor in his masticatory apparatus.

Chronic traumatic arthritis

Major trauma to the temporomandibular joint such as fracture, severe dislocation or sprain resulting from a direct blow can be responsible for arthritis of the joint. As a contributing factor to the later development of degenerative joint disease or as a complicating factor in rheumatoid arthritis it is perhaps not as important as continued microtraumas that result from masticatory dysfunction and malfunction. In other joints of the body, minor but continued trauma has been recognized as a more important etiological agent in the production of joint disease than a major single trauma. The view is held that the joint selected for localization of arthritis may be the one that has been subjected to repeated but intrinsically minor trauma. It is therefore apparent that this places treatment of dysfunction and malfunction of the temporomandibular joint and the mechanisms of the masticatory apparatus in the category of preventive therapy. It is impossible to predict whether a patient will develop degenerative joint disease or rheumatoid arthritis, but it is possible to eliminate to a large degree the incidence of these diseases in the temporomandibular articulation by first preserving the dentition and by restoring it in part or in whole, with proper attention to normal and vigorous function.

Psychogenic rheumatism

It has been well established that emotional disease affects the clinical course of all chronic joint disease and in the case of the temporomandibular joint may initiate the symptoms of joint pain without the presence of observable local or systemic pathology. It has been demonstrated by Kydd in 30 subjects with temporomandibular joint syndrome that 23 were emotionally disturbed and that in 29 abnormal electromyographic patterns were eliminated, even without occlusal equilibration, when the subject was relaxed, comfortable, and not faced by a situation threatening his security.[11] This excellent study further points out that "intrinsic oral trauma from malocclusion appears to have an enhanced etiological significance in the origin of temporomandibular joint syndrome when it took place in the setting of a threatening life situation emanating from difficulties in social and interpersonal adjustments which engendered generalized skeletal muscle hyperfunction."*

This type of problem in which there are symptoms but no objective clinical or laboratory findings and which occurs in patients with emotional problems or frank emotional disease was frequently encountered among young men in military service during World War II. One of the factors that may tend to confuse the picture is that many of these patients give a familial history of joint disease. The treatment of these pa-

---

*Kydd, W. L.: Psychosomatic aspects of temporomandibular joint dysfunction, J.A.D.A. **59**:31, 1959.

tients consists of the removal of all interfering occlusal abnormalities, but this often does not eliminate the problem and may even aggravate it. The underlying emotional disease needs to be dealt with, but the dentist will find it extremely difficult to suggest psychiatric treatment until he has established a doctor-patient relationship marked by confidence and understanding. The main problem is how swiftly one can move in this direction without giving the patient the impression of wanting to abandon or reject him. However, a common mistake is to increase the frequency of visits and the number of treatments. This will reinforce the idea that the dentist is dealing with significant physical disease and will make future psychiatric referral more difficult.

The dentist must also consider the economic factor since these patients will waste a great deal of time. It is also important to consider, in this connection, the effect upon the dentist who often becomes the victim of frustration and finally terminates the treatment in a burst of hostility and rejection. The sooner the nature of the disease is recognized the better. The sooner the basic occlusal problem is dealt with expeditiously the better. A well-directed, well-rationalized treatment plan, ending with a clear statement on the part of the therapist that he has removed the contributing physical cause of the difficulty but that definitive treatment will depend on relief of tensions and anxieties will clear the air and bring the treatment closer to the reality factors involved. There is danger in this approach, if it is made without kindness and real concern for the patient's emotional state. It is better to delay this phase and not to treat than to treat in the absence of such a clear mutual understanding. It goes without saying that it would be disastrous to deal with a case of actual joint disease in this fashion. On the other hand, one must be prepared to deal with the element of emotional disease in the presence of clinically observable joint disease. Other chapters in this book deal with the need to thoroughly investigate the nature of the patient's complaint.

Puzzling and unusual causes of arthritis in the temporomandibular joint

Telephone syndrome. Patients occasionally give the following puzzling set of symptoms: pain in the temporomandibular joint, usually the left; sometimes tingling and numbness of the fingers, especially the little finger on the same side; pain in the shoulder or side of the neck on the same side; and tingling or numbness of one or more of the toes on the same side. After listening to these complaints the physician is likely to consider his patient either demented or a victim of a rare or perhaps unknown disease. Because the only objective sign is tenderness over the affected temporomandibular joint, the examining clinician, usually a physician, refers the patient to a dentist in the belief that this is an example of joint disease secondary to malocclusion. The other complaints are brushed aside as confirming evidence that many patients with temporomandibular joint complaints are well known to be neurotic.

The whole puzzling train of symptoms begins to make sense when a history of continued use of the telephone is elicited. The disease is found in persons whose occupation requires them to use a telephone for the better part of a working day, especially if this involves them in situations of tension, high pressure, and competition. These illustrative cases are reported here for the first time.

Case A. R. This young executive with a chief complaint of pain and tenderness over the left temporomandibular joint and tingling of his left little finger stated that he had recently been involved in a promotional program that required almost continual use of the telephone. He assumed a position at his desk in which the telephone was pressed firmly against his left ear while he leaned on his elbow. After his symptoms were explained, he reported that he had "caught himself" pressing the telephone against his ear with greater force when he was annoyed or anxious to impress his listener. His elbow rested against the end of a desk pad and so the symptom of tingling could be explained by the resultant compression of the ulnar nerve which passes superficially over the medial condyle of the humerus in the elbow joint, the funny bone. Use of a microphone device instead of a hand telephone resulted in disappearance of his complaint.

Case W. K. This 47-year-old director of a division of a large company complained of pain and tenderness over the left temporomandibular joint, pain in the shoulder and neck on the left side, and numbness and tingling of the little and ring fingers. He used the telephone almost continuously while sitting in a swivel chair with the telephone pressed hard against his ear and his elbow braced against the arm of the chair. The patient's symptoms disappeared when he became conscious of the habit and took corrective measures.

Case G. W. This 37-year-old woman, administrator of a trade union, was referred to her dentist by her physician with the request that she be examined for possible malocclusion to explain a Costen's syndrome. CBC and blood chemistry were normal as was the physical examination except for tenderness over the left temporomandibular joint and the tip of the left coronoid process when the mouth was open. The patient complained of pain over the left temporomandibular joint, behind the left ear, numbness and tingling over the left cheek and malar bone area, numbness in the fingers of the left hand, pain in the neck and shoulder, pain and numbness of some of the toes of the left foot, and pain in the rump. She was able to open her mouth over 6 cm. without pain and without any bruit in the joint. Dental examination revealed tenderness intraorally over the insertion of the temporal muscle, the internal pterygoids, and extraorally over the masseter muscle, pain on palpation over the insertion of the sternomastoid muscle and the superior surface of the trapezius muscle. The patient had been told by her physician prior to her visit that her almost constant use of the telephone and tight brassiere straps might be responsible for her symptoms. She loosened the straps and began to hold the telephone in her right hand, and at the time she was seen by the dentist the severity of her symptoms had decreased. Massage and local heat applications were advised and gave good results.

Postural arthritis. Occasionally adolescent patients complain of pain over one temporomandibular joint with the infrequent occurrence of a single sound at the beginning of opening and deviation of the mandible to the affected side. In some of these patients mixed dentition makes it difficult to evaluate the occlusal factor, but the deviations from normal are not remarkable. The patient gives a history of long periods of study at a desk or table with the head cocked to one side leaning upon the elbow-supported hand or fist. If the condition is of long duration, fatigue upon prolonged chewing will occasionally be a presenting symptom and the clicking will also occur upon closure. The following case is typical.

Case S. P. This 17-year-old student was in excellent health and in no acute distress. Her chief complaint was pain over both temporomandibular joints which was more severe over the left one. She had clicking of the joints when she opened her mouth wide and after doing so felt that the jaw was fatigued. She also described a spontaneous click when she bit into an apple and jaw fatigue after prolonged chewing. She gave a history of long periods of study during which she supported her chin with her hand. The symptoms were relieved with minor occlusal adjustment. In addition, she responded well to midline mandibular exercises and rest. She was more aware of her study habit and tried to correct it. Her condition was markedly relieved.

Arthritis due to an occult single trauma. This condition is puzzling because the interval between the occurrence of the injury and the appearance of the symptoms may be such that the patient does not associate the pain with the event. Careful history taking will uncover the specific incident. Examination will reveal a point of tenderness rather than general pain in the joint itself. The location of this area of pain is consistent and may be elicited in the same way as one would elicit pain in the area of a bruise. The occlusion may be abnormal, however the short history and sudden appearance should help in making a differential diagnosis. Persons who have pain in a joint due to an injury acquired from body contact sports do not usually seek to consultation or treatment since the pain is clearly associated with the injury and the individual expects it to gradually disappear along with his other bruises, as indeed it does. The following case illustrates the typical problem resulting from an occult single trauma.

Case H. W. This 53-year-old housewife's chief complaint was pain in the right temporomandibular joint which annoyed her and made it difficult for her to sleep on her right side. She was able to point to a specific point of tenderness anterior to the head of the right mandible and stated that there was some pain on moderate opening but only mild pain on chewing. Five years before, she had had rheumatoid arthritis but was presently in remission. She wore complete dentures which were excellently constructed and no obvious functional abnormality was noted. After careful questioning she stated that her first symptoms appeared when she awoke one morning three days before the consultation. Her first feeling was that her arthritis had flared up, but she was puzzled by this since she felt exceptionally well, so well in fact, that she had done more housecleaning in the past week than she had attempted to do in the past year. Further exploration revealed that in storing heavy winter clothing she had struck the side of her face against the corner of a clothes cabinet inside a closet. She did not consider the injury severe and had forgotten it. When this fact was revealed the patient immediately understood the origin of her pain. Radiographs were negative. The pain gradually subsided in about two weeks and left no residual handicap. The rather slow recovery may have possibly been due to the underlying rheumatoid state. Salicylates (aspirin 0.6 Gm.) three or four times daily helped to reduce the discomfort, especially during sleep.

NEOPLASTIC DISEASE

Tumors of the temporomandibular joint and the head of the mandible are considered to be rare. This is borne out by the sparse reporting of tumors of this area in the existing literature. In the past seven years additional case material has been reported, but the occurrence of tumors of the temporomandibular joint and the head of the mandible is still rather infrequent. Some writers, in particular Thoma, believe that this scarcity may be due to difficulty in diagnosis. In the seven years since he stated this opinion, greater interest has been shown in the temporomandibular joint without any commensurate increase in the reports of cases of neoplasia. Therefore the infrequency may reflect a fact.

Benign

Cyst. One case was reported by Ivy in 1927.[23] This appears as a radiolucent area, but the diagnosis can be made only by biopsy. Other lesions also produce osteolytic areas.

Osteoma. McNichol and Roger reported thirty cases in 1946.[23] Previously Gruca and Meisels reported thirteen cases in 1926.[23] This is by far the most frequent tumor of the head of the mandible, but it must be distinguished from hypertrophy. In osteoma the enlargement is essentially of the articular condyle itself, whereas in hypertrophy the entire condylar process is enlarged. In both instances a deformity of the entire jaw results with accompanying disturbances in the occlusion and sometimes in total mandibular function. Thoma states that blocking of function is to be expected more frequently in osteoma.

Chondroma. Ivy reported one cartilage containing tumor of the condyle in 1927, and Shackelford and Brown reported two cases of osteochondroma in 1943.[23] In spite of the fact that the condylar portion of the mandible is enchondral bone, it is surprising that this tumor is so rare. The symptoms are the same as for osteoma, and the diagnosis is essentially histopathological.

Myxoma. One case of myxoma of the condyle was reported by Thoma in 1947.[23] This was an expanding trabeculated lesion which caused progressive deafness and injury to the vestibular nerve (Meniere's syndrome).

Benign giant cell tumor. Hofer reported two cases in 1952 both of which occurred in young patients in their second decade.[23]

Fibro-osteoma (ossifying fibroma and myxoma). Miles in 1951 reported a case of a solitary lesion which was osteolytic in nature but showed trabeculation.[23] Thoma in 1954 reported a large cystic area in a 27-year-old woman who gave a history of a blow to the jaw. The pathological examination showed myxomatous tissue in which bone trabeculae were in the process of formation, hence the diagnosis of ossifying myxoma.[22]

Fibrous dysplasia. Thoma reported one case in 1960. This tumor involved the neck of the condyle of a 28-year old woman and was responsible for facial asymmetry and a marked cross-bite. The body of the mandible of this patient showed other areas of radiolucency.[23]

Malignant

Fibrosarcoma. Thoma saw a 58-year-old man in 1947 with a soft, tender, fluctuant tumor in the right preauricular area which after excision was diagnosed as a fibrosarcoma of the joint capsule. Local excision resulted in a 7-year cure.[22]

Chondrosarcoma. This extremely rare tumor was reported by Gingrass in 1954.[23] This tumor appeared as a swelling in front of the ear and displaced the head of the mandible posteriorly. The anterior surface of the condyle was eroded while the articular surface showed bone deposition.

Metastatic carcinoma. Zimmer reported a case in 1941 of a 53-year-old patient.[23] The tumor, a basiloma, was responsible for extensive destruction of the glenoid fossa as well as the condyle. Thoma reported a similar case in 1947. In 1956 Blackwood reported a case in a woman aged 24, whose primary tumor was in the breast. Blackwood cites Box and Cahn to support his contention that it is because of the presence of red marrow in the head of the adult condyle that this area is more susceptible to metastatic tumor. Salman and Langel in 1954 reported metastatic carcinoma of the head and the neck of the mandibular condyle as a result of metastasis from primary carcinoma of the uterus.[1]

Metastatic melanosarcoma. T. Cholnoki of Columbia University Postgraduate Hospital reported a case of melanosarcoma of the condyle arising from a primary melanosarcoma of the toe.[22, 23]

Multiple myeloma. Hoeppel reported one case in 1938, and Cohen and Meyers reported a case in 1956. These cases were incidental to generalized systemic disease.[23]

Metastatic adenocarcinoma. Thoma reports a case in a 49-year-old man who gave a history of pain of four months' duration. The preoperative diagnosis was osteomyelitis which the clinical and radiographic evidence seemed to support. The true nature of the condition was established at operation and was confirmed by pathological study.[22]

Transitional cell carcinoma. A 51-year-old woman treated by Holland and reported by Thoma came to treatment because of pain and swelling in the temporomandibular joint that had been treated with immobilization and heat. At operation, in spite of the fact that the radiograph showed no destruction of the temporomandibular joint, extensive malignant invasion of the glenoid fossa, the condyle, and the zygomatic arch was found.[22]

SUMMARY

In Thoma and Goldman's textbook *Oral pathology*,[23] an excellent treatment of the diseases of the temporomandibular joint appears in greater detail. In Thoma's review of tumors of the condyle and temporomandibular joint he states the following:

"Tumors of the mandibular joint are considered rare. They produce symptoms which are often difficult to distinguish from those caused by the more common arthroses. Therefore, the diagnostician must be alert, keeping in mind the occurrence of primary and metastatic tumors in this region."*

To this might be added a note of caution which pertains to the reliance upon radiographs of the joint which are limited to the area of the articulation by means of masking. These views are useful and convenient; however, if any intrinsic disease of the joint is present, lateral plates of the entire area including the adjacent structures and tomography may be necessary to make a diagnosis.

REFERENCES

1. Blackwood, H. J. J.: Metastatic carcinoma of the mandibular condyle, Oral Surg., Oral Med. & Oral Path. **9**:1318, 1956.
2. Choukas, N. C., and Sicher, H.: The structure of the temporomandibular joint, Oral Surg., Oral Med. & Oral Path. **13**:1203, 1960.
3. Cohen, B. C., and Meyers, H. A.: Multiple myeloma involving the

---

*Thoma, K. H.: Tumors of the condyle and temporomandibular joint, Oral Surg., Oral Med. & Oral Path. **7**:1091, 1954.

temporomandibular joint, Oral Surg., Oral Med. & Oral Path. **9**: 1274, 1956.

4. Gorlin, R. J., Chaudry, A. P., Kelln, E. E.: Oral manifestations of the Fitzgerald-Gardner, Pringle-Bourneville, Robin, adrenogenital, and Hurler-Pfaundler syndromes, Oral Surg., Oral Med. & Oral Path. **13**:1233-1243, 1960.
5. Harrison, T. R.: Principles of internal medicine, New York, 1953, The Blakiston Co.
6. Hayashi, T.: How cells move, Scient. Am. **202**:184, 1961.
7. Holter, H.: How things get into cells, Scient. Am. **202**:167, 1961.
8. Johnson, B. W.: New method of reduction of acute dislocation of the temporomandibular articulations, J. Oral Surg. **16**:501, 1958.
9. Katz, B.: How cells communicate, Scient. Am. **202**:209, 1961.
10. Kwanamara, Y.: Neuromuscular mechanisms of jaw and tongue movement, J.A.D.A. **62**:545, 1961.
11. Kydd, W. L.: Psychosomatic aspects of temporomandibular joint dysfunction, J.A.D.A. **59**:31, 1959.
12. McCall, C. M., Szmyd, L., and Ritter, R. M.: Personality characteristics in patients with temporomandibular joint symptoms, J.A.D.A. **62**:694, 1961.
13. Miller, W. H., Ratliff, F., and Hartline, H. K.: How cells receive stimuli, Scient. Am. **202**:222, 1961.
14. Ogle, M. W.: Odontogenic synalgia and electroencephalograph-recorded muscle action potentials, J.A.D.A. **60**:687, 1961.
15. Pancoast, H. K., Pendergrass, E. P., and Schaeffer, J. P.: The head and neck in roentgen diagnosis, Springfield, Ill., 1942, Charles C Thomas, Publisher.
16. Perry, H. T., Lammie, G. A., Main, J., and Teuscher, G. W.: Occlusion in a stress situation, J.A.D.A. **60**:627, 1960.
17. Raffel, S.: Immunity, ed. 2, New York, 1961, Appleton-Century-Crofts, Inc.
18. Ramfjord, S. P.: Bruxism, a clinical and electromyographic study, J.A.D.A. **62**:21, 1961.
19. Sheffield, F. J., Gregg, R. A., and Mastellione, A. F.: Electric stimulation in treatment of mandibular trismus and periarticular fibrosis of temporomandibular joint, Am. J. Phys. Med. **34**:612, 1955.
20. Sherrington, Charles: Man—on his nature, New York, 1953, Doubleday & Co., pp. 229-231.
21. Thoma, K. H.: Oral surgery, St. Louis, 1952, The C. V. Mosby Co., vol. 2.
22. Thoma, K. H.: Tumors of the condyle and temporomandibular joint, Oral Surg., Oral Med. & Oral Path. **7**:1091, 1954.

23. Thoma, K. H., and Goldman, H. M.: Oral pathology, ed. 5, St. Louis, 1960, The C. V. Mosby Co.
24. Wilensky, A. O.: Osteomyelitis, its pathogenesis, symptomatology and treatment, New York, 1934, The Macmillan Co.

CHAPTER 5

THE DIFFERENTIAL DIAGNOSIS OF TEMPOROMANDIBULAR JOINT PAIN

DIAGNOSTIC CLASSIFICATION OF TEMPOROMANDIBULAR JOINT PAIN

Pain is the disturbance of the temporomandibular joint that most often causes patients to seek treatment. They are often unaware of clicking and other functional disturbances of the joint. Temporomandibular joint pain therefore is a separate clinical entity and for purposes of diagnosis and treatment should be considered as such. For diagnostic purposes, it can be classified as follows:

1. Temporomandibular joint pain of local origin: this is pain due to local pathology.
2. Temporomandibular joint pain of referred origin: this is pain that appears in the joint but is caused by pathological or pathophysiological processes elsewhere.
3. Temporomandibular joint pain of psychogenic or neurogenic origin: this is pain caused by central or peripheral nervous disease.

Pain of local origin. Stresses, diseases, and dysfunctions of the temporomandibular joint are discussed in detail in Chapter 4. The following is only a classification and a general summary of the symptoms and differential diagnosis:

1. *Traumatic.* The symptoms are essentially pain, swelling, muscle spasm, and limitation of motion. The history and clinical and roentgenographic examinations will

usually suffice for a diagnosis. These symptoms may also be produced by a traumatogenic occlusion, which will be seen on clinical examination.

2. *Infectious.* The symptoms may include pain, swelling, limitation of motion, and on occasion may be associated with systemic disease. This is relatively rare and is usually an extension from an infectious process in neighboring structures.
3. *Neoplastic.* The symptoms may include pain and may simulate other conditions. This too is very rare (see Chapter 4). Roentgenographic examination will indicate the diagnosis, which can then be confirmed by biopsy.
4. *Arthritic.* This is the commonest disturbance of the temporomandibular joint and may be either rheumatoid arthritis or degenerative joint disease. These are impossible to differentiate in their early stages by either clinical or roentgenographic examination although the systemic nature of rheumatoid arthritis will indicate the diagnosis. The pain is usually an aching type, and it is relieved by rest. However, prolonged rest as in sleeping usually results in stiffness. Joint sounds are present and there may be tenderness or swelling. In severe cases the musculature may go into spasm in an attempt to splint the joint. Roentgenography is of only limited value in diagnosing this condition; the stethoscope is the instrument to be depended on.

Pain of referred origin. The temporomandibular joint is a common site of referred pain. Obviously it is essential that such pain be differentiated from pain of local origin. Pain referred here can be produced by muscle spasm and by myofascial trigger areas which can of themselves also produce muscle spasm. In our experience the masseter muscle is by far the commonest site of referred pain. These myofascial problems are discussed in detail in Chapter 7. When this condition is present there is always some mandibular dysfunction.

The mandibular dysfunction will appear either as a trismus of varying degrees or a midline deviation of the mandible on opening. Palpation of the muscles of mastication will reveal spasm or trigger areas with referral of pain to the temporomandibular joint. Since myofascial trigger areas will produce deep tenderness in their zones of reference, the joint may exhibit tenderness even though there is no pathology present.

Pain of psychogenic or neurogenic origin. Pain of neurogenic origin is the rarest type of temporomandibular joint pain, but it must always be considered as a possibility. Only a neurologic examination can establish the diagnosis. Within the experience of most clinicians, however, pain in the preauricular area adjacent to the joint has often been associated with disease of the lower third molar. Less frequently, coronary disease causes referral of pain to the area of the temporomandibular joint.

Temporomandibular joint pain of psychogenic origin is also extremely rare. However, hysterical trismus has been noted not infrequently. It can only be considered after the possibility of any pathological or pathophysiological condition has been completely eliminated, but this should never be merely a diagnosis of elimination. Later in this chapter techniques whereby a positive diagnosis can be made are discussed. See Table 1 and the following discussion.

THE DIFFERENTIAL DIAGNOSIS OF SOMATIC AND PSYCHOGENIC DISEASE

So long as there are diseases of unknown etiology, a certain part of clinical therapy will consist of the application of empirical methods. In the area of diseases of the temporomandibular articulation the "art" of treatment will continue to play an important role since patients will require relief from pain and other distressing symptoms.

In the absence of specific findings with demonstrable etiological significance there is a tendency to seek psychological explanations. Under the general heading of hysteria there are many recorded case histories in which it is clearly illustrated that psychological stress may produce symptoms of disease that are amenable to treatment only after the underlying psychological cause is resolved.

The burden of proof is of course upon the therapist who decides that there is no physical disease. In most instances this proof will be the disappearance of symptoms or marked amelioration of the disease after psychotherapy. Nevertheless many diagnostic errors have been made; serious physical disease has been fruitlessly treated by psychological methods and psychological disease has been treated vainly by physical methods. It is useful therefore, particularly in the area of temporomandibular diseases, to examine some of the ways in which the practitioner may hope to distinguish between diseases of psychological origin and those due to physical or physical-environmental stress.

Since the end result of severe continued stress of all kinds is physical alteration of the organism (Selye et al.), the patient will obviously reach the same end point in any untreated disease. The following discussion will deal with disease before this common end point is reached.

Taking a proper history. To establish a clear position of concern and interest in the patient's problem, a careful exploration of his chief complaint and of his medical and surgical histories must be undertaken.

Use of standard history forms. Use of standard history forms, often a sheet visible to the patient, will more often than not introduce an impersonal note that will hinder free communication with the patient. On the other hand, extremely long and detailed questioning carefully recorded with great attention on such a form may impress some patients with the thoroughness of the examiner. However, an air of detachment must be avoided if such forms are used.

Patient interview without the use of standard forms. Although detailed records on forms are not decried as such (they can always be completed later from notes), it is far better to ask a leading question so general in nature that a great deal of information will be elicited spontaneously. From discussions with articulate patients one can learn that the difference lies in the fact that there appears to be a definite and impending end to a "form" approach after which the delayed dental or other treatment will of necessity begin. In the undirected approach the patient is master of the length as well as the content of the interview.

A question such as "When did you have your last physical examination and for what reason?" will elicit a great deal of information with little accompanying anxiety. From this point specific questions pertaining to the chief complaint will be accepted more readily since the therapist has a more knowledgeable approach to the problem and he can relate it to the patient's previous experience.

Suggested leading questions. The following questions have been found to provide a maximum of information without appreciable anxiety, except in patients with special emotional problems.

1. When did you have your last physical examination and for what reason?
2. What did your physician tell you?
3. Are you receiving treatment for any disorder at the present time?
4. Are you taking any medication? If so, what?
5. Are you sensitive or allergic to anything?

The answers to these questions will provide the first indication of significant psychological components. Unlike the directed interview the patient is free to offer information beyond the categories of the "standard form" and hence the likelihood of eliciting emotional problems and attitudes is better.

A special diagnostic question. If the content of the answers to the first group of questions suggests emotional disease, it is important not to come to any conclusion at this point. Emotionally disturbed patients do not always have symptoms referable to every organ system and while the oral cavity and the joint that moves it are emotionally supercharged the problem can still be, and more often is, physical. However, in the presence of baffling symptoms or bizarre language and, more important, failure to find any meaningful sign or symptom in spite of a thorough examination, a special question may be asked. Namely, "If I could cure you right now; if I could free you of pain and/or discomfort right now, how would your life be changed?"

This question appears to separate the broad categories of emotionally conditioned and determined disease from physical ailment. The patient who is not using a symptom or disability to deal with the problems of his life and environment will state that he does not see how his life would be measurably changed, except that he would be more comfortable and would be glad to be free of his distress. The patient for whom the disease is a way of meeting the problems of life and often of manipulating environment and people, including the therapist, will proceed to describe how it would then be possible for him to get a job, to marry, or return to writing or art, etc. In short, the patient believes that the disease is the stumbling block in his efforts to adjust to life and is responsible for his failure to solve its problems.

Patients with temporomandibular joint problems are most interesting in respect to neurotic use of their symptoms as are the "denture-problem" patients.

Where is your pain? The answer to this question, which is almost universally asked, is not always understood. In the past too much attention has been paid to the verbal content of the answer and too little to any accompanying gestures, i.e., the nonverbal communication. In answering such a question most patients will indicate with their hands or fingers the location of the site or area of pain. It seems to make a great deal of difference whether they point to a spot with one finger or whether they apply their palm or whole hand to a large

Table 1. Physical signs in clinical examination of temporomandibular articulation*

EXAMINING PROCEDURE	FINDING	DISORDER
Visual inspection from in front of patient and at midline of patient's face	Asymmetry	Congenital deformity (agenesis) Severe trauma or untreated fracture before age 19 Productive or destructive tumor Parotid tumor (inflammatory or neoplastic) Infantile osteomyelitis (rare) Previous surgery (resection)
Light palpation	Asymmetry	All of preceding plus joint fluid due to inflammation
Firm palpation anterior and posterior to temporomandibular joint in closed position and during opening	Pain Crepitus Heat	Inflammation Fracture Inflammation of tissues over but not in joint
Pull ear back and out	Pain	Otitis externa (furunculosis of external ear)
Push mandible back with heel of hand	Pain	Subacute inflammation of joint due to early osteo-arthritis Reparative stage of acute trauma Fluid in synovial cavities
Patient asked to open mouth	Deviation from the midline	Trauma Fracture Muscle dysfunction
	Complete in-ability to open (com-plete trismus)	Inflammation of middle belly of temporal muscle due to (1) erupting third molar, (2) infected third molar, (3) needle trauma

*Chief complaint—pain in the region of the joint.

Continued on next page.

Table 1. Physical signs in clinical examination of temporomandibular articulation—cont'd

EXAMINING PROCEDURE	FINDING	DISORDER
		Tetanus (masseter and temporal) Hysterical spasm Depressed zygomatic arch
	Ability to open very slightly	Hematoma caused by needle injury to internal pterygoid muscle or to temporal muscle Spasm of masseter muscle Depressed zygomatic arch
Patient asked to close mouth	Inability to close mouth	Extrusion or premature contact of posterior teeth Mandibular fracture Maxillary fracture Zygomatic arch fracture Anterior dislocation Defensive reaction to pericementitis of a molar
Palpation of muscles with tip of finger	Tenderness in temporal muscle Tenderness in masseter muscle Tenderness in external pterygoid muscle Tenderness in internal pterygoid muscle Tenderness in sternomastoid muscle Tenderness in trapezius muscle	Pain referred to temporomandibular joint does not always originate in joint (see Chapter 7)

Table 1. Physical signs in clinical examination of temporomandibular articulation—cont'd

EXAMINING PROCEDURE	FINDING	DISORDER
Patient asked to bite lightly until first tooth contact is made	Patient indicates one tooth	Premature occlusal contact—pathogenic if there is joint or tooth pain
Patient asked to bite hard	Mandible shifts after first contact, either observed or reported by patient	Disharmony of occlusal planes or premature occlusal contact
Patient asked to point to pain	Patient uses finger to indicate pain	Pain almost always has physical basis
	Patient uses hand to show an area of pain, indicating no consistent distribution	Physical cause should be sought but emotional factor or factors should be considered

area. It likewise is significant if they fix the motion of hand or finger in one spot or area or if they describe with a sweeping or restless motion a sizable area in indicating the site of the pain. Furthermore, it is of some importance if they cross the midline of the face or confine themselves to the sensory distribution of one half of the face. Physical pain except in the case of bilateral disease is confined to an anatomically determined nerve distribution. In our experience during more than a decade of dealing with emotionally disturbed patients for oral surgery whose presenting symptom was pain, we have never found a psychologically caused pain if the patient indicated it with a finger, definitely pointing to a spot and not crossing the midline of the face. Often it was not easy to find the cause, but in every instance a cause was found with varying degrees of effort.

Obviously it is necessary to be convinced of the physical origin of a pain to expend the additional and often tenacious effort required to discover it. It is easy to understand that once this conviction is weakened the way is open to end the diagnostic exploration for the sake of adopting the attitude that the pain may be psychologically caused.

Denial of disease. Denial of disease is a feature of certain neurotic and psychotic states. However, in some relatively normal individuals it may occur in the dental situation. These patients may deny symptoms and even pain in order to escape the unpleasantness of treatment. This situation is encountered most frequently in children, but many adults behave in the same manner. However, in the adult the event that engendered his anxiety is discovered in the history or the oral examination and is evidenced by advanced dental disease which must have caused severe pain and discomfort in the past. Paradoxically, these patients who are capable of suffering and denying untold tortures until they are forced to seek treatment almost never have psychologically caused oral disease. The reason perhaps lies in the fact that their anxiety is reality oriented as far as the specific oral condition is concerned. Their fear of treatment may have a neurotic basis, but the disease itself is recognized for what it is, decayed or abscessed teeth or perhaps an oral tumor that is growing.

The patient who is overconcerned with his teeth and mouth, who goes to the dentist for frequent checkups, each time with some complaint for which minimal cause is found, is the more likely candidate for emotionally conditioned oral disease. These patients must not be treated casually since they seek dental treatment for the gratification of some need other than dental. They must be given a thorough examination, and some form of treatment must be instituted even if this is limited to roentgenographs, prophylaxis, or correction of a defective margin or roughened area in a restoration.

Similar "maintenance work" must also be performed for the "joint" patient.

The dentist's responsibility. So long as the mouth continues to be an organ of gratification and aggression, patients will suffer from psychological disease of the oral cavity and the temporomandibular articulation. The dentist will be sought by patient and psychiatrist for the final determination of the question of causality. If the dentist can find no physical disease and if this is based on reliable criteria, the psychiatrist will then feel free to pursue emotional etiology with greater assurance and vigor.

When examining these patients, the dentist must be prepared to institute the most complete oral examination that modern dental practice affords. The following list indicates the essential procedures of such an examination:

1. Careful and complete history of the chief complaint
2. Roentgenographs of all oral and extraoral structures
3. Instrument examination and pulp testing of all existing teeth
4. Visual examination and careful palpation of all of the soft tissues and oral structures, including the salivary glands and regional lymph nodes
5. Examination and palpation of the muscles of mastication to discover points of tenderness and spasm
6. Examination of occlusal disharmonies and the temporomandibular articulation
7. Investigation of diet, dietary and masticatory habits, degree of salivary flow and nocturnal oral activity (that is, bruxism, sleeping with hand against the jaw, eating before retiring, etc.), daytime habits affecting mouth and jaw function, etc.
8. History of previous experience with dentists and dentistry

This represents a partial list of the general requirements of a good examination of oral function. Specific findings may of course indicate special tests.

Hyperesthesia and Libman's sign. This method of determining the degree of a patient's reaction to pain is a useful and simple tool in the diagnostic armamentarium of the clinician. With his fingers the clinician presses firmly upon the tips of the mastoid process on both sides for a few seconds. In hyperesthetic and anxious patients a positive finding will be their complaint of intense pain when the pressure is applied and a lasting ache after the pressure is released. Phlegmatic individuals will be scarcely discomfited. It is important to conduct the test in as simple and direct a manner as possible. Initiating the test by saying simply "What do you feel when I press here?" will avoid false positives that may occur if the patient is told in advance that it is a test for pain response.

REFERENCES

1. Block, L. S.: Muscular tensions in denture construction, J. Pros. Den. **2**:198, 1952.
2. Block, L. S.: Preparing and conditioning the patient for intermaxillary relations, J. Pros. Den. **2**:599, 1952.
3. Borland, L. R.: Hysterical symptoms as a factor in oral diagnosis, Oral Surg., Oral Med. & Oral Path. **6**:444, 1953.
4. Collett, H. A.: Psychodynamic study of abnormal reactions to dentures, J.A.D.A. **51**:541, 1955.
5. Collett, H. A., and Briggs, D. L.: Personality factors relating to overadaption to dentures, J. Pros. Den. **4**:269, 1954.
6. Donnelly, John: Review, psychomatics in dentistry, J. Connecticut D. A. **29**:4, 1955.
7. Edwards, A. T.: Psychiatric implications in dentistry, D. J. Australia **22**:589, 1950.
8. Elfenbaum, Arthur: Causalgia in dentistry, an abandoned syndrome, Oral Surg., Oral Med. & Oral Path. **7**:594, 1954.
9. Ewen, S. J.: Dental interview, guided psychological process, New York J. Den. **21**:392, 1951.
10. Fischer, Granville: Theoretical aspects of fear, J. Den. Children **22**:38, 1955.
11. Foster, H. C.: Abnormal mouth habits, J. New Jersey D. Soc. **22**:7, 1951.
12. Friend, M. R.: Everyday psychiatric problems of dentistry, New York J. Den. **23**:252, 1953.

13. Gibbs, F. G.: Psychosomatic aspects of dentistry, D. Record **70:** 241, 1950.
14. Gross, H. N.: Functional oral pain in menopause; dental conditions caused by menopause, D. Students Mag. **31**:22, 1952.
15. Haiman, J. A.: Vasomotor disturbances of especial importance to dentists, New York J. Den. **25**:224, 1955.
16. Hammerman, Steven: Psychiatrist looks at the dentist and his psychoneurotic problems, Pennsylvania D. J. **21**:3, 1954.
17. Hammerman, Steven: Some psychiatric aspects of management of the dental patient, J. Connecticut D. A. **29**:14, 1955.
18. January, J. W.: Psychosomatics in patient management, Angle Orthodont. **21**:155, 1951.
19. Jarabak, J. P.: Practical aspects of psychosomatic dentistry, Oral Surg., Oral Med. & Oral Path. **6**:425, 1953.
20. Jensen, M. B.: Muscular tensions and prosthetic dentistry, J. Pros. Den. **2**:604, 1952.
21. Kelsten, L. B.: Significance and effects of oral habits, Bull. New Jersey Soc. Den. Child. **2**:4, 1954.
22. Kucera, Lew: Of the tongue (psychological preparation for dentures), Chron. Omaha Dist. D. Soc. **19**:20, 1955.
23. Kuehner, G. F.: Role and scope of psychosomatic dentistry, Northwest Den. **30**:245, 1951.
24. Kutscher, A. H.: Psychosomatic diagnosis, Bull. Midtown D. Soc. **29**:1, 1955.
25. Laband, P. F.: Conversion hysteria manifested by anesthesia of the right face, report of a case, J. California D. A. & Nevada D. Soc. **31**:333, 1955.
26. Landa, J. S.: Stomatopyrosis and glossopyrosis syndrome, J. Den. Med. **6**:17, 1951.
27. Landa, J. S.: Temporomandibular joint syndrome viewed from the psychosomatic standpoint, J. Den. Med. **6**:53, 1951.
28. Lefer, Leon: Correlation between gastrointestinal disorders and psychosomatic pathology manifested in the mouth, J. Den. Med. **7**:59, 1952 (abstract).
29. Leigh, Denis: Psychosomatic medicine, D. Practitioner **5**:355, 1955.
30. Manhold, J. H., and Manhold, V. W.: Preliminary report on the relationship of psychosomatics to oral conditions, relationship of personality to periodontal condition, J. D. Res. **30**:459, 1951 (abstract).
31. Mellars, N. W., and Herms, F. W.: Investigations of neuropathologic manifestations of oral tissues, Tufts D. Outlook **24**:20, 1951.
32. Moulton, Ruth E.: Psychiatric considerations in maxillofacial pain, J.A.D.A. **51**:408, 1955.

33. Protell, M. R., and Markham, S.: Psychodynamic approach to immediate denture prosthesis, Oral Surg., Oral Med. & Oral Path. **8**:3, 1955.
34. Raginsky, B. B.: Psychosomatic dentistry, J. Canad. D. A. **20**:479, 1954.
35. Robinson, H. G.: Psychology in dentistry, Temple D. Rev. **21**:7, 1951.
36. Ross, I. F.: Effects of tensional clenching upon the structures of the neck, J. Periodont. **25**:46, 1954.
37. Selye, H.: Stress, Canada, 1949, ACTA Endocronologica, Inc.
38. Stern, E. S.: Some psychiatric aspects of dentistry, D. Practitioner **1**:245, 1951.
39. Stolzenberg, J.: Case report on periodic hysterical trismus, Oral Surg., Oral Med. & Oral Path. **6**:453, 1953.
40. Stroubant, R. E.: Dentist-patient relationships, New Zealand D. J. **49**:164, 1953.
41. Theriault, J. C.: Dental psychology, J. Canad. D. A. **21**:565, 1955.
42. Thoma, K. H.: Trismus hystericus, Oral Surg., Oral Med. & Oral Path. **6**:449, 1953.
43. Walsh, J. P.: Psychogenic symptoms in dental practice, Oral Surg., Oral Med. & Oral Path. **6**:437, 1953.
44. Warren, J. LeB., and Reich, J.: Intractable dental pain of psychogenic origin, Australian J. Den. **56**:94, 1952.
45. Weedin, J. B.: A phase of diagnosis: reciprocal relations between psyche and oral disturbances, Texas D. J. **71**:478, 1953.
46. Weiss, J. K.: Some psychological aspects of dentistry, Tufts D. Outlook **24**:2, 1951.
47. Zeidens, S. H.: Psychosomatic disorders of the mouth, New York J. Den. **24**:218, 1954.
48. Zeikert, M.: Psychiatric aspects of dentistry, J. California D. A. & Nevada D. Soc. **29**:316, 1953.

CHAPTER 6

DISEASES AND DISORDERS CAUSING REFERRED PAIN IN THE REGION OF THE TEMPOROMANDIBULAR ARTICULATION

Referred pain is the subject of much speculation, but the exact physiological mechanism is unknown. A theory, based upon neuromuscular phenomena, of one type of pain referred to the temporomandibular joint is described in Chapter 7. In this chapter other causes for pain in the region of the temporomandibular articulation are discussed. Not all pain in an area that is not coincidental with the site of the disease process is referred pain. Much of this pain is proper to the distribution of the sensory nerves involved and some is due to inability to localize the pain because of its objective severity. The failure to localize may be due to inadequate perception and to many subjective factors among which anxiety is foremost. Other factors are cultural patterns of pain response, previous experience with pain, and the significance to the patient of the site of pain as a threat to life. For example, a highly emotional patient with a fear of brain tumor will ascribe more meaning to and will suffer more anguish from pain in his head.[5] Most patients either ignore pain in the region of the temporomandibular articulation or seek consultation for relief of acute discomfort. Patients often consult friends and relatives before they seek professional advice. It is for this reason that even an emotionally balanced individual will often have anxiety about temporomandibular joint pain since their nonprofessional colleagues can find no precedent for the pain or ready stories of treatment and cure. A purposeful and ordered investigation of the area for the causes of the pain as evidenced by a thorough examination will go a long way toward the initial allaying of the patient's anxiety. Familiarity with some of the other less usual causes of pain in the temporomandibular joint is essential to such an ordered and thorough initial examination.

OTITIS EXTERNA[2]

When the external ear is involved by infection, a relatively minor cellulitis or superficial epidermal abscess may cause severe pain during mandibular movements. The close attachment of the skin to the cartilaginous external ear canal leaves little room for expansion of even a small locus of infection. As a result, mandibular movements that bring about tension upon these closely contiguous structures will cause pain. It will appear to the patient that the pain is related to movement of the jaw and therefore he will assume that the disease is in the jaw. The differential diagnosis between otitis externa and interarticular disease is made by pulling the pinna of the ear upward and backward. Pain caused by this maneuver is indicative of an infection in the external ear canal. Patients with this disorder should be reassured that their difficulty is not in the jaw but in the ear. Prompt referral to an otolaryngologist or their physician is indicated.

CARCINOMA OF THE NASOPHARYNX[2]

At the other extreme of seriousness is carcinoma of the nasopharynx which, because of its location, will cause deafness, immobility of the palate on the affected side, and severe pain in the distribution of the third division of the trigeminal (fifth) nerve, including the area of the temporomandibular articulation. This combination of symptoms is known as Trotter's syndrome. The important symptom is that the pain is severe and persistent and is not controlled easily by the usual analgesics. The patient may also give a history of recurrent nosebleed and may show signs of involvement of other cranial nerves. Palpation of the oropharynx and nasopharynx will reveal the tumor.[2] Prompt referral is essential. Carcinoma of the tonsil will sometimes cause pain in the region of the ear and the joint.

LESIONS OF THE TONGUE

Because of the close association of the lingual nerve with the auriculotemporal nerve, pain from many lesions of the posterior part of the tongue are referred to the area of the temporomandibular joint. These will vary from traumatic ulcers and recurrent aphthae to carcinoma. The tongue should always be examined carefully by pulling its tip gently forward and to one side, with gauze, so that the lateral and posterior borders can be seen clearly. The entire tongue should be palpated for areas of induration (hardness) and for changes from normal color and consistency. Fortunately pain in the temporomandibular joint area caused by lesions of the tongue is usually of minor significance. The patient will be reassured and happy to learn that the tongue lesion will in most cases be transitory and that the pain in the ear and joint will disappear. If the pain is severe and intractable, the possibility of carcinoma should be considered although some cases of severe pain are due to lingual overextension of denture borders and one should not insist upon maintaining their length if this is consistent with a good prosthetic result. It would, on the other hand, be a mistake to adjust the degree of vertical opening or the occlusion if the problem of joint pain were due to a lingual ulcer or abrasion or to insist on lingual extension of the denture in the presence of severe pain.

INJURY TO THE AURICULOTEMPORAL NERVE (FREY'S SYNDROME)[2]

With the influx of immigrants from eastern Europe where suppurative parotitis is more common, the disorder known as the auriculotemporal syndrome or Frey's syndrome is sometimes encountered in the United States. The patient complains of pain in the area of distribution of the auriculotemporal nerve. This may be the outstanding symptom for a time. Later there is unilateral flushing of the face over the temple, the lateral border of the mandible, and the cheek, and there is gustatory sweating over the temple in front of the ear and over the angle of the mandible. These patients may give a history of having had typhus. In some instances patients who have had postanesthetic parotitis may have pain in the auriculotemporal area. The cause of postanesthetic parotitis is unknown, but if this condition results in suppuration, the incision for drainage may injure the auriculotemporal nerve and bring about Frey's syndrome. One patient who had undergone plastic surgery for face-lifting to correct "bags" under the eyes presented with this syndrome. The incision for this plastic procedure is made on the hairline, and since its inferior extension is in front of the ear the auriculotemporal nerve may be injured. This problem must be considered in all open reductions of condylar fractures. In all of these conditions one of the outstanding symptoms is gustatory sweating. A patient in India, an eastern European refugee medical officer in the British army, had profuse sweating over the temples and pain in his right temporomandibular joint when he ate onions or curry. He responded well to atropine and a bland diet. He gave a history of typhus and an incision for suppurative parotitis. Patients with Frey's syndrome should be referred to an internist or neurologist for definitive diagnosis and treatment.

OSSIFICATION OF THE STYLOHYOID LIGAMENT

In birds the stylohyoid ligaments are a chain of ossicles known as the epihyal bone. In human beings they are rarely seen except as abnormal elongations of the styloid process. Occasionally, injury to the tip of the styloid process during tonsillectomy may be a cause for prolonged postoperative

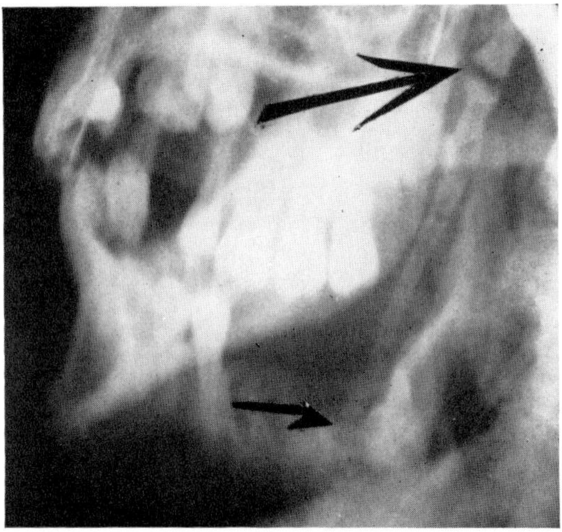

Fig. 34. Lateral roentgenograph of mandible showing pseudoarticulation of the stylohyoid ligament (large arrow) and the abnormal length of this structure (small arrow).

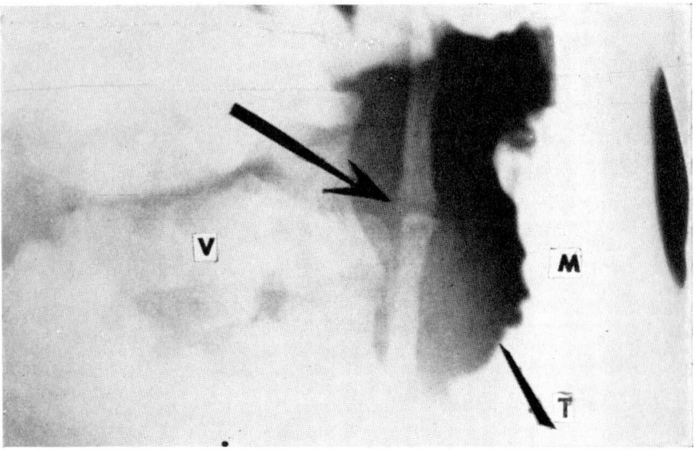

Fig. 35. Special roentgenographic view of the stylohyoid ligament taken through the open mouth (anteroposterior), showing the pseudoarthrosis of this structure. **M,** Mandible; **T,** teeth; **V,** vertebral column.

pain. Since temporomandibular joint pain is not usual in children this should not be a source of confusion, but in the young adult who has had a recent tonsillectomy this possibility should be considered. In the older adult with pain in the temporomandibular joint, roentgenography will sometimes reveal an ossified stylohyoid ligament which may show definite articulations (Fig. 34). These pseudoarticulations (or are they actual vestigial articulations?) are subject to the disorders that all joints are heir to. The pseudoarthroses that result from nonunion of a fracture or from failure of a spinal bone graft come to the attention of the orthopedic surgeon primarily because of pain.[4] Certainly a joint in the area of the mandible adapted phylogenetically to the bill movements of a bird would be subject to abnormal motion in man whose

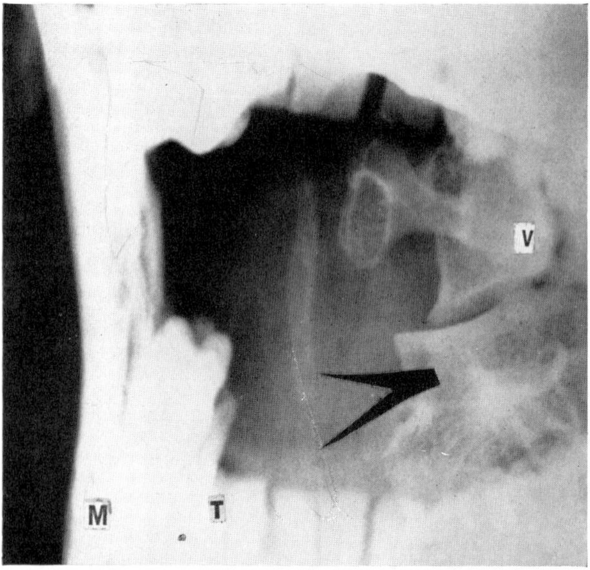

Fig. 36. Blunt fork points to the two segments of a calcified stylohyoid ligament; special roentgenograph taken through the open mouth anteroposteriorly. **M,** Mandible; **T,** teeth; **V,** vertebral column.

pattern of motion is of a higher order of complexity. In Fig. 35 the pseudoarticulation (pseudoarthrosis) is seen clearly in a special anteroposterior roentgenograph taken through the open mouth with the film at the back of the head. Occasionally the stylohyoid ligament appears calcified (less dense and without trabeculation), but several sections may still be seen as if this were an earlier stage in the process of eventual ossification. As a matter of fact, the patient in Fig. 36 was younger (45 years of age) than the patient in Figs. 34 and 35 (60 years of age). Although surgical intervention appears to be indicated, no approach at present has been deemed suitable.

FRACTURE OF THE STYLOID PROCESS

This accident is reported infrequently, and the mechanics of its occurrence in the absence of any other fracture is difficult to understand. A blow to the side of the mandible, if it is relaxed, may possibly result in a fracture of the styloid process because of the presence of the stylomandibular ligament as a limiting structure. Although this is a rare occurrence, at least a rarely reported occurrence, it is a cause of pain in the region of the temporomandibular articulation as well as in the neck. The patient gives a history of a blow to the mandible usually while in a drunken condition caused by alcoholic drink. Possibly the mechanism involved may be that when the mandible is relaxed by the anesthetic effect of alcohol a blow delivered from the side (a right or left cross) may move the mandible sufficiently to cause a break in this slender structure. No treatment other than reassurance and rest is required. In the case illustrated in Fig. 37, the patient complained of pain four weeks after the traumatic incident. The roentgenograph shows a fracture of the styloid process. A case of fracture of the styloid process is reported by Armao[1] for which partial (the patient was instructed to remove the elastics at mealtime) intermaxillary fixation was used. The value of fixation is doubtful.

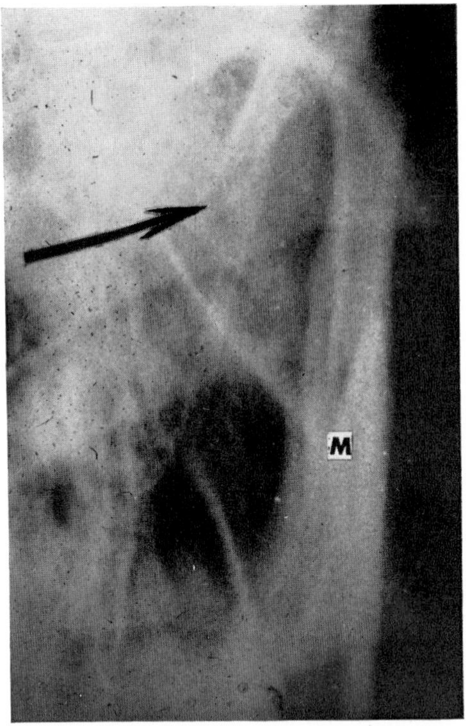

Fig. 37. Posteroanterior view of the skull (detail) showing a fracture of the styloid process (arrow). **M,** Ascending ramus of the mandible.

CHANGES IN AIR PRESSURE[3]

With more people participating in aviation and skin diving, more people are subject to significant alterations in air pressure. Rapid changes or prolonged exposure to higher or lower pressures that are not accompanied by equalization through the eustachian tubes may result in an aero-otitis media, especially if there is pre-existing infection in the nasopharynx. The pain that results may be localized in the temporomandibular joint. In professional airmen aerodontalgia may result from high altitude flying or as the result of experience in a compression chamber. It is important to be aware of such relationships in order to make a proper diagnosis. Treatment of the pain is not different from the usual treatment of the same condition resulting from other more common etiological factors.

CORONARY OCCLUSION

It is important to note that a certain number of patients with angina pectoris (coronary artery insufficiency) and those in various stages of coronary occlusion will complain of pain in the region of the left mandibular third molar as well as pain in front of the left ear, sometimes localizing the pain in the left joint. If the patient has angina pectoris, the pain will disappear when he takes nitroglycerine, which such patients usually have with them. However, it is not necessary to administer this drug to make the diagnosis. Any pain in the region of the ear that improves or disappears upon the administration of oxygen or that requires morphine or meperidine (Demerol) for relief should be looked upon with grave suspicion and the patient should be promptly referred to his physician. The possibility of coronary heart disease in a young adult must not be disregarded. The administration of oxygen is a safe and simple clinical test which, if positive, i.e., the pain is relieved, provides a high order of proof of pre-existing poor cardiac muscle oxygenation.

TEMPORAL ARTERITIS[5]

Because of the location of the superficial temporal artery, anterior to the tragus of the ear, an inflammatory lesion in this vessel will cause a throbbing pain sometimes aggravated by wide opening of the mouth and by hard clenching of the teeth. The diagnosis is made by palpating the area of the vessel and noting the wider distribution of pain over the side of the entire temple and over the eye. In addition this condition is often bilateral, and the patient will often point to or apply pressure to the exact area of tenderness. A thorough physical examination is indicated. Generally, temporal arteritis is a condition found in aged persons.

REFERENCES

1. Armao, Thomas A.: Diagnosis and treatment of a styloid fracture, Oral Surg., Oral Med. & Oral Path. 13:1423, 1960.
2. Bailey, Hamilton: Demonstrations of physical signs in clinical surgery, Baltimore, 1960, The Williams & Wilkins Co.
3. Behnke, A. R.: Principles of internal medicine, New York, 1950, The Blakiston Co.
4. Scheman, Louis: Personal communication.
5. Stead, Eugene A., Jr.: Principles of internal medicine, New York, 1950, The Blakiston Co.

CHAPTER 7

ANTERIOR DISLOCATIONS OF THE TEMPOROMANDIBULAR ARTICULATION

DIAGNOSIS

The chief signs of anterior dislocation of the temporomandibular joint are (1) marked lack of contact of the teeth anteriorly, (2) a protrusive relationship of an otherwise normally placed mandible, (3) pain in varying degrees, and (4) inability to close the jaws.

Palpation of the posterior aspect of the head of the mandible will reveal a depression anterior to the tragus of the ear. The masseter muscle appears as a prominent and spastic bulge just posterior to the inferior margin of the malar bone. If the patient gives a history of a blow, the possibility of a depressed zygomatic arch, which will give similar symptoms, must be considered.

CHIEF CAUSES

Yawning is the commonest cause of spontaneous anterior dislocation of the temporomandibular joint, but it may also appear as an idiopathic event in some forms of hysteria and in elderly persons. In elderly patients there is often little pain. In the younger patient an attempt to bite off more food than can be chewed will sometimes cause a dislocation. Third molar elevation has been a cause as has prolonged dental treatment during one sitting. A complicating factor in all these cases is the anxiety that accompanies inability to close the jaws, and early reassurance that the condition will respond to treatment will spare the patient a period of panic.

TREATMENT

In the light of present knowledge of the temporomandibular articulation, it is not proper to apply force to reduce these dislocations. The chief obstacle to relocation of the mandible is spasticity of the external pterygoid muscle, particularly of its inferior belly. Attempts to forcibly depress the head of the mandible and move it bodily into its fossa will cause greater spasm and may induce more damage in the joint structures.

Dislocations of the temporomandibular joint will correct themselves if methods are used to reduce the spasm and in particular to break the cycle of pain which in turn causes pain and more spasm. This objective can be accomplished readily by injecting 1 to 2 ml. of a suitable regional anesthetic into the insertion of the external pterygoid muscle just anterior to the head of the mandible. The relief of spasm will result in spontaneous relocation of the mandible. Often it is not necessary to inject bilaterally; the mandible may relocate itself before the other side can be injected. The occasional transient paralysis of the facial nerve that sometimes occurs when lidocaine hydrochloride (Xylocaine) is used should not be a cause for alarm.

Occasionally if dislocation is habitual, especially in elderly persons, it may be necessary to use a large towel as a sling over the chin and by twisting it over the occiput gently pull and guide the mandible into position as the spasm is relieved by the effects of the regional anesthetic.

If the method described does not easily reduce the dislocation, relaxation under general anesthesia is indicated. Halothane (Fluothane) is ideally suited for this purpose as are intravenous barbiturates and succinylcholine.

POSTOPERATIVE AFTERCARE

Dislocations that are reduced promptly, that is within one half to three fourths of an hour after they occur, cause little discomfort and require only subsequent regulation of the diet. This need not be a liquid diet or even a soft diet. A regular diet may be eaten, but the amount of food taken in each mouthful should be smaller than usual. The patient may be instructed to eat a soft diet if there is pain on mastication. If there is *considerable* pain, the length of time during which the dislocation existed should be questioned and a liquid diet and a period of rest varying from several days to a week should be prescribed.

For dislocations that have lasted several hours or even several days, light intermaxillary fixation is indicated. This is best accomplished by the use of orthodontic bands with small hooks for intermaxillary elastic traction. After periods varying from one to two weeks the traction can be removed and the patient can resume a regular diet taken in small portions.

Additional treatment may consist of the local application of moist heat and the use of muscle-blocking agents such as orphenadrine citrate (Norflec) 100 mg. in the morning and in the evening, without regard to the age or sex of the patient, or mephenesin carbamate (Tolseram) 2 to 3 Gm. three to five times daily, and adjusted to the age and weight of the patient. The latter drug should be given after meals or after milk or juice.

CHAPTER 8

ROLE OF THE MYOFASCIAL TRIGGER MECHANISM IN THE NEUROMUSCULAR PHYSIOLOGY AND PATHOLOGY OF THE TOTAL TEMPOROMANDIBULAR ARTICULATION

In speaking of the problem of myofascial trigger mechanisms, Bonica[1] said that "they constitute one of the most important clinical problems confronting the physician." The dentist who is interested in either the temporomandibular joint (merely a junction between two bones) or the temporomandibular articulation, which includes not only the joint but all the elements that play a role in the functioning of that joint (the joint itself, the mandible including its entire neuromuscular and vascular mechanisms, and the teeth in the mandible and maxillae), also will find the myofascial trigger mechanism one of his most important clinical problems. In fact, in many cases it will be the most important clinical problem he encounters in the whole group of dysfunctions located in both the joint itself and the myofascial elements of the total articulation and extending into all the elements of the total articulation. It thus behooves us to define precisely this mechanism and also to learn something of its historical background.

Myofascial pain is the term applied to those pain syndromes originating in myofascial structures.

A *myofascial trigger area* is a small, circumscribed, very hypersensitive area in myofascial tissues from which impulses arise to bombard the central nervous system and produce referred pain. This area exhibits deep hyperalgesia, fasciculation, and referred pain. It should be emphasized that it is a physical sign, not a symptom, and the patient is usually unaware of it.

The *zone of reference* is the region in which pain, hyperalgesia, muscle spasm, and certain autonomic concomitants are produced by a myofascial trigger area. Patients can localize referred pain with surprising accuracy, distinguishing between reference zones even a half inch apart.[12] Travell and Rinzler[12] have charted the zones of reference for the commonly affected skeletal muscles throughout the body. They found the zones of reference to be either "essential zones," those zones of reference found in 100 per cent of the subjects, or "spillover" zones, which were found in less than 100 per cent of the subjects. The zones of reference of myofascial trigger areas in the neck and head muscles, those of interest to the dentist, are shown in Fig. 38. Note how many muscles have the temporomandibular joint and the ear as zones of reference and how almost all of these muscles have some part of the total temporomandibular articulation as a zone of reference.

It is possible for the nonpainful symptoms to be the dominant ones. The muscle spasm may lead to an apparent shortening of the muscle with limited motion and weakness. However, once the myofascial trigger mechanism is blocked, the muscle returns to normal no matter how long the shortening, limited motion, and weakness have lasted. Possibly the most dramatic and alarming condition produced by these muscle spasms and the consequent shortening of the muscles of mastication when they are in the zone of reference is the patient's inability to open his mouth normally; opening is sometimes limited to as little as a few millimeters. Blocking the trigger mechanism will restore the muscles to normal and therefore will allow the degree of opening to return to normal.

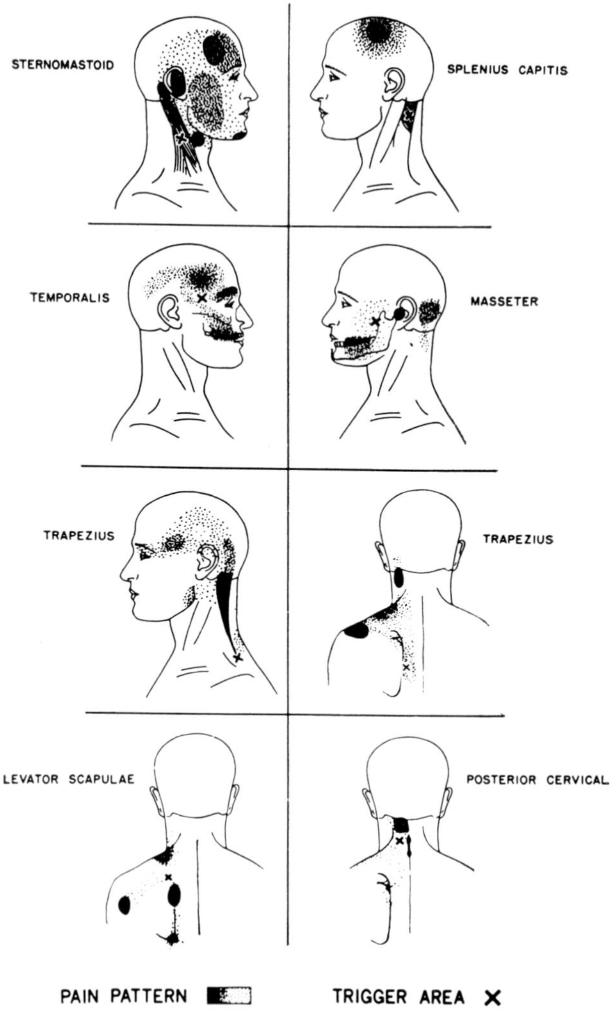

Fig. 38. Zones of reference in the head and neck. Solid black areas indicate "essential zones" and the stippled areas indicate "spillover zones"; the heavier the stippling, the more frequent this area is a zone of reference. (From Travell, J., and Rinzler, S. H.: Postgrad. Med. **11**:425-427, 1952.)

The *mechanism of myofascial pain* is unknown. It is a type of pathophysiological disorder producing a self-perpetuating pain cycle, possibly a feedback neuron circuit. It is evidently based on fixed anatomic circuits, since the zone of reference is the same for all patients and can be accurately charted, as Travell and Rinzler[12] have done.

HISTORICAL REVIEW

The term "trigger zone" was first used in 1936 by Edeiken and Wolferth.[2] In 1938 Steindler and Luck[7] found what they called "trigger points" in the muscle of the lower part of the back to be sources of pain referred to the leg. They pointed out that contact with the needle in the course of an injection of procaine into these "trigger points" produced local pain and referred pain, both of which disappeared on the injection of the procaine. In 1940 Steindler[8] found that many patients with sciatic pain of purely reflex origin were immediately and permanently relieved by the injection of procaine. In 1940 Outland and Hanlon[6] reported on the use of procaine in patients with various of these pain syndromes.

There was no systematic investigation into the myofascial trigger mechanism until the work of Travell, Rinzler, and Herman[9] in 1942. In 1949 Travell[11] published the techniques for blocking the mechanism by ethyl chloride spray and procaine infiltration.

ACTIVATING STIMULI, CAUSES, AND OCCURRENCE

The myofascial trigger area can be activated by the following stimuli: (1) any motion that stretches the structure containing the trigger area, (2) needling, (3) pressure, (4) intense heat or cold, (5) prolonged cooling, and (6) drafts. It should be noted that while pressure activates this mechanism, strong sustained pressure can block it, and diathermy will often increase the pain.

The practitioner of dentistry, should note that such routine procedures as having the patient open his mouth (which involves the stretching of a number of myofascial structures) or administering a local anesthetic (which involves needling) may activate dormant myofascial trigger areas. Consequently, the appearance of an active myofascial trigger mechanism following routine dental procedures does not necessarily mean that the practitioner has produced it but only that he may have activated a dormant condition.

Travell[13] classifies the causes of the myofascial trigger mechanism as precipitating and predisposing.

Events that commonly precipitate the condition are as follows: "(1) sudden trauma to musculoskeletal structures, (2) unusual or excessive exercise, (3) chilling of the body, (4) immobilization, (5) an acute visceral lesion such as myocardial infarction or appendicitis, with localized reflex spasm of the skeletal musculature, (6) acute arterial closure in the extremities, as in popliteal thrombosis, (7) rupture of an intervertebral disk with nerve root pressure, and (8) acute emotional distress."*

The conditions predisposing to myofascial trigger mechanisms are as follows: "(1) chronic muscular strain, produced by repetitive movement frequently performed over a long period of time, (2) general fatigue, (3) acute infectious illness, e.g. infectious mononucleosis, acute hepatitis, or an acute upper respiratory infection (postinfectious myalgias), (4) a chronic focus of infection, (5) nutritional deficiencies, (6) a progressive lesion of the nervous system, (7) nervous tension, (8) syndromes of the menopause and male climacteric, and (9) hypometabolism with creatinuria."*

To the dental practitioner many of these have a direct and immediate relevance. Among the precipitating causes, the first two sound a warning as to the kind of dental treat-

---

*From Travell, J.: Referred pain from skeletal muscle; the pectoralis major syndrome of breast pain and soreness and the sternomastoid syndrome of headache and dizziness, New York J. Med. **55:** 331-340, 1955.

ment the patient should be subjected to. The first predisposing cause mentioned is as good a description of grinding and clenching as we know. The practitioner must keep the problems of the myofascial trigger mechanism in mind when treating the emotionally disturbed patient and must be aware of the possible presence of these problems in the patient suffering from a nutritional deficiency or who exhibits either the syndrome of the menopause or the male climacteric.

The myofascial trigger mechanism has implications that extend far beyond the area we are interested in—in fact, to all areas of the body. As Travell[13] has pointed out, myofascial trigger areas have been found in the skeletal muscles of patients with disorders as different as tension headache, acute painful torticollis, calcific bursitis and other painful shoulder syndromes, myocardial infarction and effort angina, musculoskeletal types of chest pain and breast pain, low back pain and sciatica, osteoarthritis of the hip, intermittent claudication, and traumatic and postoperative pain syndromes including those of the abdominal musculature. A syndrome of postural vertigo and headache[14] is also due to a myofascial trigger mechanism. Travell and Bigelow[10] have shown that the patterns of hysteria are associated with myofascial trigger areas. However, a strong warning is in order here: clearing up the symptoms of patterns of hysteria by blocking the myofascial trigger mechanism can lead to disintegration of the ego. Hysteria must be treated only by psychotherapy.

DYSFUNCTIONS OF THE TOTAL TEMPOROMANDIBULAR ARTICULATION

Once again it must be emphasized that the total temporomandibular articulation embraces all the elements that play a role both anatomically and functionally in the temporomandibular joint—namely, the elements of the joint itself, the mandible (including its entire neuromuscular and vascular mechanisms), and the teeth in both the mandible and the maxillae.

Following is a list of temporomandibular joint disturbances classified[3] for diagnostic purposes:

1. *Traumatic.* The symptoms are pain, swelling, limitation of motion, and muscle spasm. The history and clinical and roentgenographic examinations will establish the diagnosis.
2. *Neoplastic.* The symptoms, which include pain, may simulate other conditions. Roentgenographic examination will establish the diagnosis, to be confirmed by biopsy. This disturbance is relatively rare and is usually a metastasis from a primary tumor elsewhere.
3. *Infectious.* The symptoms are pain, swelling, limitation of motion, and, on occasion, systemic involvement. This disturbance also is relatively rare and is usually an extension from an infectious process in the neighboring structures.
4. *Arthritic.* This is either degenerative joint disease (osteoarthritis) or rheumatoid arthritis. The symptoms are pain, stiffness, and joint sounds. In the early stages it is impossible to make a differential diagnosis on the basis of either clinical or roentgenographic examination. Since rheumatoid arthritis is a systemic condition, a differential diagnosis can be made on the basis of medical findings. Arthroses are the most common temporomandibular joint disturbances. In a study of arthritic patients selected at random, arthrosis of the temporomandibular joint was found in 73.8 per cent.[4]

From a clinical and diagnostic point of view it is advantageous to classify the pains that affect the tissues comprising the total temporomandibular articulation. The following classification is based first on the tissues affected and then on whether the tissue is the primary source of pain or only the site of referred pain.[5]

1. *Pain in the teeth.* Pain in and about the teeth may be due to pathology of the hard and soft tissues of the teeth and periodontal tissues. In rare cases it may be

psychogenic in origin. In one patient a nondirected type of history elicited the information that whenever the patient had serious emotional problems "the teeth would ache." (The technique and value of the nondirected history are discussed in detail in Chapter 5.

2. *Pain in the mouth and throat.* Pain in the mouth and throat may be due to local pathology or it may be referred. The dentist and physician must cooperate to determine whether there is local pathology. Myofascial trigger areas in the pterygoid muscles can refer pain to ger areas in the pterygoid muscles can refer pain to the throat; trigger areas in the digastric and geniohyoid muscles can refer pain to the tongue.
3. *Pain in the face and head.* Only the physician can determine the possibility of local or systemic pathology. Referred pain can be due to dental pathology which must be checked and determined by the dentist. After pathology and referred pain have been eliminated, zones of reference and the myofascial trigger areas producing them must be investigated.
4. *Pain in the ears.* The physician must eliminate the possibility of local pathology. Pain referred to the ears can arise from dental pathology, but the most common cause by far is pain referred from the temporomandibular joint or a myofascial trigger area.
5. *Pain in the temporomandibular joint.* The joint must be checked for local pathology (see list of its disturbances given on page 122). This pain can also be the pain of a zone of reference produced by the myofascial trigger mechanism and this is the cause of much confusion in making the diagnosis. As has been noted, zones of reference exhibit deep hyperalgesia, therefore, the temporomandibular joint can exhibit both pain and deep hyperalgesia and yet be completely free of pathology. This often leads to the local treatment of a temporo-

mandibular joint which is perfectly normal. Locating and blocking the myofascial trigger area is the only way to treat this condition and is done without touching a normal temporomandibular joint. Pain referred from the tissues of a joint is usually referred close by, while that referred from muscles is usually referred a considerable distance away. This explains why pain referred from the temporomandibular joint is usually referred to the ear.

TREATMENT

As clinicians, we are vitally concerned with the treatment of the myofascial trigger mechanism, but it must be emphasized that the mechanism must be completely blocked or it will become clinically latent or dormant, only to reappear when any activating stimulus acts upon it.

There are two methods of treatment. A local anesthetic without a vasoconstrictor can be injected directly into the trigger area, and it does not seem to matter what the anesthetic is—procaine, lidocaine, Pontocaine, etc. Ethyl chloride spray is also an effective method of treatment. The bottle is held just far enough away so that there is no whitening of the skin. The spray is used in long, slow, sweeping strokes over the muscle involved until there is no pain on stimulation of the trigger area.

We prefer ethyl chloride because there is so often an emotional basis for myofascial trigger areas in the mandibular musculature, and an injection will produce further anxiety in the patient.

REFERENCES

1. Bonica, J. J.: The management of pain, Philadelphia, 1953, Lea & Febiger.
2. Edeiken, J., and Wolferth, C. C.: Persistent pain in the shoulder region following myocardial infarction, Am. J. M. Sc. **191**:201-210, 1936.

3. Freese, A. S.: Mandibular muscle spasms and temporomandibular joint disturbances, J. Pros. Den. **8**:831-836, 1958.
4. Freese, A. S.: The occurrence of temporomandibular joint arthroses in arthritic patients: a preliminary report. Unpublished.
5. Freese, A. S.: The temporomandibular joint and myofascial trigger areas in the dental diagnosis of pain, J.A.D.A. **59**:449-453, 1959.
6. Outland, T., and Hanlon, C. R.: The use of procaine hydrochloride as a therapeutic agent, J.A.M.A. **114**:1330-1333, 1940.
7. Steindler, A., and Luck, J. V.: Differential diagnosis of pain low in the back, J.A.M.A., **110**:106-113, 1938.
8. Steindler, A.: The interpretation of sciatic radiation and the syndrome of low-back pain, J. Bone & Joint Surg. **22**:28-34, 1940.
9. Travell, J., Rinzler, S. H., and Herman, M.: Pain and disability of the shoulder and arm; treatment by intramuscular infiltration with procaine hydrochloride, J.A.M.A. **120**:417-422, 1942.
10. Travell, J., and Bigelow, N. H.: Role of somatic trigger areas in the patterns of hysteria, Psychosom. Med. **9**:353-363, 1947.
11. Travell, J.: Basis for the multiple uses of local block of somatic trigger areas (procaine infiltration and ethyl chloride spray), Mississippi Valley M. J. **71**:13-21, 1949.
12. Travell, J., and Rinzler, S. H.: Scientific exhibit: the myofascial genesis of pain, Postgrad. Med. **11**:425-434, 1952.
13. Travell, J.: Referred pain from skeletal muscle; the pectoralis major syndrome of breast pain and soreness and the sternomastoid syndrome of headache and dizziness, New York J. M. **55**:331-340, 1955.
14. Weeks, V. D., and Travell, J.: Postural vertigo due to trigger areas in the sternocleidomastoid muscle, J. Pediat. **47**:315-327, 1955.

CHAPTER 9

COSTEN'S SYNDROME—A NEW CONCEPT

A syndrome is a symptom-complex—a group of symptoms that occur together in a morbid state. Neither etiology nor treatment has a diagnostic place in any description of the symptom-complex that constitutes a syndrome. The accepted etiology and treatment of almost all diseases have been metamorphosed through the centuries, but the description of a syndrome has often gone practically unchanged. Certainly the validity of a syndrome should not be made to stand or fall on the correctness of either etiology or treatment or both as originally described; yet this has happened to Costen's syndrome with such resultant bewilderment and obfuscation that for the past twenty-eight years the literature has been almost choked with "proofs" and "disproofs" all based not on the symptoms but on the etiology or treatment. The first step out of this jungle of confusion is to eliminate both etiology and treatment, respectively "overclosure of the mandible" and "opening the bite," from any role in the proof or disproof of the validity of the syndrome James B. Costen first described in 1934.[1]

HISTORY

Not until 1918 was any attention paid to the role of the dental apparatus in disturbances of the temporomandibular joint. Both Prentiss[22] and Summa[24] in that year pointed out that malocclusion and loss of teeth without replacement caused damage to the temporomandibular joint. In 1920

Wright[27] reported deafness due to malposition of the mandible. Also in 1920 and again in 1921 Monson[20, 21] claimed that both overclosure of the mandible and malocclusion of the teeth can force the condyle back in the articular fossa and thereby can reduce the diameter of the auditory canal thus producing deafness. Beginning in 1932, two years before Costen's first paper, Goodfriend reported his series of studies.[17-19] Goodfriend's work paralleled and agreed with Costen's theories. Since 1934[1] Costen has written extensively on the syndrome that bears his name, and with some modification in emphasis he has continued his writing up to the present time.[2-6]

SYMPTOMS

We[7-9] first suggested further clarification of Costen's syndrome by breaking the syndrome down into groups of related symptoms. With this procedure, a totally new picture emerges and the path is open to proper study and evaluation of this suggested concurrence of symptoms. No longer do seemingly unrelated symptoms float around in a vague sea of uncertain relationships. These symptoms can be summarized as follows:

1. *Otological symptoms:* stuffiness in the ears, tinnitus aurium, loss of hearing
2. *Pain in head and neck:* pain in and about the ears, headaches in the vertex and occipital regions, pains typical of "sinus disease"
3. *Miscellaneous symptoms:* vertigo, tenderness of the temporomandibular joint, burning sensations in the tongue and throat, metallic taste.

Otological symptoms. Costen[1] described tinnitus aurium, stuffiness in the ears, and loss of hearing as symptoms of his syndrome and attributed them to overclosure of the mandible. Here again this symptom-complex suffered from the "all or nothing" attitude: if Costen's etiology could be disproved, the syndrome should be discarded and there certainly has been ample disproof of his etiology. No one had taken a fresh view until 1958 when we[9] offered a new explanation for the majority of the symptoms, and no one had been willing to accept the validity of the syndrome if even a few of the symptoms were not present at all times.

We were the first to report,[9] in 1958, that blocking a myofascial trigger mechanism in the mandibular musculature eliminated loss of hearing, stuffiness, and tinnitus aurium in a number of patients. We have found that this only occurs when the masseter muscle is involved. This finding was confirmed in 1960 by Travell[26] when she reported that blocking a myofascial trigger area in the masseter muscle mediated stuffiness and tinnitus of the ear. The mechanism of this phenomenon is obscure and should prove to be an interesting and fertile field for future investigation.

Young[28] showed that lymph channels run from the internal ear through the petrotympanic fissure, the tissues of the articular fossa, and down the neck of the condyle. Seldin[23] pointed out that interference with flow of lymph could produce ear dysfunction. Muscle spasms could interfere with this flow of lymph and could also constrict the lumen of the eustachian tube. A myofascial trigger area could have as its zone of reference those muscles which, when thrown into spasm, would produce these results.

Pain in head and neck. The head and neck pain described by Costen[1] includes a miscellany of pain that must be examined in detail. If we discard Costen's etiology and think in terms of the myofascial trigger mechanism, discussed in considerable detail in Chapter 5, a new and scientifically acceptable picture emerges. In the myofascial trigger mechanism we find an explanation of the head and neck pain described by Costen, as we have also found an explanation for the otological symptoms. Thus a new and unified understanding of these symptoms as well as the miscellaneous symptoms (discussed subsequently) appears, and it is evident that the concurrence of these symptoms is due not to chance but to the fact that a pathophysiological condition causes them to occur together in this symptom-complex, which has come to be known as Costen's syndrome.

Pain in and about the ears, headaches in the vertex and occipital regions, and pain typical of "sinus disease" are conditions described by Costen. However, these are vague and unscientific terms which overlap and leave much to be desired in both accuracy and descriptiveness. When they occur as part of Costen's syndrome, they are due to the same myofascial trigger mechanism that produces the other symptoms. The necessary differential diagnosis is so complex and far-reaching that it is beyond the scope of this chapter but can be found in Chapter 6. Details can also be found in other of our published papers.[10-16]

Miscellaneous symptoms. Vertigo can be produced by a myofascial trigger area in the sternocleidomastoid muscle—the sternomastoid syndrome described by Travell.[25] It must be remembered that a myofascial trigger area can produce another trigger area in its zone of reference.

A zone of reference of a myofascial trigger area presents deep tenderness; thus the temporomandibular joint may be tender to palpation when the joint itself is a zone of reference but may be completely free of disease. Here again we find a myofascial trigger mechanism capable of producing another of the symptoms in Costen's syndrome.

Fixed anatomic circuits cause pain in the digastric and geniohyoid muscles to be referred to the tongue and pain in the pterygoid muscles to be referred to the throat. Thus myofascial trigger areas or referred pain in these muscles can produce the pain or "burning sensations" in tongue and throat mentioned by Costen.

The "metallic taste" Costen includes in his syndrome is so vague and so subjective that it is impossible to either evaluate or measure in anything remotely approaching a scientific manner. Because this symptom is too vague and indefinite to be adequately studied, we feel that it alone of all the symptoms in this complex must be discarded. The myofascial trigger mechanism can easily account for metallic taste, but the entire subject is too uncertain to warrant evaluation or even speculation.

EVALUATION

Costen's syndrome is a symptom-complex and this alone. It has fallen into disrepute in recent years only because Costen's theories of its etiology and treatment have been completely disproved. The syndrome does exist, but the etiology is far from that offered by Costen and the pathophysiological disorder causing it was not reported in any systematic fashion until 1942. The myofascial trigger mechanism provides a thorough explanation of this symptom-complex.

Thus Costen's syndrome once again finds its place in modern scientific medicine and dentistry.

REFERENCES

1. Costen, J. B.: A syndrome of ear and sinus symptoms dependent upon disturbed function of the temporomandibular joint, Ann. Otol. Rhin. & Laryng. **43**:1-15, 1934.
2. Costen, J. B.: Glossodynia: reflex irritation from the mandibular joint as the principal etiologic factor, A.M.A. Arch. Otolaryng. **22**: 554-564, 1935.
3. Costen, J. B.: Neuralgias and ear symptoms associated with disturbed function of the temporomandibular joint, J.A.M.A. **107**: 252-264, 1936.
4. Costen, J. B.: The mechanism of trismus and its occurrence in mandibular joint dysfunction, Ann. Otol. Rhin. & Laryng. **48**:499-515, 1939.
5. Costen, J. B.: Correlation of x-ray findings in the mandibular joint with clinical signs, especially trismus, J.A.D.A. **26**:405-407, 1939.
6. Costen, J. B.: Diagnosis and treatment of mandibular joint reactions, J. M. A. Alabama **29**:45-48, 1959.
7. Freese, A. S: Degenerative joint disease of the temporomandibular joint, J. Pros. Den. **7**:663-673, 1957.
8. Freese, A. S: Etiology and symptomatology of temporomandibular joint disturbances, New York J. M. **57**:2837-2841, 1957.

9. Freese, A. S: Costen's syndrome: a reinterpretation, A.M.A. Arch. Otolaryng. **67**:410-416, 1958.
10. Freese, A. S: Head and neck pain in temporomandibular joint disease and muscle spasm, A.M.A. Arch. Otolaryng. **67**:410-416, 1958.
11. Freese, A. S: Mandibular muscle spasms and temporomandibular joint disturbances, J. Pros. Den. **8**:831-836, 1958.
12. Freese, A. S: Myofascial trigger mechanisms and temporomandibular joint disturbances in head and neck pain, New York J. M. **59**:2554-2558, 1959.
13. Freese, A. S: The temporomandibular joint and myofascial trigger areas in the dental diagnosis of pain, J.A.D.A. **59**:448-453, 1959.
14. Freese, A. S: Temporomandibular joint pain: etiology, symptom and diagnosis, J. Pros. Den. **10**:1078-1085, 1960.
15. Freese, A. S: The differential diagnosis of temporomandibular joint pain, A.M.A. Arch. Otolaryng. **71**:789-792, 1960.
16. Freese, A. S: The myofascial trigger mechanism in temporomandibular joint and allied disturbances, J. Oral Surg., Oral Med. & Oral Path. **14**:933-937, 1961.
17. Goodfriend, D. J: Dysarthrosis and subarthrosis of the mandibular articulation, D. Cosmos **74**:523-535, 1932.
18. Goodfriend, D. J: Symptomatology and treatment of abnormalities of the mandibular articulation, D. Cosmos **75**:844-852, 1933; **75**: 947-957, 1933; **75**:1106-1111, 1933.
19. Goodfriend, D. J: The role of dental factors in the cause and treatment of ear symptoms and disease, D. Cosmos **78**:1292, 1936.
20. Monson, G. S.: Occlusion supplied to crown and bridgework, J. Nat. D. A. **7**:399, 1920.
21. Monson, G. S.: Impaired function as a result of closed bite, J. Nat. D. A. **8**:833, 1921.
22. Prentiss, H. J: Preliminary report upon the temporomandibular articulation, D. Cosmos **60**:505-512, 1918.
23. Seldin, H. M: Traumatic temporomandibular arthritis, New York D. J. **21**:313-318, 1955.
24. Summa, R: The importance of the interarticular fibrocartilage of the temporomandibular articulation, D. Cosmos **50**:512-514, 1918.
25. Travell, J: Referred pain from skeletal muscles; the pectoralis major syndrome of breast pain and soreness and the sternomastoid syndrome of headache and dizziness, New York J. M. **55**:331-339, 1955.
26. Travell, J: Temporomandibular joint dysfunction, J. Pros. Den. **10**:745-763, 1960.

27. Wright, W. H: Deafness as influenced by malposition of the jaw, J. Nat. D. A. **7**:979-992, 1920.
28. Young, M. W: Anatomical and functional relationships between the jaw and ear, Anat. Rec. **109**:102, 1952 (abstract).

CHAPTER 10

TEMPOROMANDIBULAR ARTICULATION PROBLEMS IN RELATION TO EVERYDAY DENTISTRY

The dentist must accept his role in the etiology of stresses, diseases, and dysfunctions of the temporomandibular articulation. Even the simplest amalgam or synthetic restoration can be a source of trauma to the entire temporomandibular articulation if that restoration is not carefully adjusted to either produce or preserve balanced occlusion. Temporomandibular articulation problems result from an accumulation of all the insults visited upon the articulation from adolescence onward, and herein lies an important consideration in all dental treatments.

DEVELOPMENT AND GROWTH ASPECTS

Preadolescent children do not have temporomandibular articulation problems despite all that happens dentally to many of them, that is, orthodontia with all its attendant changes of maxillomandibular relations in all planes, restorative dentistry, loss of deciduous and permanent teeth, bruxism, etc. The cartilage of the head of the mandible is the most important site of growth in the mandible and is unique in that the condylar cartilage is covered by connective tissue. Prior to adolescence the relation of the head of the mandible to the articular tubercle is flexible and allows for any necessary adjustments. During the period of growth, the growth itself makes the adjustments but as the child grows into the adolescent (earlier in girls than in boys) growth reaches completion and ceases, and temporomandibular articulation disturbances first appear after this time.

CLINICAL IMPLICATIONS

The stresses, diseases, and dysfunctions of the temporomandibular articulation represent a summation of all the dentistry improperly performed throughout the life of the patient. In the child the amalgam restoration treats caries, but in the adult it also treats the occlusion. Any operative or restorative procedure must be approached in this light. The simplest occlusal amalgam or lingual silicate restoration is capable of causing as much damage to the total articulation as an extensive prosthesis. The dentist who would not dream of inserting a three-unit fixed partial prosthesis without carefully checking and correcting all centric and eccentric relations may place an amalgam or silicate restoration and then forget about it. We have seen acute traumatic injury to the mandibular musculature and the temporomandibular joint resulting from such carelessness.

It is essential that any restoration, even a simple occlusal amalgam restoration, placed in a patient's mouth be equilibrated with the same care and thoroughness as would be given an extensive prosthesis. The approach to the patient is discussed in detail in the section on equilibrating the occlusion in Chapter 11. Complete dentures usually do not cause damage to the mandibular joint because the residual bone resorbs rapidly to produce what might almost be called a "natural" occlusal equilibration, and the residual bone rather than the joint is damaged.

The clinician must realize that patients react in various ways. There is the patient who will accept almost anything in order to get the procedure finished and to escape from the dentist's office. There is the patient who is so desirous of pleasing the dentist that he will say anything he thinks the dentist wants to hear, and there is the patient who will feel and do just the opposite of this. It is thus essential to avoid any word or action that might indicate a desired answer. It is best for the dentist to reassure the patient that he is seeking only to determine whether the restoration is correct and that the patient's answer will make no difference in his feelings. Certainly every clinician should be familiar with the sigh of relief and the instant assured response from the patient when the occlusion is correct. There is no mistaking the patient's reaction when he finally finds his correct occlusal relationships restored.

CHAPTER 11

ROLE OF OCCLUSION IN TEMPOROMANDIBULAR JOINT PROBLEMS

The study of any disease, dysfunction, or disability must begin with an examination of the signs and symptoms that evidence its presence. An occlusal problem exists only if the occlusion presents a problem, that is, produces disease. The importance of this fact cannot be overemphasized, because vast damage is done through failure to recognize this obvious truism. To correct an occlusion that has produced no disease or dysfunction is comparable to performing an appendectomy or hysterectomy when there is no disease in the organ.

PATHOGENIC OCCLUSION

It is only the pathogenic, not the pathological, occlusion that requires correction. The distinction is vital and of the same nature as the distinction between traumatogenic and traumatic occlusion.

Pathologic: "Indicative of or caused by a morbid condition."*
Pathogenic: "Giving origin to disease or to morbid symptoms."*
Traumatic occlusion: "Occlusion in which the contact relation of the masticatory surfaces of the teeth is directly the result of trauma."*
Traumatogenic occlusion: "Occlusion which, under biting pressure, produces injury to the periodontal tissues."*

*From Dorland's illustrated medical dictionary, ed. 23, Philadelphia, 1957, W. B. Saunders Co.

The vital distinction lies in the relationship of cause and effect. Thus traumatic or pathological conditions are the results of causes, whereas traumatogenic or pathogenic conditions produce the trauma or ultimate disease.

At this point we are concerned only with the traumatogenic or pathogenic occlusion. Here then arises the question of diagnosis, or how to recognize what we prefer to call pathogenic occlusion because the term is more inclusive but not synonymous with traumatogenic occlusion. The occlusal problem is thus narrowed down to the symptoms and diagnosis of the pathogenic occlusion.

Pathogenic occlusion must by definition produce disease or dysfunction or both. There may be prematurities in centric or eccentric relations or in gliding into or out of these positions. The vertical dimension may be increased or decreased from the correct physiological dimension either in occlusion or in an open position or both. Malocclusion or pathologic occlusion thus may or may not be pathogenic.

The pathogenic occlusion causes damage to any or all or a combination of the following elements of the temporomandibular articulation and can be recognized by the morbid conditions produced in these elements:

1. *Teeth and periodontal tissues.* Effects of a pathogenic occlusion are disease or destruction of the periodontal tissues, loosening of the teeth, and pathological attrition and abrasion with facet formation. These are actually the least of the effects of a pathogenic occlusion on the temporomandibular articulation and the total patient.
2. *Neuromuscular mechanism of the mandible.* The muscles of mastication can readily be thrown into spasm by a pathogenic occlusion and a myofascial trigger area produced. The ramifications of this are wide (see Chapter 8 on the myofascial trigger mechanism). Myofascial trigger areas and spasms of the mandibular musculature, under certain circumstances, can also cause loosening of the teeth.

3. *Temporomandibular joint.* The effects of a pathogenic occlusion on the temporomandibular joint are both direct and indirect. It can produce degenerative joint disease and traumatic arthritis as a result of the microtraumas to the joint. Indirectly the pathogenic occlusion can produce these same morbid conditions by its effect on the neuromuscular mechanism. A detailed discussion of these conditions is found in Chapters 4 and 8.

Grinding and clenching (bruxism). In almost all patients who exhibit these symptoms the etiology is psychophysiological. However, occasionally a pathogenic occlusion, particularly a prematurity or increased vertical dimension, will produce grinding or clenching for the first time. Correction of this problem is ordinarily simple because it usually arises suddenly from an obvious and minor occlusal problem often produced in the course of dental treatment. As a protective action, the muscles of mastication will try to reduce or remove whatever is in the way of the mandible's normal functional movements and this grinding or clenching may cause the muscles to go into spasm or may initiate a myofascial trigger mechanism with all of its attendant problems. If this condition is allowed to continue, a neuromuscular pattern will be established. Correction is then too late, for the patient either will have established a permanent pattern or at best will revert to this pattern under stresses encountered in his life situation.

CHAPTER 12

EQUILIBRATION OF THE OCCLUSION

It is impossible to overemphasize the importance of using physiological in preference to arbitrary techniques when equilibrating the occlusion. This should be considered axiomatic. Occlusal equilibration should be performed so that the muscles themselves determine the final tooth, muscle, and joint relationships. The practitioner should never impose his arbitrary will upon the teeth, muscles, and joints to produce a theoretical relationship.

Equilibrating the occlusion is a worse than useless procedure when performed on a patient who has any spasm of the mandibular musculature, inequality of muscular contraction, or a myofascial trigger area in the mandibular musculature. Other patients who should not undergo this procedure are those who have had recent trauma or surgery involving the mandibular musculature (see Chapter 8). In these patients the occlusion would be corrected at a temporary and changing mandibular position, and as soon as the position either changed or returned to normal the occlusion would then be pathological at the patient's normal mandibular positions.

TECHNIQUES

While standing clear of anything against which he can lean or rest and with his hands hanging down freely, the patient is instructed to look at some selected object that is on a level with his eyes. This induces a relaxed postural position. It is essential that the practitioner be calm and relaxed, preferably sitting with his arms folded, because this makes him neutral in the situation and he is no longer a threatening figure to the patient.[1] The practitioner should never be anxious or concerned or have a desire to obtain any predetermined reaction except the true expression of the patient's responses. Full confidence must be expressed in the patient's ability to perform his task correctly, and reassurance is of great help to the patient.

With the patient in this relaxed postural position, he is instructed thusly: "open your mouth just a little and slowly let your teeth come together." The phraseology is most important both to obtain the exact movements and, since some patients will try to tell the practitioner what they think he wants to hear and some will try to tell him the opposite, to prevent the patient from sensing, rightly or wrongly, what response is wanted or expected. After this action has been practiced until the patient performs it properly, allowing the teeth to close in centric relation, he can then be asked which tooth hits first. Almost invariably the patient will indicate the tooth that makes the premature contact. It then becomes a simple matter to locate the spot with articulating paper since the patient has shown the tooth involved. Step by step this is continued until the patient appears a bit surprised and puzzled and remarks that all the teeth seem to hit at the same time or that he cannot tell which tooth hits first.

Should it be necessary to check the patient or to proceed without his cooperation as described, there are physiological methods for this also. If the practitioner places the ball of his forefinger on the buccal or labial surfaces of the teeth while the patient opens and closes in centric relations or moves into eccentric relations, he can feel the tooth that makes a premature contact. It is often difficult for a patient to move his mandible in certain ways, such as closing in centric relation, upon instruction and when he is consciously trying. Some patients can learn this readily, but for most it is difficult and many cannot do so. If the patient cannot move his mandible as instructed, it is useful to have him chatter his teeth lightly, starting at a small degree of opening; the rapid movement usually prevents him from making strained movements and so these movements are performed in centric relation. If articulating paper is placed between the teeth and the patient is told to chatter his teeth lightly, the points of premature contact in centric relation show up as more heavily marked spots.

When articulating paper is used, it is essential that the instrument used to hold the paper place a minimum of bulk in the patient's mouth because bulk makes it more difficult for the patient to close in centric relation. Foreign objects in the mouth produce proprioceptive impulses that are translated into muscular activity and thus affect the maxillomandibular relationships. Therefore, it is important to keep proprioceptor stimulation to an absolute minimum when the patient is to demonstrate any muscular relations such as centric. The late

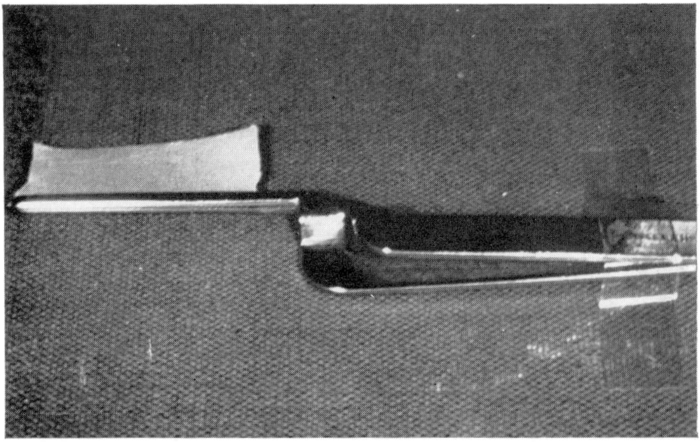

Fig. 39. Dr. S. C. Miller's articulating forceps. The thin long beaks make it possible to hold articulating paper as far posteriorly as desired, yet the amount of bulk in the mouth is kept to a minimum.

Dr. S. C. Miller's forceps for placing articulating paper are particularly well adapted. Miller's forceps (Fig. 39) make it possible to hold the articulating paper between the teeth by narrow forceps blades which minimize the amount of bulk in the mouth.

This procedure ordinarily is spread over five visits because after a while the patient usually becomes confused and unable to tell which tooth makes the first contact. The muscles tire also and, if this is continued too long, the patient may have much discomfort later. On the first visit, centric occlusion is corrected; on subsequent visits, right and then left lateral, and then protrusive occlusions are corrected; finally, on the fifth visit the previous work is rechecked and the ground surfaces are polished. Should much grinding be necessary, it is wiser to spread it over as many visits as needed to prevent too much trauma to the pulp and too much sensitivity afterward. Additional visits are needed if it is also necessary to reduce markedly or reshape the occlusal table or even to recarve the occlusal surfaces of the posterior teeth to provide more sluiceways or cutting planes. For these purposes, handpiece and right-angle diamond stones of the shape and size most convenient to the individual operator and used at ultra high speeds with very light pressure will keep unpleasant sensations at a minimum.

Radical techniques. When replacements are necessary, occlusal equilibration must be followed by prostheses, but in some cases even this cannot resolve the occlusal problem. For these patients it may be necessary to fall back on a complete occlusal reconstruction. This must be recognized as a very radical procedure and should be avoided whenever more conservative techniques will accomplish the desired ends. This is discussed in greater detail in Chapters 11 and 13.

New techniques and methods. The patient can accurately inform the operator which tooth makes a premature contact, but the problem then is to find the point of contact.

The prematurely contacting tooth can be checked by

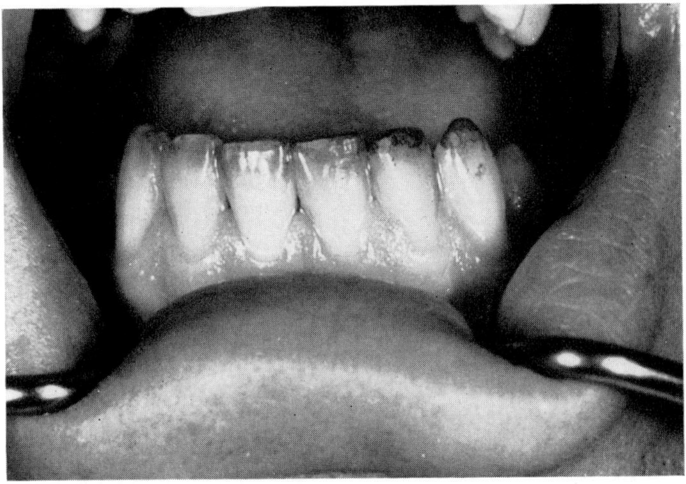

Fig. 40. Points of premature contact revealed by disclosing ink on lower anterior teeth. The ink was painted on the lower anterior teeth, and opening and closing in centric relation wears off the ink. Note areas where ink has been worn off.

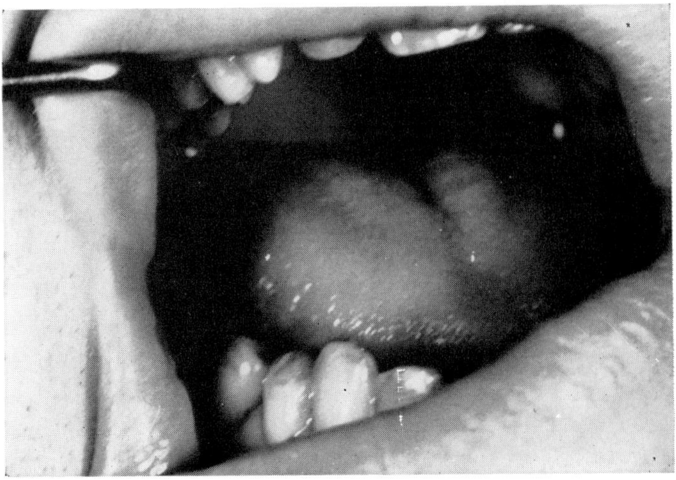

Fig. 41. Premature contact revealed in centric relation by disclosing ink.

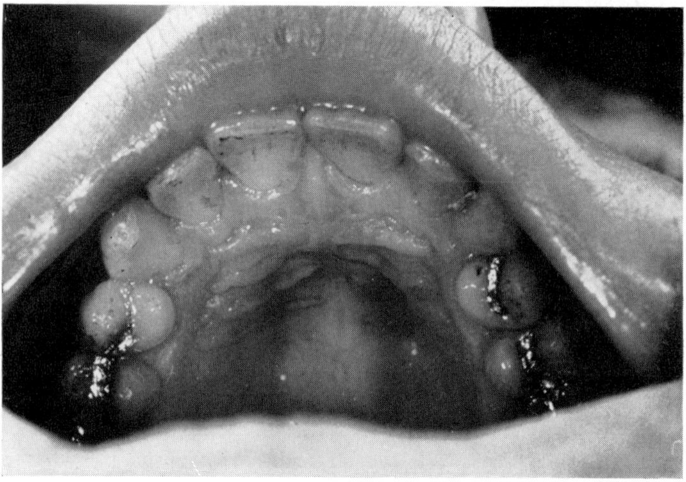

Fig. 42. Points of contact in various movements revealed on upper teeth by disclosing ink. (The ink was painted on the lower teeth.)

holding the ball of one finger against two teeth at a time while the patient closes into occlusion; the operator can feel the premature pressure against one tooth. Articulating paper will disclose the point of contact. Both these techniques introduce foreign objects into the mouth and thus make it difficult, and for some patients impossible, to obtain unstrained recordings. We have had the opportunity of working with a new material, a disclosing ink that can be painted on the teeth and is worn off in the particular mandibular movement (Figs. 40 to 42).* This utilizes a technique that is hoary with age in the tool and diemaking industry. It obtains markings without introducing any foreign bodies into the mouth and thus permits recordings of contact in movements which can be truly free and unstrained.

---

*Product supplied for experimental purposes by the manufacturer (Parkell Co.).

DANGERS AND CONTRAINDICATIONS OF OCCLUSAL EQUILIBRATION

It is most important that the practitioner think of occlusal equilibration in terms of the radical treatment it essentially is. The widespread proprioceptive changes inaugurated are only a small part of the total emotional impact of this procedure on the patient. To see this treatment in its true perspective requires broadening of our field of vision from that limited area illuminated by the powerful mouth lights to include the total patient seated so expectantly and usually so fearfully in the dental chair. This is not just a set of teeth with perhaps two jaws and a joint or two. This is a total human being and his teeth are only a small part of him and a part not nearly as essential as many others.

It is necessary to approach this problem from a psychodynamic point of view. The mouth is the infant's first means of expressing his emotions—he accepts food, he rejects food, he bites, he laughs, he cries, he makes sounds, later he kisses. Later in life he will change these sounds into words that express love and hostility. The mouth is of tremendous importance sexually throughout the life of the individual. Its role is clearly expressed in language such as the person swallows his anger, chokes it back, grits his teeth, clenches his teeth, sets his jaw, spits out words, uses cutting words, etc. Herein lies the probable basis of grinding and clenching, and also the fear of dentistry, for the dentist is assaulting a sexually supercharged part of the patient. With so much of the emotional life of the individual centering upon his mouth it becomes obvious how, in an emotionally disturbed individual, radical dental treatments can wreak havoc and how even in a well-adjusted patient severe damage can be done by ill-advised or ill-timed radical dental treatments.

Occlusal equilibration must be practiced with the greatest of care on any patient and only when the occlusion is pathogenic. In a patient with a pathological occlusion nothing need be done to correct a situation that is doing no harm. There are even times when a pathogenic occlusion must be ignored because the damage to the total patient would be far worse than any damage that could result from the pathogenic occlusion. Occlusal equilibration on the wrong patient can focus his attention on his mouth or make an existing preoccupation far worse. Occlusal equilibration can produce grinding and clenching, muscle spasms of the mandibular musculature, myofascial trigger areas in the mandibular musculature, a veritable host of other difficulties ranging from slight to severe pain and from simple vague complaints to bizarre difficulties, and has even resulted in the precipitation of an emotional collapse.

Occlusal equilibration is definitely a two-edged sword and one that is capable of outright destruction. It should only be used with utmost care and with a deep respect for the capacity of a potent weapon both for good and for evil.

SIGNIFICANT CASE HISTORIES

The following case histories are presented because they offer much in diagnosis, treatment, and technique. By illustrating an approach to the problems and opportunities of occlusal equilibration, they will help in developing a way of thinking that will make it possible for the practitioner to approach his occlusal problems regardless of how they may vary.

Case L. B. This man, approximately 60 years of age with no significant dental history beyond the loss of teeth over a period of many years beginning at approximately 18 years of age, had no history of any temporomandibular joint disturbances but had the traditional "bulldog" jaw. On examination he could only open and close the mandible in one position (Fig. 43). Thus he had only one relationship with no ability to make lateral or protrusive movements.

When a condition of this kind occurs, it is necessary to determine whether this is the patient's true centric relationship or whether it is a convenience centric relationship developed in response to pathological changes in the masticatory apparatus. The pathological changes producing an extreme relationship of this type can be either changes in

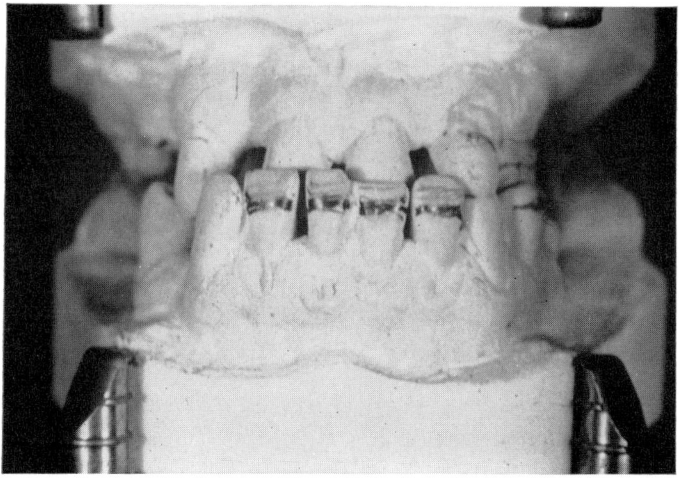

Fig. 43. Articulated study casts showing a convenience centric relationship. The line on the lower anterior teeth shows the level of the incisal edges of the upper anterior teeth.

the dentition which force the mandibular musculature into compliance or changes in the mandibular musculature which force the mandible into compliance. Very gently pressing one finger posteriorly (without force) against the point of the chin and asking the patient to close his mouth is usually the best way to find true centric relationship, and it may help to shake the finger laterally as the patient closes. In this particular patient, as only rarely happens, it was necessary to exert light pressure distally against the point of the chin during closing to find that the anterior teeth met in an edge-to-edge relationship, but immediately following this forced closure the patient was able to close in an edge-to-edge relationship with only the gentle pressure of one finger as described above. However, in this position the vertical dimension was increased so severely that it could be seen on the most casual examination and the patient could not maintain it for more than a few minutes without sensations of strain and discomfort.

When gentle pressure is sufficient to guide the musculature into a new centric relation, the convenience centric relation is almost invariably due to pathologic changes in the dentition and is maintained by the tooth relationship thus produced. In these cases if the necessary tooth planes are freed, the mandibular musculature will of itself restore the true centric relationship. When changes in the centric rela-

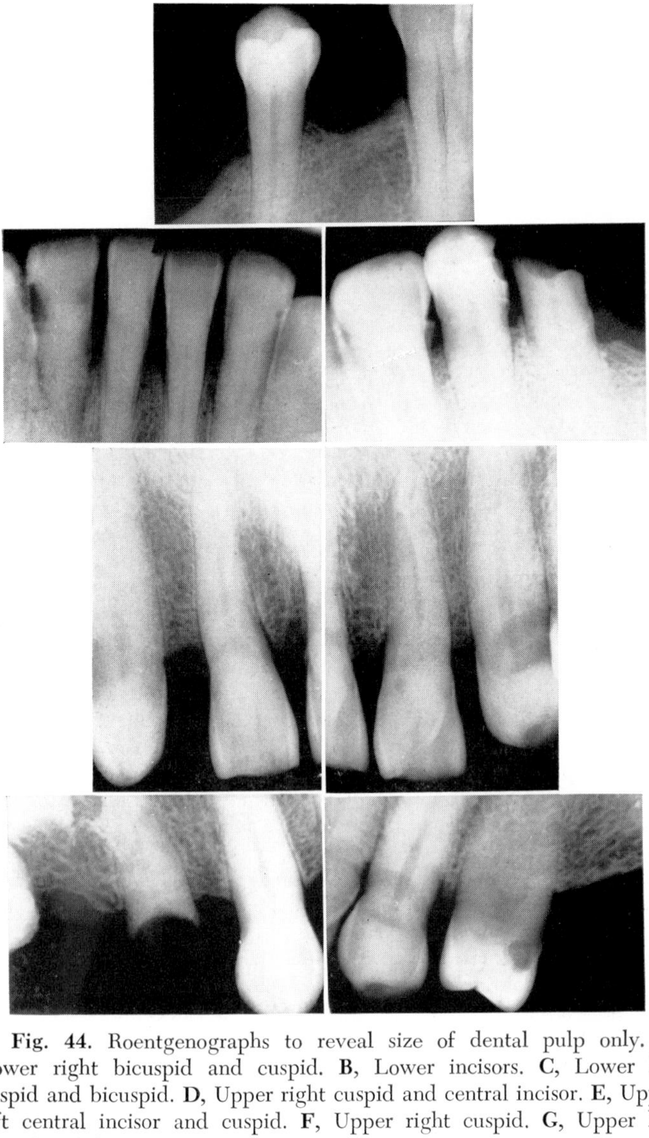

Fig. 44. Roentgenographs to reveal size of dental pulp only. **A,** Lower right bicuspid and cuspid. **B,** Lower incisors. **C,** Lower left cuspid and bicuspid. **D,** Upper right cuspid and central incisor. **E,** Upper left central incisor and cuspid. **F,** Upper right cuspid. **G,** Upper left cuspid and bicuspid.

tionship are due to changes in the mandibular musculature, the situation is completely different and is discussed in detail in Chapters 8 and 11.

In this particular patient it was obvious that considerable reduction of the incisal edges and occlusal surfaces would be necessary. The patient could not afford dental care beyond the simplest and least expensive. The whole success of the treatment plan depended on what the roentgenographs revealed, and two series were taken: (1) the usual full-mouth periapical roentgenographs and (2) roentgenographs taken at such angulations as to show without distortion the size of the dental pulp in each tooth (Fig. 44). The marked resorption of the pulp in each of the teeth showed that the considerable reduction of tooth structure necessary would be safe, and this was done but done in very slow stages. When this much reduction is required, and particularly when no protection of the teeth by means of restorations is possible, the procedure must be done in very slow stages and must be spread over a considerable period of time (in this case, 8 weeks) to avoid too much shock to the pulps and too much pain and aftersensitivity.

To begin with, the incisal edges of the incisors were reduced. The articulating paper showed the points of contact and the incisors were reduced incisally on a flat plane labiolingually until the cuspids

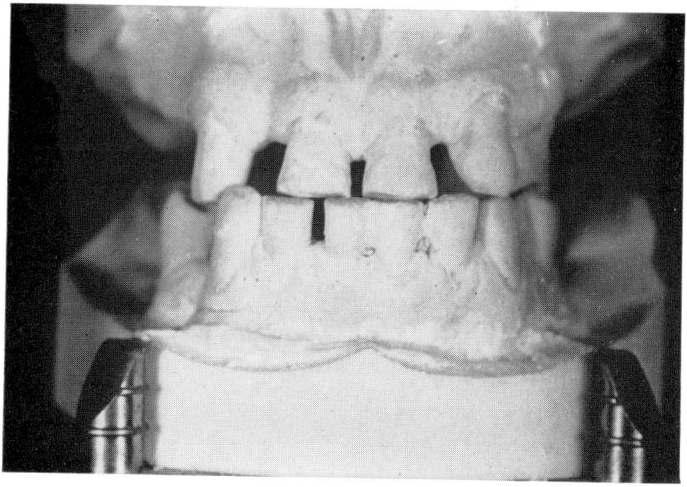

Fig. 45. Articulated study casts showing the final and true centric relationship. Compare with Fig. 43. Note in particular the changes in the inclined planes of the cusps of cuspids and bicuspids.

and bicuspids made contact. At this point the reduction of the cuspids and bicuspids began and these teeth were reduced in a different manner. To begin with, the inclined planes of the cusps were such (see Fig. 43) as to hold the mandible in its protruded position. A new set of inclined planes had to be developed so that they would help hold the mandible in the position that the mandibular musculature showed to be the true centric relation (see Fig. 45). As the work, which took approximately 8 weeks, was being completed, the patient found it more and more difficult to go back to his original convenient centric relationship and eventually it became impossible.

The final result can be seen in Fig. 45. Although an edge-to-edge bite is not theoretically ideal, the important and deciding factor is what the patient's musculature requires rather than any theoretical concept arbitrarily set by a particular school of thought.

After the patient had found his true centric relationship, simple upper and lower removable partial dentures were constructed. Thus without great expense or complicated extensive dental procedures, a patient's mouth was restored to health and function. This case is extremely important in that it shows how much can be accomplished

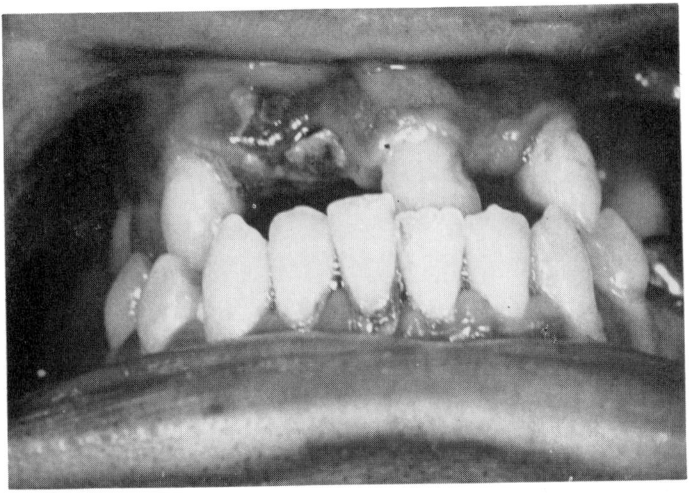

Fig. 46. Convenience centric relation as presented by patient. Note extrusion of lower right central and lateral incisors and unworn incisal surfaces of all lower incisors. Note cuspal relationships of cuspids and posterior teeth.

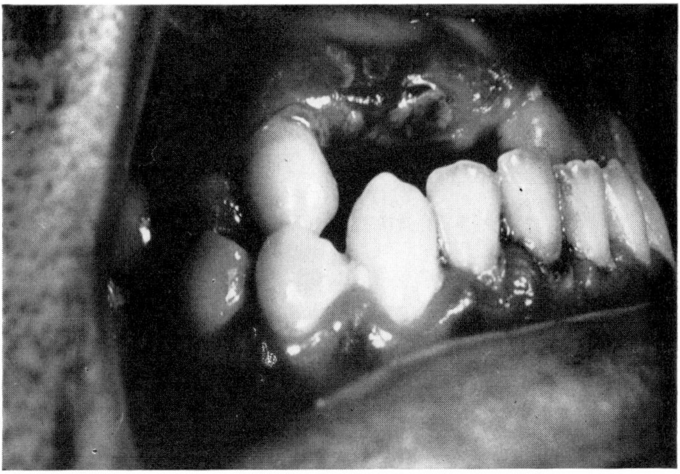

Fig. 47. Lateral view of mouth seen in Fig. 46. Again note incisal surfaces of lower incisor teeth and cuspal relationships.

even when the economic or the emotional condition of the patient may prevent the extensive procedures associated with occlusal rehabilitation by means of full coverage of all teeth.

Case M. E. This patient, a man in his late forties, had no significant dental history beyond obvious neglect. The mandibular teeth closed anteriorly to the maxillary teeth in the centric occlusion in which he closed by himself (Figs. 46 and 47). It is important to note here that both the lower right central and lateral incisors had extruded. This was proved by the fact that the anatomy of the left central incisor showed definitely that it had not worn to any great extent. Also the cusp of the upper right cuspid articulated with the distal slope of the cusp of the lower right first bicuspid. The cusp of the lower left cuspid slid upward past the lingual surface of the upper left cuspid and onto the mesial surface.

With the tip of the finger placed very lightly against the point of the chin, the patient was directed to close the mandible. Fig. 48 shows the vastly different position the patient assumed. When this happens without pressure forcing the mandible back, we know that this position must be approaching the patient's true centric relation although when the patient has been accustomed to a convenience centric relation for many years, it may take some time for the mandible

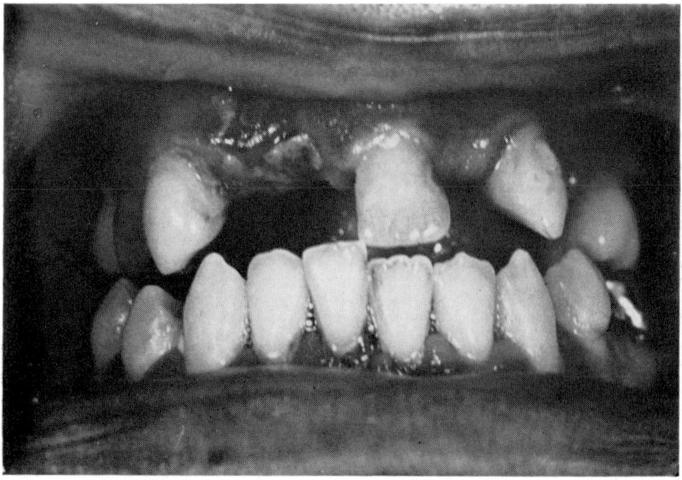

Fig. 48. Position assumed by patient in Figs. 46 and 47 when patient closes with tip of operator's finger against his chin. This is true centric relation. Note how incisal surface of lower left incisor has been protected so that mamelons are still present even though patient is in mid-forties. The extrusion of the lower right central incisor prevents any other contact.

to find (and it should be allowed to do so unaided) its correct position.

With closure in true centric relation, note (Fig. 48) that the vertical dimension is vastly increased. Maintaining this centric relation under these conditions would subject the patient to all the disabilities that a vastly increased vertical dimension of pathogenic proportions would. However, note that the mesioincisal corners of the upper left and lower right central incisors are maintaining this vertical dimension. As in Case L. B., an economic problem limited severely our planning and we were limited in essence to an acrylic resin veneer on the upper left cuspid and two removable partial dentures.

The same procedure was followed as in Case L. B., that is, reduction of occluding surfaces and realignment of cusp planes, since these were the factors maintaining the malocclusion. After reduction and realignment (Fig. 49), the upper incisor was in an edge-to-edge relationship with the lower incisors. The upper right cuspid articulated with the lower cuspid and with the mesial slope of the cusp of the lower right first bicuspid. The lingual surface of the upper left cuspid

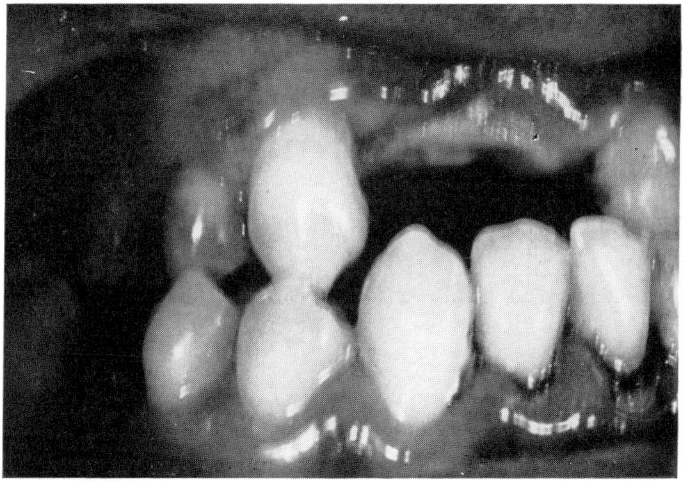

Fig. 49. Position assumed by patient unaided in simple occlusal equilibration. Compare with Figs. 47 and 48. Note cuspal relationships.

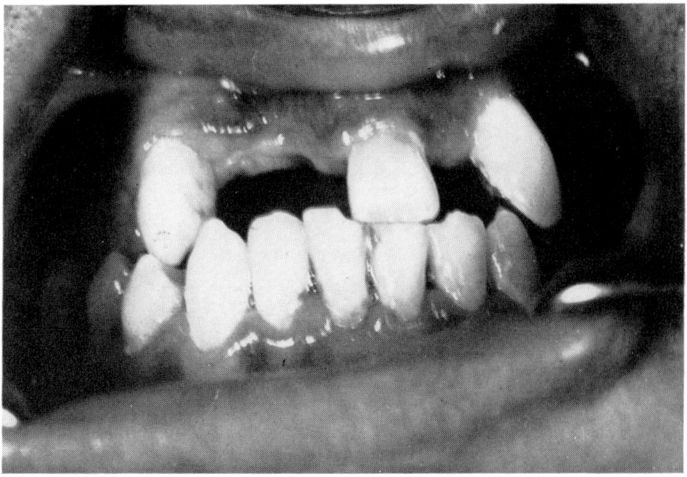

Fig. 50. Taken two weeks after Fig. 49. An acrylic resin veneer crown has been placed on the upper left cuspid.

was directly over the cusp of the opposing lower cuspid, but there was no contact with either lower cuspid or first bicuspid and for this reason an acrylic resin veneer was necessary. The posterior teeth were related in a similar manner. Two weeks after the teeth had been adjusted so that the mandible was freed to find the true centric relation as determined by the patient's musculature, the central incisor returned to a position labial to the lower incisors (Fig. 50).

REFERENCE

1. Scheman, P.: A preliminary report on the role of the dentist in a mental hospital, J. Hillside Hosp. **5**: 488-494, 1956.

CHAPTER 13

OCCLUSAL REHABILITATION

Occlusal rehabilitation presents an even greater problem than does occlusal equilibration. It is not a procedure to be undertaken lightly. A more perfect occlusion can be obtained with occlusal rehabilitation than with occlusal equilibration, but much more damage can be done. Occlusal rehabilitation must be recognized as the extensive and radical procedure it is. It should be used only with the greatest care and restraint and only when it alone can solve the problem. Like occlusal equilibration it should be used only when there is a pathogenic occlusion evidenced by definite disease in some element of the temporomandibular articulation, namely, the teeth, periodontal tissues, temporomandibular joint, or the neuromuscular mechanism of the mandible. When a pathogenic occlusion cannot be corrected sufficiently by occlusal equilibration, then and only then should the practitioner think in terms of occlusal rehabilitation. Such a situation may arise for several reasons:

1. When the grinding necessesary to equilibrate the occlusion would cause extensive loss of tooth structure to so many of the teeth that complete full coverage would be necessary to prevent widespread caries and such extreme sensitivity that eating would become well-nigh impossible and when the grinding would damage pulps.
2. When teeth are missing and the remaining teeth so

shifted that only occlusal rehabilitation can restore both the missing teeth and the occlusion.

3. When the teeth have so loosened that splinting the remaining teeth offers the only hope of preserving them; under these circumstances a fine point of diagnosis is involved, and consultations with and treatment by a periodontist may be indicated.

TECHNIQUE

In occlusal rehabilitation all the teeth receive full coverage and commonly are splinted as well. Whenever teeth are splinted, the opposing teeth must also be splinted or the unsplinted teeth will loosen. This principle is applicable even to a simple three-tooth fixed partial denture. The practitioner should be sure that the opposing teeth are in particularly good health periodontally before he inserts a fixed partial denture or ties together as few as two or three abutments for replacement purposes. It is sometimes advisable to make a fixed partial denture by soldering the pontic to one abutment and attaching it by means of a lock-in attachment to the other abutment to avoid the rigidity of two soldered joints.

When a patient is to have occlusal rehabilitation, it is essential that the whole mouth be prepared and all restorations and replacements be fabricated in conjunction with each other. To complete one section or quadrant at a time is equivalent to fitting a new door into an old and warped doorframe, thus perpetuating instead of correcting the defects.

The teeth are prepared in four visits. Any other necessary treatments such as root canal therapy, periodontal treatments, orthodontic movements, and any necessary extractions or surgery, should be completed prior to this procedure. At each of these four visits the teeth in a whole quadrant are prepared, the impressions are made, and the teeth are covered with temporary acrylic resin jackets, which are either fused together or individually fabricated depending on whether the teeth are to be splinted. The occlusion of the temporary jackets is made a simple flat one at the patient's original vertical dimension.

Preparations. The preparations should be done with an ultra high-speed handpiece. So extensive a procedure as occlusal rehabilitation is very straining on a patient, but with handpiece speeds in excess of 100,000 revolutions per minute vibration is eliminated and the time required is reduced, thus making the procedure far less traumatic. Ultra high speed also reduces the strain on the operator by reducing the time and thus decreasing his fatigue. The saving in time arises primarily from simplification in instrumentation. With one diamond stone, at most two, a tooth can be prepared completely.

Full coverage should serve two purposes, namely, function and esthetics. Only two types of crowns, porcelain fused to iridio-platinum or gold, and acrylic resin veneer crowns, provide both. Porcelain fused to iridio-platinum provides better esthetics but acrylic resin veneers are slightly stronger. Preparation of the tooth is essentially the same. The amount of tooth structure removed for the iridio-platinum crown is the same as that removed for a porcelain jacket crown plus the thickness of one layer of 29-gauge wax. The preparation can be shoulderless, chamfer, or shoulder (Figs. 57 and 58). If the shoulderless preparation is used, better esthetics can be obtained by making a chamfer or shoulder on the buccal or labial surface extending one third of the width of the proximal surfaces. This preparation can be completed with diamond stones (Fig. 59). A round-ended stone is capable of completely preparing a tooth for a chamfered preparation, whereas a thin pointed stone can make a shoulderless preparation. A square-ended stone in conjunction with a pointed stone to make a bevel can prepare a tooth for a shoulder preparation. A small wheel or ball stone is particularly useful for the lingual surfaces of the anterior teeth and also for the occlusal surface of the posterior teeth, if so desired.

Impressions of preparations. Impressions can be made in

several ways and with several different materials. Individual copper band impressions can be made with mercaptan rubber-base impression material or with modeling composition. These bands must be handled very carefully, otherwise serious damage can be done to the gingival attachment, causing later pocket formation or marked recession or both. Impressions of preparations en masse can be made with mercaptan rubber-base impression material, silicone impression material, or reversible or irreversible hydrocolloid. All these materials will produce satisfactory results in the hands of an operator who is familiar with the particular material and technique. It is wisest for each operator to adhere to the materials and techniques with which he can produce the most consistent results.

Transfer copings. Transfer coping may be of hard acrylic resin, nonprecious metal, or the precious metal to form the

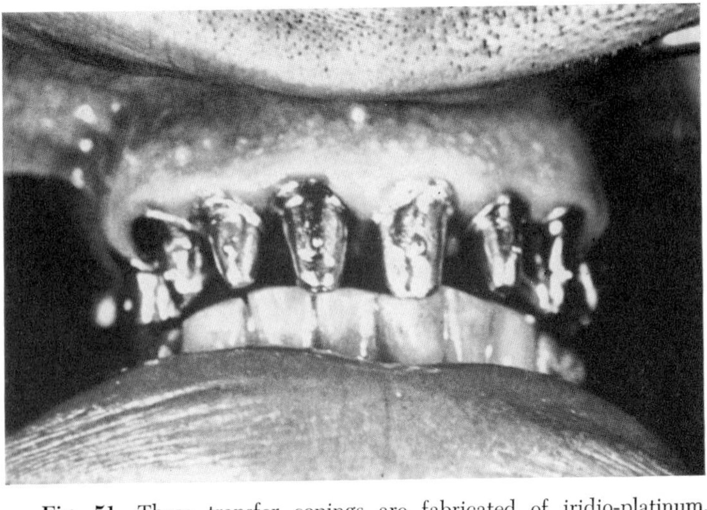

Fig. 51. These transfer copings are fabricated of iridio-platinum. They are fabricated directly on the dies obtained from copper band impressions. The plaster impression to be taken will be the only one needed since the porcelain will be fused to these castings. Thus a patient visit and another plaster impression are avoided.

final restoration depending on the circumstances (Figs. 51, 68, and 70). If a hole is left on the buccal or labial surface at the occlusal or incisal end of the preparation, it is possible to see directly the seating of the transfer coping. Since plaster is necessary for the final impressions, a lower tray should be used for the impression of the upper teeth—this will make the patient more comfortable by eliminating the plaster on the palate which serves no purpose.

If the restorations are to be acrylic resin veneer crowns, one visit and a full procedure can be eliminated. Gold thimbles carried accurately to the finishing lines of the preparations are used as transfer copings, the necessary relations and dimensions are established, and the master impression is taken. On this cast the final assembly is fabricated, assembled, and finished, and then returned to the operator for cementation.

For restorations of porcelain fused to iridio-platinum crowns, two different techniques are used. If the restorations are individual crowns, iridio-platinum castings are used as transfer copings and registrations and the final impression are taken. The crowns are then returned in the biscuit bake stage for adjustments, primarily for esthetics, and then are finished. When the restorations are to be soldered or are to be abutments for fixed or removable dentures, the transfer coping techniques described on pages 177 to 182 must be used. Iridio-platinum castings are returned to the operator, registrations and final impressions are taken and proceeded with as above.

Temporary coverage. When a tooth is prepared for full coverage, it must be protected from thermal shock and the patient's appearance must be maintained until the final restoration is placed. Acrylic resin jacket crowns accomplish both these purposes and also make it possible to splint teeth if desired. If there is any question about the vertical dimension, it can be tested by establishing it in temporary acrylic jacket crowns for a sufficient period of time.

Temporary acrylic jacket crowns can be fabricated in one

of several ways. The teeth on a stone cast of the patient's mouth can be cut down to a lesser extent than the planned preparations, and the laboratory technician can then fabricate acrylic resin jacket crowns on these stone pseudopreparations. When the teeth are prepared, self-curing acrylic resin is placed inside the prepared thimbles and then seated to place on the teeth which are full of undercuts and liberally coated with cocoa butter. This is allowed to set, is removed, smoothed, and polished, and then is cemented with a temporary zinc oxide and eugenol cement.

Another technique is to take impressions of the teeth before preparation, using irreversible hydrocolloid, mercaptan rubber-base impression material, or a hard baseplate wax. The impressions of the prepared teeth are then filled with self-curing acrylic resin of the correct shade and are seated to place on the prepared teeth which have been liberally coated with cocoa butter after making certain that there are no undercuts. This is maintained in position until the resin has set hard. The crown or crowns are then tapped off with a reverse mallet, polished, and cemented with temporary zinc oxide and eugenol cement. This yields an exact reproduction of the original tooth and occlusion. A variation of this is also possible. If the impressions are taken prior to the visit during which the preparations are made, thin thimbles are made by painting self-curing acrylic resin into the impressions of the teeth to be prepared. When the preparations have been completed, self-curing acrylic resin is placed in these thimbles which are then seated to place and are allowed to harden. The crowns are then removed, polished, and cemented to place with temporary zinc oxide and eugenol cement.

DETERMINATION AND REGISTRATION OF VERTICAL DIMENSION AND OF CENTRIC AND WORKING RELATIONS

To speak of vertical dimension is meaningless unless the speaker specifies which vertical dimension, whether in occlusion or in rest position. In the same way, centric relation is meaningless unless we specify the centric relation at a particular vertical dimension. Vertical dimension and centric relation are actually descriptions of maxillomandibular relation in two different planes, namely, the vertical and the horizontal.

If the patient presents with a correct occlusal vertical dimension, it should be measured with a Willis gauge (Figs. 94 and 95) and the measurement should be recorded on the patient's chart. A correct vertical dimension should never be changed. The advantage of the Willis gauge is that in measuring from the nasion to the gnathion it permits measurement by pressing against firm unyielding structures rather than against easily movable soft tissues as is done with adhesive tape or tattoo marks. It is best to determine the vertical dimension at the initial examination before the radical operative procedures may confuse the muscle sense or make recording more difficult. A simple way to check is to place a small ball of equalizing wax over the buccal cusp and onto the buccal surface of a lower bicuspid. The patient is then instructed to swallow several times. If only a thin layer of wax is left, the vertical dimension is correct. If the wax is completely cut through, there is an increased vertical dimension. If a thick layer of wax remains, there is a reduced vertical dimension. This test can be checked in turn by any one of several phonetic methods. A simple one is to have the patient say "hum" or make a steady humming sound and while he is doing so look into his mouth for at this time the mandible is in its physiological rest position. When a person swallows, his mandible rises to occlusion, moves posteriorly into centric relation, and then drops to the physiological rest position. These positions can be measured and recorded with a Willis gauge. To calculate occlusal vertical dimension by subtracting an arbitrary figure from rest vertical dimension only introduces an unnecessary element of guesswork into the determination of occlusal vertical dimension because the interocclusal space varies widely between individuals and must be determined separately for each individual. Wax bites should never be used because they are too treacherous. Quick-curing acrylic resin is the ideal material used as demonstrated in Figs. 52 and 53.

Centric relation is a neuromuscular relationship, a functional relationship. It can only be determined on a physiological basis. It should never be determined by arbitrary means, and this is true for all maxillomandibular relationships. When Gothic-arch tracings cannot be used to determine centric relation, the swallowing reflex is an accurate physiological means of checking and even of recording centric relation. Tapping teeth together rapidly also gives an accurate centric relation.

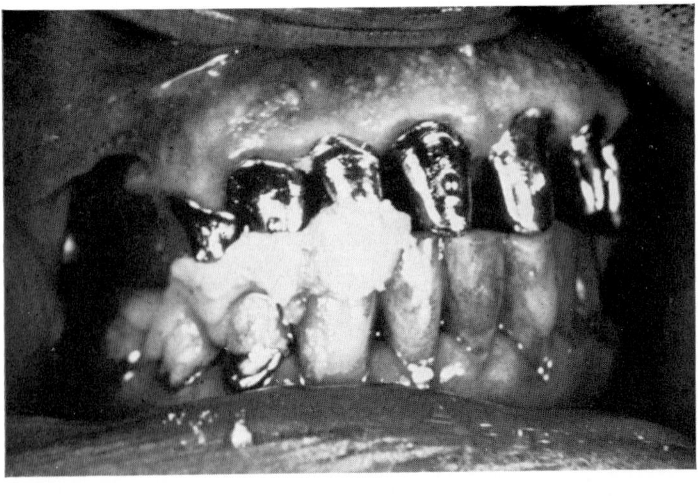

Fig. 52. Quick-curing acrylic resin is applied to the transfer copings, either upper or lower—in this case the lower. The resin here was thinned out on the lower copings to demonstrate more clearly the extent to which the copings are covered. This is the only technique for an accurate and unchanging registration.

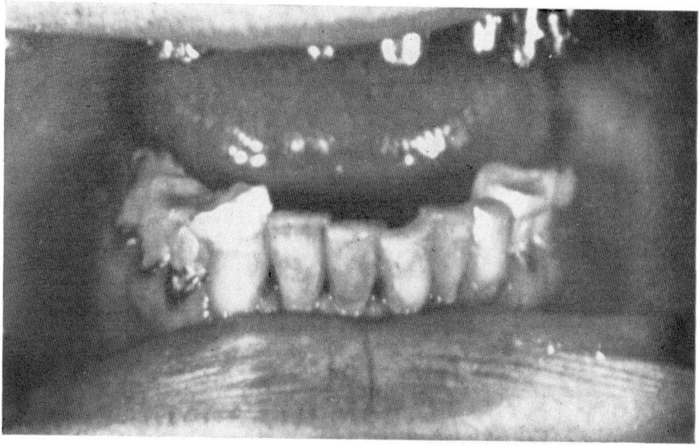

Fig. 53. Occlusal view of the quick-curing acrylic resin registration shown in Fig. 52. This should be checked as carefully as the relationships of the final appliance. When the patient taps his teeth together rapidly, he automatically does so in centric relation and will give an accurate relation. Articulating paper or 28-gauge wax can be used to check the above registration.

OCCLUSAL SURFACE ANATOMY

In occlusal rehabilitation, the anatomy of the occlusal surfaces should follow within limits that in the patient's own natural dentition when present to an extent sufficient to set a definite pattern of occlusal cusp relationship. When the occlusal cusp relationship is so defective that there is no definite pattern, the operator must perforce establish one. The patient who needs occlusal rehabilitation is almost never a young patient and the teeth have almost always suffered periodontal damage to a greater or lesser degree thus making a reduced amount of masticatory pressure advisable. This is attained in two ways: (1) by the use of flat cusps with accentuated sluiceways similar to many of the teeth now available for artificial dentures, and with a limited area of occlusal contact and (2) by a reduced occlusal table obtained by eliminating the second or third molars or by narrowing the buccolingual width or both.

Steep cusps should always be avoided in occlusal rehabilitation (Figs. 54 and 55), for the dentition is morbid rather than young and healthy. The steeper the cusps the more exact the occlusal centric relation necessary to prevent doing damage and also the less the ability of the mechanism to sustain any change, however slight, in centric relation. The patient who requires occlusal rehabilitation is a patient whose occlusion has degenerated to a point at which the entire neuromuscular system of the mandible is affected. Centric relation is no longer a fixed precise and extremely stable position but is transitory and shifting. Flat cusped teeth permit a change in occlusal centric relation without causing injury to the teeth, periodontal tissues, muscles, or temporomandibular joint.

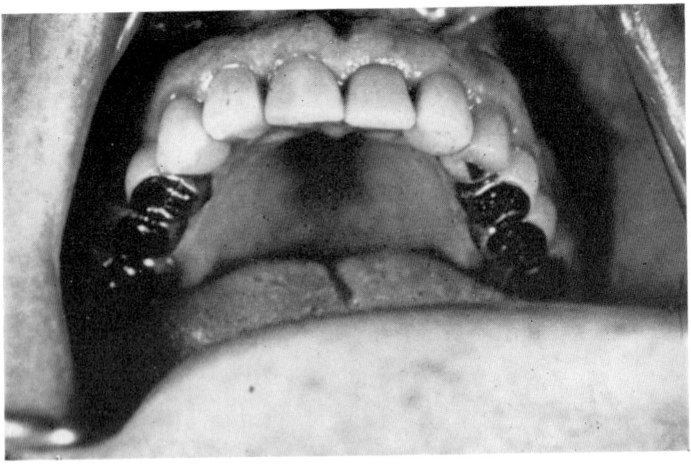

Fig. 54. The occlusal anatomy is almost flat with only the barest hint of cusps. This patient had an extremely well-developed mandibular musculature, and suffered from both clenching and grinding. The reconstruction was performed to prevent further loosening of the posterior teeth. Note the healthy condition of the gingiva.

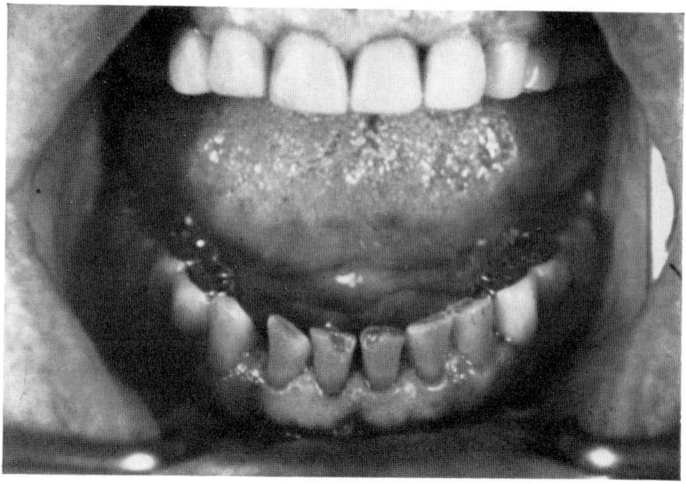

Fig. 55. This is the lower reconstruction for the patient in Fig. 54. Note the occlusal anatomy and the condition of the gingiva. Wherever possible the acrylic resin should terminate short of the gingival margin. Note that the lower acrylic facing is terminated short of the gingiva because here it can be done buccally without sacrificing the esthetics since this patient did not show this area in normal lip movements. Also note that the buccolingual width has been markedly reduced, thus sharply reducing the total occlusal table.

MATERIALS

In full-mouth occlusal rehabilitation only two materials are satisfactory for full coverage, namely, acrylic resin veneer crowns and porcelain fused to iridio-platinum crowns. Acrylic resin veneer crowns are completely satisfactory from the standpoints of strength and function, but they leave much to be desired esthetically, particularly in the left bicuspid to right bicuspid area where they are freely seen.

Crowns made of porcelain fused to iridio-platinum are the ultimate in modern dentistry (Fig. 56). They are comparable in strength, equal in function, and markedly superior in esthetics to acrylic resin veneer crowns, and produce the perfection of the porcelain jacket crown esthetically. The

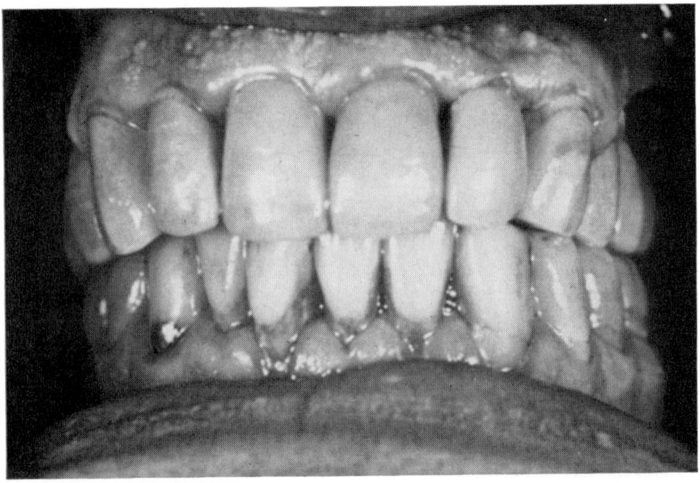

Fig. 56. Completed reconstruction of teeth shown in Figs. 51 to 53. Note how staining is used in all the upper teeth and the lower posterior teeth (the lower anterior teeth being the patient's own). Also note the healthy condition of the gingival tissues.

metal is no mysterious or patented material, being 90 per cent platinum and 10 per cent iridium, but it is difficult to handle. When a gold and a porcelain combination can be developed to give the proper esthetics consistently, this will be preferable because gold is much easier to handle.

Handling of porcelain. The esthetics of the porcelain jacket crown in any form depends on the operator, not on the technician. When the crowns are in the biscuit bake stage, the operator can perform a service that is richly rewarding both to the patient and to himself because it permits him the deep satisfaction that comes only from being truly creative. These crowns should be reshaped in every dimension—the incisal edge, the proximal surfaces, and the labial surface most of all. The labial surface must be shaped and carved from the mesial to the distal surface and from the incisal to the gingival surface. In this way restorations are produced that truly belong in the individual patient's mouth; that is, they will be in keeping with his age, sex, and personality. Finally the operator must determine the staining of the crown, that is, the locations to be stained in each individual tooth, the shade and depth of the stain and whether it is to be broad and heavy or so subtle as to be almost unnoticed except for the effect it produces. This is a most rewarding experience for the conscientious operator.

Cementation. Permanent cementation is no different from cementation of any restoration or fixed partial denture. A zinc phosphate cement is mixed to a loose consistency for two reasons: (1) it is more adherent and less likely to prevent complete seating of the restorations and (2) less heat is produced in setting and it causes less irritation or damage to the pulp. If the teeth are considerably sensitive after preparation or if they are prepared deeper than usual, a layer of calcium hydroxide will protect the pulp, but this layer must be kept free of the margins of the restoration.

If there is any doubt as to the condition of any of the teeth or the accuracy of any of the relations or dimensions, temporary cementation is advisable. For this purpose, experimentation with the various zinc oxide and eugenol temporary cements will soon reveal the best one for the operator. Cocoa butter should be incorporated in the mix to permit easier removal. On rare occasions it may be impossible to remove a restoration or appliance that has been temporarily cemented. If a crown and bridge reverse mallet will not budge the restoration or appliance, it should be observed and tested regularly at intervals of four to six months, but should cause no concern. It may eventually prove to be a permanent cementation. However, it is now possible and, we believe, preferable to do permanent cementation with special zinc oxide and eugenol cements.

CONTRAINDICATIONS

An extensive procedure such as occlusal rehabilitation is warranted only when the abutment teeth have a reasonable life expectancy, that is, a minimum of seven to ten years. This procedure should be carried out only if it will contribute materially to the health of the elements of the total temporomandibular articulation. Should it threaten the health of any of these elements, the procedure is contraindicated.

One other factor and an overriding one that must be carefully and thoroughly considered is the emotional welfare of the patient. Occlusal rehabilitation presents the patient with emotional problems of considerable magnitude. The emotional status of the patient must be thoroughly considered before embarking on this project because, done on the wrong patient, serious emotional problems and severe damage can result. Under certain circumstances it is even possible for the procedure to cause an emotional disturbance so serious as to require hospitalization. If the patient's emotional stability is at all uncertain, a consultation with someone trained to assess both the dental and the emotional problems is urgently indicated. We have seen patients for whom even small fixed partial dentures have been enough to produce severe grinding and clenching. In one of these patients extensive dental treatments would have caused long and possibly permanent hospitalization for mental disturbance.

CHAIRSIDE OPERATIVE PROCEDURES FOR OCCLUSAL REHABILITATION

Occlusal rehabilitation or any other restorative procedure is destined for total failure unless every tooth involved is first restored to its correct functional position. This is similarly true of occlusal equilibration and periodontal treatment. Thus to restore teeth, perform periodontal treatments, correct occlusion, or create a new occlusion are worthless procedures unless the teeth are in their correctly functioning position or are first so positioned. For the final result to be successful the teeth must have the correct relationship of the clinical crown to the root; that is, the relationship that will transmit the occlusal forces in the long axis of the tooth and the length of the clinical crown must be in correct proportion to that of the root. Thus it is frequently essential to move teeth orthodontically in order to perform periodontal treatments, occlusal rehabilitation, or occlusal equilibration successfully. This is just as true for the individual restoration and the simple replacement of one or more teeth.

Preparation and instrumentation

There are three basic types of tooth preparation for full coverage: (1) shoulderless, (2) chamfered, and (3) shoulder either with or without a bevel (Fig. 57). The shoulder preparation without a bevel is limited strictly to the porcelain jacket crown, but the others are universal preparations. However, when the shoulderless preparation is used for acrylic resin veneer or porcelain fused to metal crowns, a slight modification is preferable, namely to make a shoulder or chamfer on the labial or buccal surface extending into the

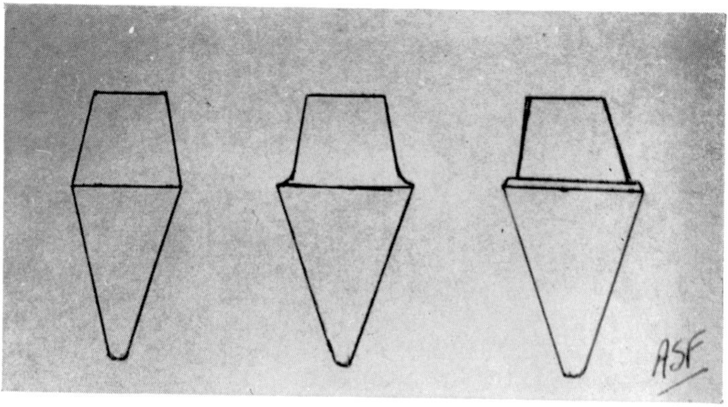

1 2 3

Fig. 57. Diagrammatic representation of buccolingual slice through a prepared tooth: **1,** shoulderless preparation; **2,** chamfered preparation (saucerlike at gingival end); **3,** shoulder preparation with a bevel (shoulder preparation without a bevel used only for porcelain jacket crowns).

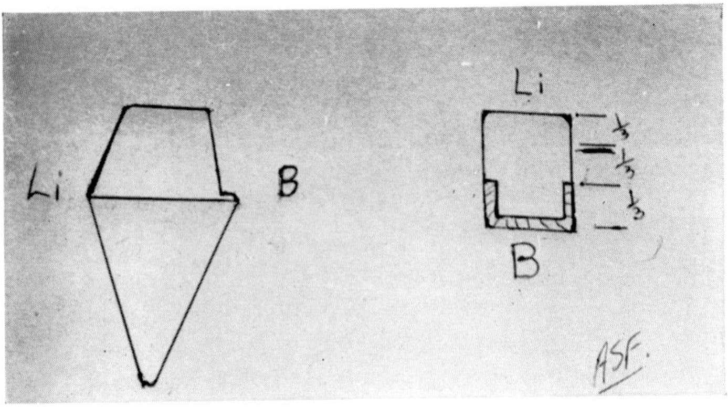

1 2

Fig. 58. Another diagrammatic representation of a slice through a prepared tooth: **1,** buccolingual slice showing shoulderless preparation with a buccal shoulder or chamfer added for acrylic resin veneer or porcelain fused to metal crown; **2,** diagram illustrating how far this shoulder or chamfer extends interproximally.

interproximal surface approximately one third its width (Fig. 58). With chamfered and shoulder preparations it is possible to check the seat of the casting conclusively with an explorer and therefore these are the preparations of choice for full coverage.

Ultra high speed instrumentation is essential for occlusal rehabilitation for two reasons: (1) speeds over 100,000 revolutions per minute eliminate vibration for the patient and (2) by proper use, the time needed for the procedures is markedly reduced and thus makes it easier for both patient and operator. Occlusal rehabilitation is a straining and fatiguing process for both patient and operator, and anything that reduces vibration and time required is of enormous importance. It must be understood that ultra high speed instrumentation saves time primarily by reducing the number of instruments used rather than by the speed of the instrument itself. The instruments in Fig. 59 constitute our full armamentarium of burs and diamond points for any full coverage preparation. We never use more than five instruments for any series of preparations, in the posterior teeth not more than four, and in many cases as few as two. The thin diamond stone (Fig. 59) is used to cut through interproximally and particularly in anterior teeth where a thicker stone might produce a pulp exposure. The barrel diamond stone (Fig. 59) can be used to make a complete preparation if the shoulder or chamfer is to be the same width as the stone, and the tapered square-end diamond stone (Fig. 59) can do the same for a shoulder preparation, followed by one of the tapered pointed diamond stones for making the bevel. The round ball diamond stone (Fig. 59) is ideal for preparing part of the lingual surface of anterior teeth which is extremely difficult to get at with any other stone. We prepare the tooth almost down to the gingival margin with coarse diamond

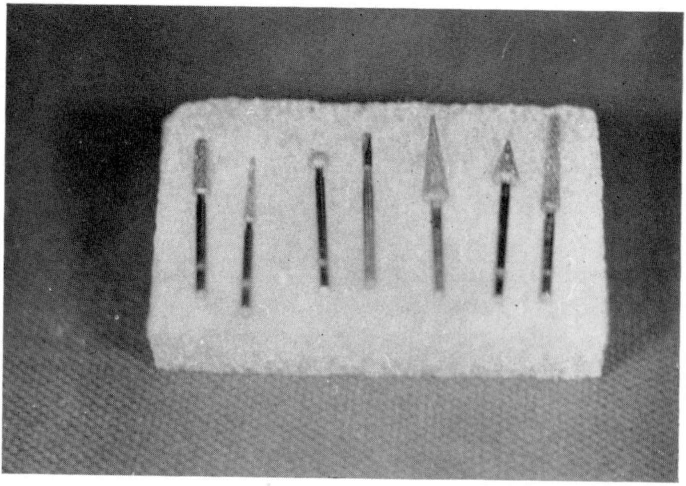

Fig. 59. Instruments used to prepare a tooth for full coverage with ultra high speed. From left to right: barrel diamond stone, thin diamond stone, round ball diamond stone, break-through bur, large and small triangular stones, and tapered square-end diamond stone.

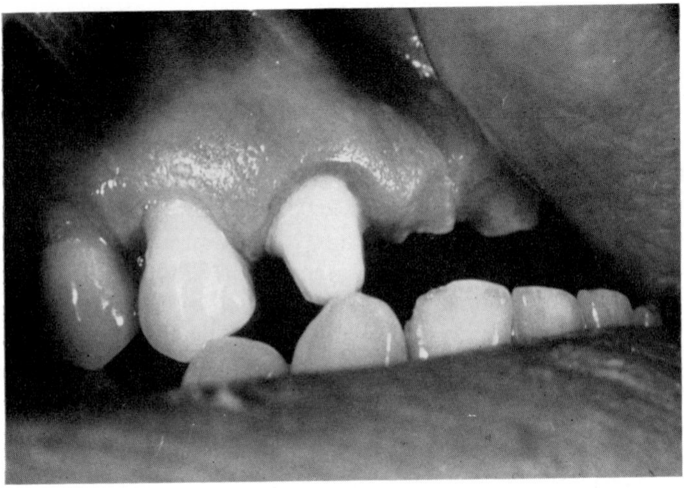

Fig. 60. Photograph taken immediately after completion of shoulder preparation with ultra high speed instrumentation; note condition of gingival tissues and lack of laceration and bleeding. Note that shoulder preparation was used.

stones and then carry the preparation below with the break-through bur (Fig. 59) making it possible to prepare under the gingival margin without injuring the gingiva or going too deeply into the body of the tooth. It is essential that the gingival margin be uninjured during the preparation since injury will cause it to recede at a later date. Injury to the gingival tissues produces a bluish rim around the gingival margin of restorations. There must be no injury to the gingival tissues during the preparation: absence of injury is evidenced by lack of bleeding (Fig. 60).

It is essential that adequate coolant be supplied to the tooth and the cutting instrument throughout the operative procedure, and the only adequate coolant is water. This means a large quantity of water enters the patient's mouth, and the high speed of the cutting instrument spins the water all about the mouth. High velocity evacuation equipment is essential to adequately remove this water and the saliva that is secreted. The routine saliva ejection system operated by the dental unit is totally inadequate for this purpose and will leave the patient most uncomfortable.

Impressions—materials and methods

Impressions of preparations are best confined to two media: (1) modeling composition and (2) mercaptan rubber-base impression material.

Modeling composition is the older material and is simpler to handle. The most important step is to festoon the thoroughly annealed copper band, the size of which must be very accurately chosen. It is essential to prevent the material from getting into the undercuts beyond the preparation for then it must be sprung in removing and this material is not elastic and will distort. It is very convenient to select the size of the band when the bulk of tooth structure has been removed

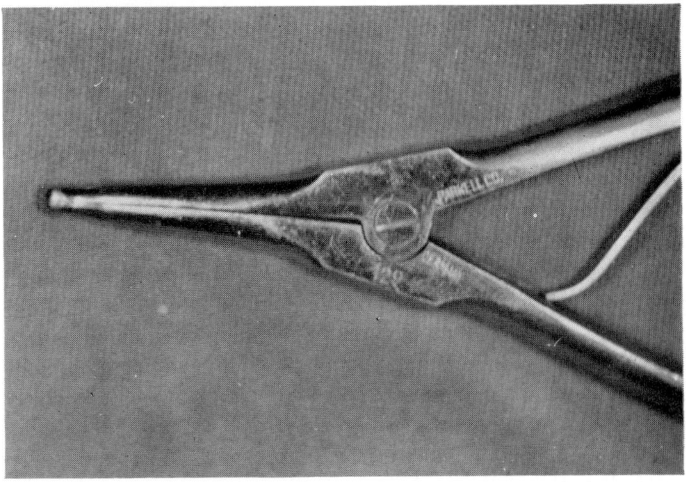

Fig. 61. Band stretcher. Copper band is placed on the beaks, and the handle is squeezed to enlarge the band as desired. To begin, the band is slipped on from the left as far as it will go.

and before the shoulder and bevel have been made. Extreme care in handling this band is essential at all times or the gingival attachment can be injured with all the permanent damage and disease that will result from this. If an in-between size is necessary, the smaller one is used and a band stretcher (Fig. 61) will bring it to correct size. In the rare instances where the band is too short, one band can be inserted inside another to give the correct length and a small amount of low-heat radio solder run around the junction to provide an adequate impression band. A curved scissors is used and a curved-beak orthodontic pliers (Fig. 62) will pinch in the end of the band to give it a tight fit and at the same time will smooth it so that there will be no sharp uneven edges to cut the gingiva as the band is slipped under it to place. Removal is easy and accurate with a pair of Baade pliers (Fig. 63) which cannot press in or distort the impression in the band

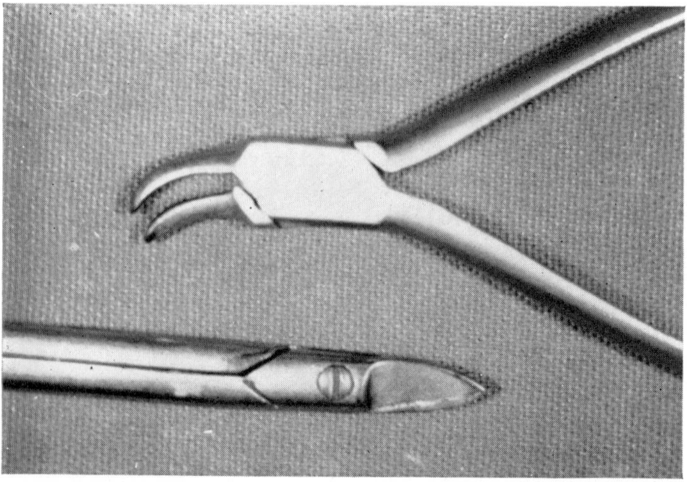

Fig. 62. The lower instrument is the curved shears of the type common in all dental armamentaria. Curved-beak orthodontic pliers permit the operator to smooth and pinch in the copper band so that it will fit snugly but will have no ragged edges to lacerate the gingiva.

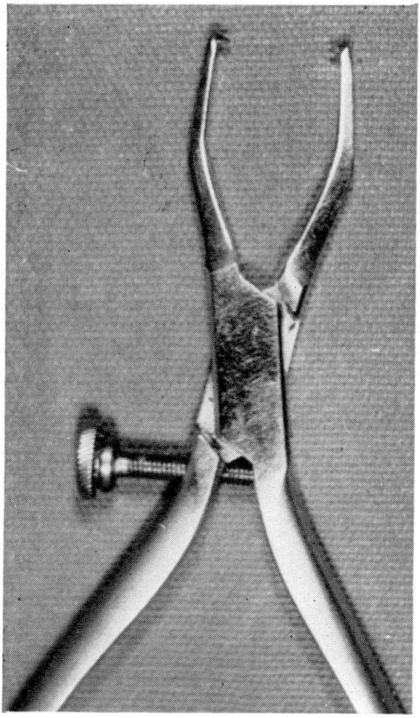

Fig. 63. Baade pliers. Needle points at ends of beaks permit a simple positive grip of the impression band without penetrating too deeply, and the screw on the handle can be adjusted so that the needle points will exert no pressure to distort the impression.

and can be used to remove the impression in a straight vertical direction in the long axis of the tooth. The screw on the handle is adjusted so that the needle-sharp beaks cut just through the copper band. The impression is then removed either with a straight pull or by using a wooden block on another tooth as a fulcrum in such a manner that the band is removed in a straight line in the long axis of the tooth.

Mercaptan rubber-base impression material can in a number of different ways shorten the time the patient must spend in the dental chair. With this material it is possible to take the final impression for both the individual preparations and the complete replacement whether it be a three-unit fixed partial denture or a fourteen-unit soldered splint replacing any number of missing teeth. The injection technique is best, and the Coe injection syringe is best in weight and design. Two types of material are used—light-bodied material is injected about the tooth and heavy-bodied material is used for the mass impression over injected material and balance of teeth on the same side. The gingival tissues around the abutment teeth should be retracted to expose the entire preparation, but this should never be done with an electrocautery since this will lead to future recession. A cord impregnated with the formula used in Gingipack wrapped around the tooth will permit an accurate impression by safely exposing the tooth down almost to the gingival attachment.

Cementation

The traditional method of cementing restorations with zinc oxyphosphate cement has been improved upon in recent years by coating the tooth with calcium hydroxide, but this should be kept well away from the margins of the preparation. Many traditional techniques should be re-examined in the light of modern knowledge. It has long been known that zinc oxyphosphate has properties that irritate the dental pulp, but no substitutes have been available.

When a sedative is necessary we have always fallen back upon zinc oxide and eugenol cements or some variation of them. For some time we have been using Temrex, a permanent zinc oxide and eugenol cement, for permanent cementation, and successfully. When the preparation has been deep into the body of the tooth, this cement gives a feeling of security so far as the health of the pulp is concerned, although we have been hesitant to use this for inlays only because of the limited experience with this material.

It is also possible to obtain temporary zinc oxide and eugenol cements in tubes. These cements make it unnecessary to use the traditional method of adding petroleum jelly or cocoa butter to facilitate removal at a later date.

Checking occlusal contacts

It is always difficult to determine which cusps are in contact by looking into the patient's mouth, regardless of whether the patient has the entire natural dentition, a complete occlusal rehabilitation, or complete dentures. Articulating paper in any form has some thickness and may show contacts when actually the teeth are separated by this thickness and the contacting cusps have cut through the articulating paper to allow markings elsewhere where there is no contact in occlusion. The use of wax introduces bulk into the mouth and causes some reaction by the patient's musculature and thus is not entirely trustworthy.

However, if a loop of dental floss is passed around the most posterior tooth present and both ends are held in front of the patient's lips, there will be no bulk and the patient is able to close until the first teeth contact. If the dental floss is pulled forward, as the loop moves forward along the occlusal table the contacts can be felt, and a sensitive touch will indicate even the degree of contact and lack of contact. This can be done also in centric occlusion. This technique provides a degree of accuracy that cannot be equalled by any other technique.

Transfer copings

Transfer copings can be made of any one of three materials: (1) hard self-curing acrylic resin, (2) nonprecious metal, or (3) precious metal to be used in the final crown. When the transfer coping can be made in the final precious metal to be used, the amount of time the patient must spend in the dental chair can be reduced because the final case can be fabricated directly and completely on the cast thus obtained since the casting can be checked in the transfer-coping stage for both fit and length. When acrylic resin transfer copings are used, the castings must first be checked on the abutment teeth, the impression must be made and then first, on the cast thus obtained, the appliance is fabricated.

Materials

Two materials are best for complete coverage in occlusal rehabilitation—acrylic resin processed to gold and porcelain fused to metal. Acrylic resin veneer crowns are too familiar to require discussion. However, when the transfer copings are made of gold, a second casting can be made over this (Figs. 64 to 67) after which solder is run around the junction of the two castings. A nonoxidizing type of investment is used for the second casting to the original coping. Once the gold copings are tried in and checked for fit and length under the gingival margin, maxillomandibular relations are registered and a final impression is made. On the cast thus obtained, the entire appliance is fabricated and carried to completion, because the accuracy of this technique is dependable. Acrylic

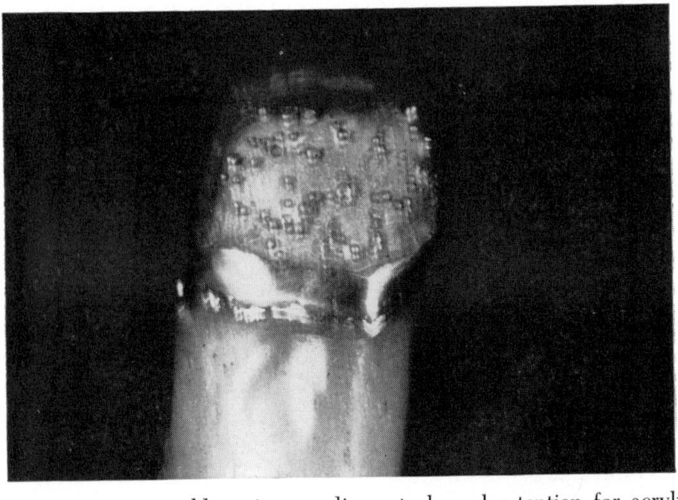

Fig. 64. Cast gold coping on die; note buccal retention for acrylic resin.

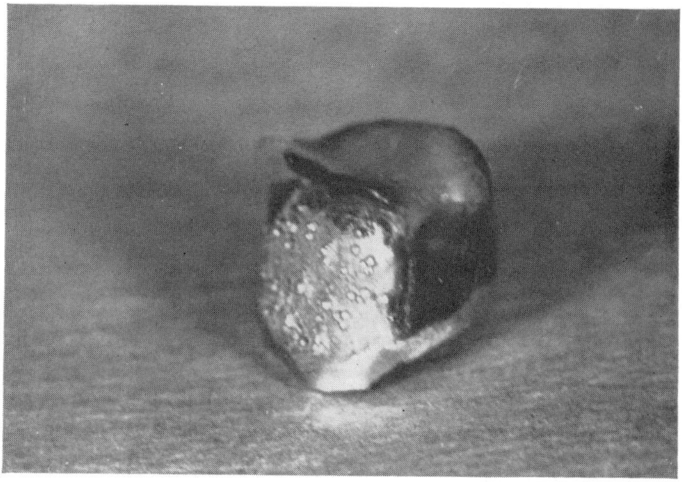

Fig. 65. Wax-up for second casting to produce gold crown for acrylic resin veneer; this wax-up was made on the coping shown in Fig. 64.

Fig. 66. Casting of wax-up in Fig. 65 with sprues and button in place; large size of casting required two sprues.

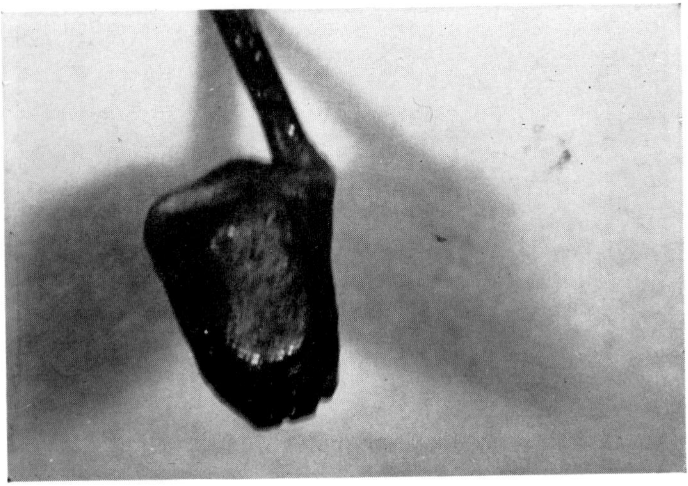

Fig. 67. Different type of wax-up on gold coping sprued for investment.

resin transfer copings allow too much chance of error and inaccuracy in fit to permit completion without first checking the final castings by themselves, and then taking the maxillo-mandibular relationships and a final impression.

When porcelain fused to metal crowns are used, the technique varies in accordance with the case. When an individual restoration is to be made, an individual copper band impression is made (if modeling composition is to be used) and the laboratory returns a casting of whatever metal is to be used, which then acts as the transfer coping (Fig. 68). When a fixed partial denture or splint is to be constructed, a different technique is necessary because the metal castings must be fabricated with flanges that come to contact or very close to it to provide for soldering. In Fig. 69 a small fixed partial denture was to be constructed. If mercaptan rubber-base impression is used, a final impression is made and the denture can be completed on the resulting cast. However, if modeling composition is to be used, individual

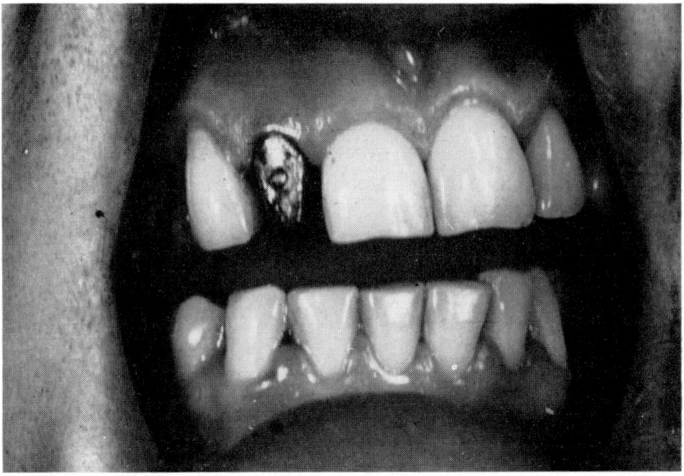

Fig. 68. Iridio-platinum casting in position; this acts as the transfer coping, but it is the final casting to which the porcelain will be fused.

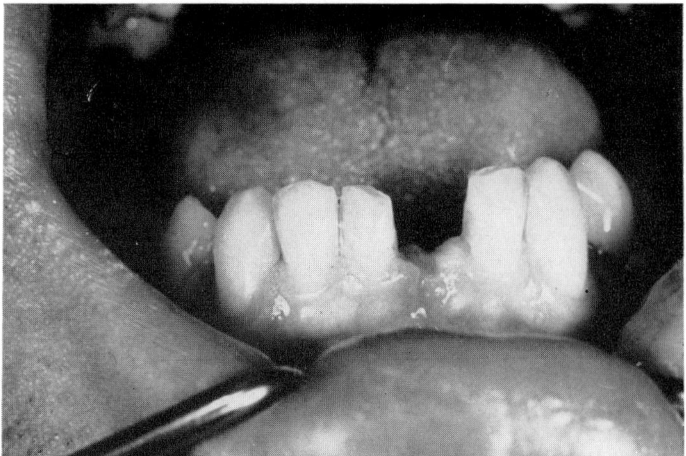

Fig. 69. A fixed partial denture is needed. Porcelain fused to iridio-platinum is ideal under these conditions. It was not possible to use a conventional shoulder preparation on all three teeth because of the large pulpal chambers and the shape of the teeth.

copper band impressions are made, then self-curing acrylic resin or nonprecious metal transfer copings, which are placed in position in the mouth. A plaster impression of the area is taken to provide a cast on which the castings are fabricated (Fig. 70). A final full-mouth plaster impression provides the cast from which the technician will fabricate and finish the denture (Fig. 71) after the frame has been checked in the mouth. This particular case illustrates the wonderful flexibility of this material because we have the esthetics of porcelain where a shoulderless preparation is needed to preclude a pulp exposure, thus combining the advantages of the acrylic resin veneer crown with those of the porcelain jacket crown.

Porcelain fused to metal is the ultimate in modern dentistry and therefore is a subject of overwhelming importance. It provides the accuracy of fit of the cast crown with the esthetics of the porcelain jacket crown, and its strength is comparable to the acrylic resin veneer crown. Only at the

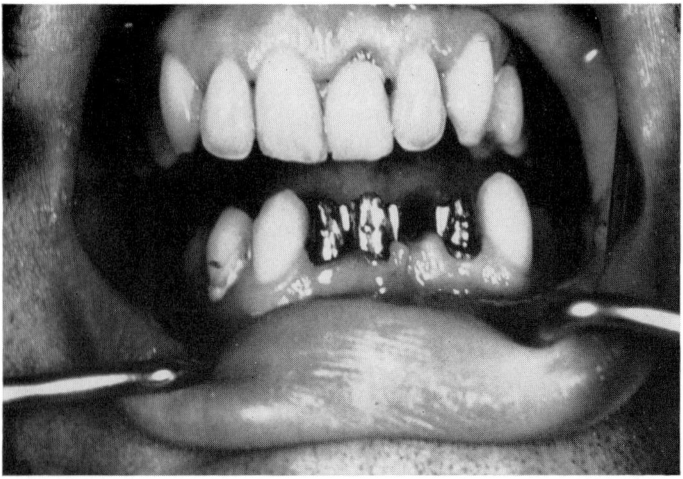

Fig. 70. Iridio-platinum castings. Note how flanges are built for soldering at contact points; this is why resin or nonprecious metal transfer copings and a sectional plaster impression are necessary.

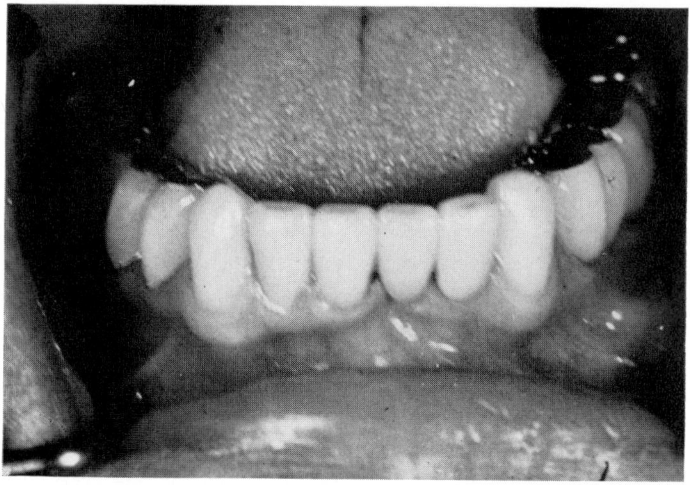

Fig. 71. Porcelain fused to iridio-platinum fixed partial denture for dentition shown in Figs. 69 and 70. Note staining of incisal edges and healthy condition of the gingival tissues even in this difficult area; also note the interproximal spaces and the contact points at the normal position. This problem can only be solved by porcelain fused to iridio-platinum crowns and is the reason it is the ultimate in modern dentistry.

buccal or labial surfaces and slightly into the interproximal surfaces should the porcelain extend (and even then only slightly) under the gingival margin; elsewhere there should be at least 2 millimeters of metal showing above the gingival margin so that this tissue is maintained as healthy as possible by having the material under it as thin as possible. With this technique it is also possible to have highly glazed porcelain (the material of choice) against the ridge lap (Fig. 72) and adequate interproximal embrasures can be provided (Figs. 71 to 74).

While the preceding considerations may seem removed from our basic consideration of temporomandibular joint problems, they actually are related closely in and of themselves. Any discomfort in the mouths of certain patients will aggravate or even produce grinding and clenching. Gingival

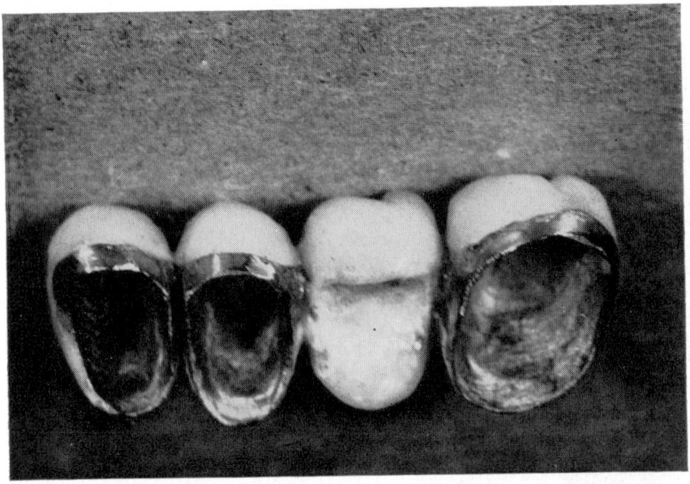

Fig. 72. Fixed partial denture of porcelain fused to iridio-platinum showing how highly glazed porcelain contacts the ridge lap; note adequate interproximal embrasures and metal at gingival margin on lingual surface (facing camera) and part of the interproximal surface. Thus material under the gingival margins is kept thin and at a minimum.

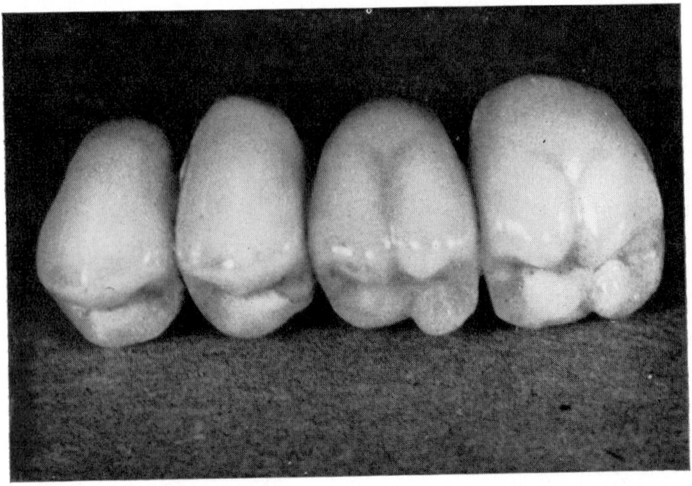

Fig. 73. Same fixed partial denture as shown in Fig. 72 but from buccal aspect showing interproximal embrasures and staining.

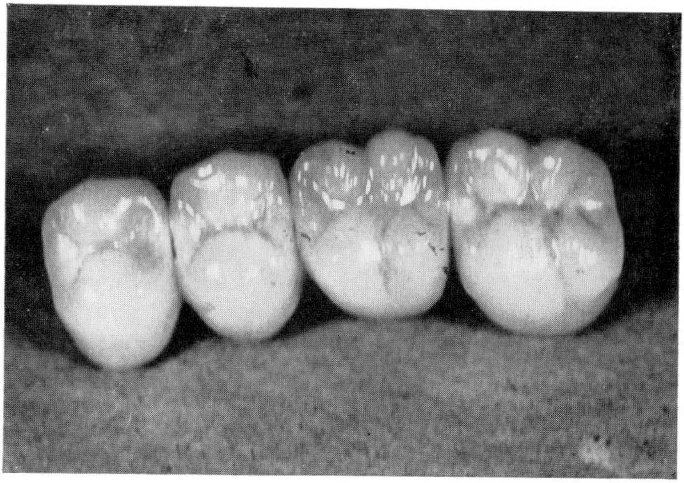

Fig. 74. Same partial denture as shown in Figs. 72 and 73 but from occlusal aspect showing the staining on the occlusal and lingual surfaces.

irritation seems to be a special offender in this respect, and even what clinically seems to be a mild gingival irritation produced by the fit of a pontic or crown can cause the patient to clench or grind. Dentistry might well begin to consider the possibility of using three-fourths crowns or inlays as abutments in fixed partial dentures when they offer sufficient strength and retention because they require less gingival irritation in operative procedures and the patient should never be subjected to any procedure that is longer than absolutely necessary.

Fixed versus removable partial dentures

The great bulk of temporomandibular joint problems have a myofascial basis. Thus the fixed removable partial denture that closely resembles the tooth or teeth it replaces is less likely to produce reactions of the tissues of the mouth and the mandibular musculature and is the preferable replacement; of course, this is not always possible. The removable partial denture introduces bulk and a large foreign body into the mouth which changes the contours of the dentition and by its very nature must move to some extent in use.

The preferable type of removable partial denture is the precision internal attachment type because it is most retentive, most stable, and thus most closely resembles the natural dentition. The precision internal attachment removable partial denture can be designed both to increase its retentiveness and to decrease later need for frequent adjustment of the male attachment. Anterior and posterior abutments are almost as necessary for this type of removable partial denture as for a fixed partial denture, and when a free-end saddle is used the abutment tooth on the same side must be splinted to at least one other tooth or the inevitable stresses placed upon it will loosen it.

A small dent is made in the lingual surface of the abutment casting at the junction of the middle and occlusal thirds of the tooth. A piece of 19-gauge gold round wire is balled at one end. In the framework casting of the denture a groove is prepared for this wire in such a way that the wire runs in the groove for a short distance and then up along the tooth so that the ball of the wire fits into the dent prepared for it; it is then soldered to the framework at the point farthest from the abutment tooth and balled end (Figs. 75 to 77). This round wire acts as a spring, snapping into the dent in the abutment casting in seating the denture and preventing the forces of mastication from loosening the denture. The denture can be loosened only when the patient actively does so in removal by hand.

There are instances when it may even be necessary to cantilever a molar pontic from abutments anterior to it. This can be done successfully if the abutments are satisfactory, the fixed partial denture is designed properly, and the opposing dentition is also properly prepared. The patient's profession may require this; for example, a singer or certain types of musicians are severely affected by any changes in the mouth

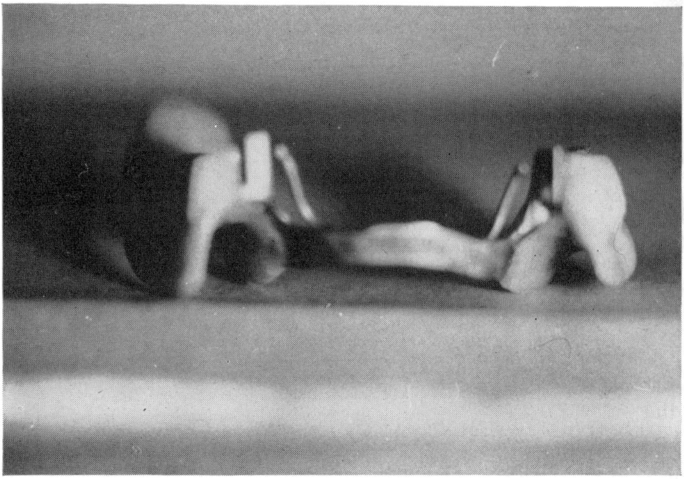

Fig. 75. View from front showing lower lingual bar precision attachment removable partial denture with balled retention wires.

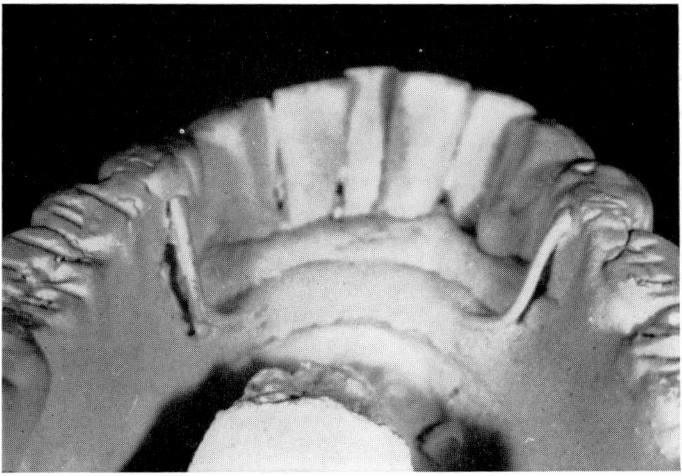

Fig. 76. Study cast of appliance in Fig. 75 illustrating how the round wires fit into the abutment castings. Note the length of wire from the point of soldering far forward on the lingual bar casting.

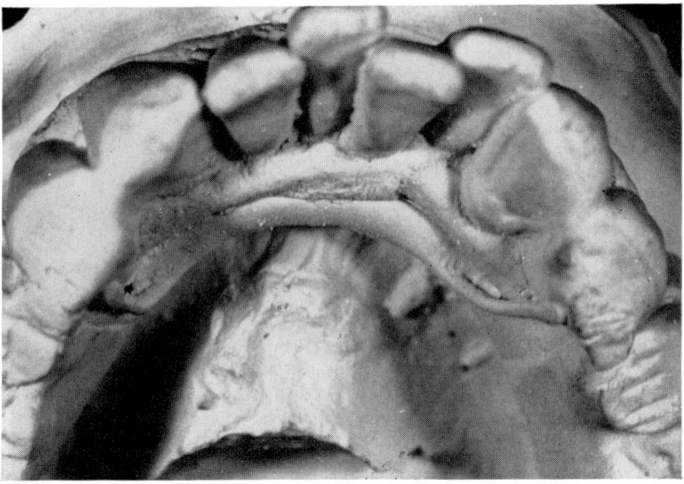

Fig. 77. Another view of study cast in Fig. 76 to show length of round wire and fit into abutment casting. Again note how far forward is the point at which the round wire is soldered to the lingual bar.

and the bulk of a removable partial denture may eliminate the patient from his profession. Also the patient's emotional make-up may negate the use of a removable partial denture; for example, one patient, an artist, believed that if he had to wear a removable partial or complete denture he would be unable to paint again. Here again the total human being must be considered for certainly such an effect is more than enough to warrant breaking the rules of dentistry.

Case histories

Case J. N. This patient, a woman in her late forties, presented with the dental condition seen in Figs. 78 to 80. Examination showed that the centric vertical dimension had decreased materially, and as a result the upper incisors were being driven labially to an extent that diastemata were present between all the incisors, particularly between the central incisors. The study casts in Figs. 79 and 80 show how all the upper incisors had been rotated in the process whereas the lower incisors remained in a position that was good for a patient of this age. To correct

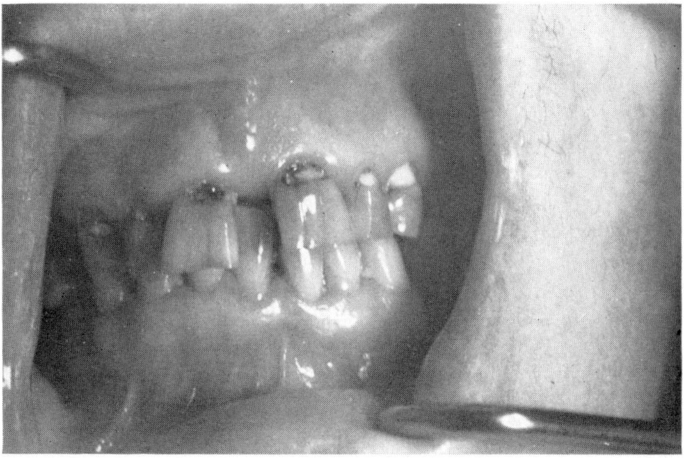

Fig. 78. Note extreme horizontal and vertical overlap, lower incisor almost touching incisive papilla, and large diastema between upper central incisors. This presents almost all the serious problems that a practitioner is likely to face.

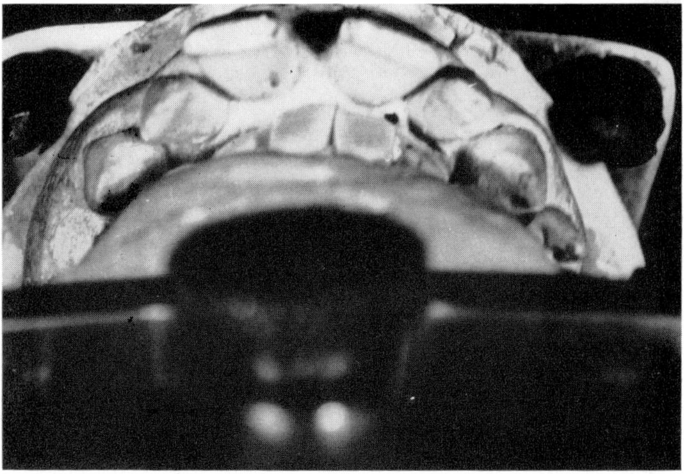

Fig. 79. Articulated study casts showing how extreme the horizontal overlap is and how far lingually lie the lower incisors.

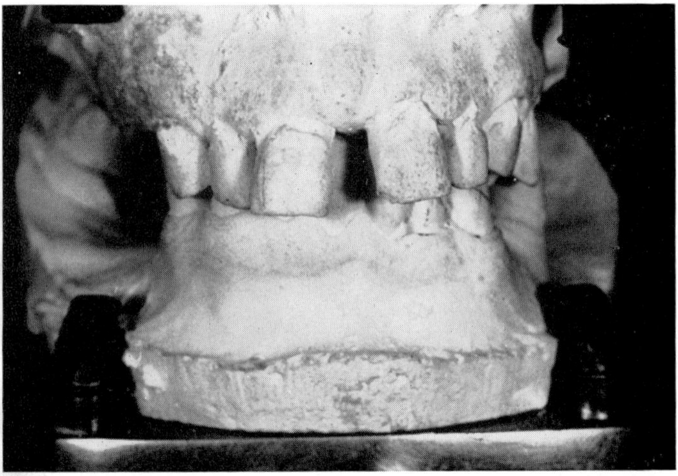

Fig. 80. Articulated study casts showing positions of incisors. Note extreme vertical overlap. This was due to a decreased vertical dimension.

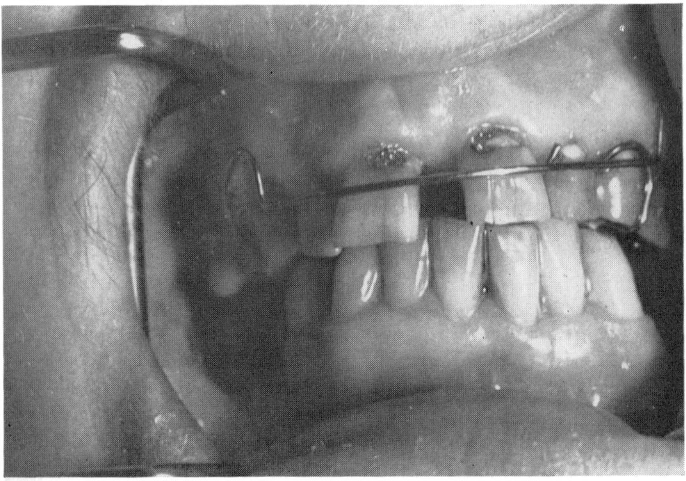

Fig. 81. Jackson crib appliance in position; note new vertical dimension found by functional techniques. Compare with Fig. 78.

this condition by full coverage of the upper anterior teeth only would put them in such poor clinical crown to root relationships that these teeth would have been lost because the clinical crowns would have extended at a sharp angle lingually from the roots. Only by first putting these teeth in their correct functional relationship could we hope to achieve a successful and permanent result.

A Jackson crib appliance was designed to accomplish the ends necessary, that is to restore the teeth to their correct functional relationships and to restore the vertical dimension and centric relation to their correct physiological position. In Fig. 81 the Jackson crib appliance is shown as it would appear to other people, which is often of paramount importance to the patient. If this photograph is compared to Fig. 78 the difference in vertical dimension can be seen clearly. When the correct centric vertical dimension is determined (physiologically as explained in detail on pages 160 to 162), the first appliance at this dimension should always be temporary to allow for changes, which are often necessary since no technique can give accurate scientific measurements if for no other reason than that the patient and his muscles are living, functioning, and constantly changing structures. The Jackson crib ap-

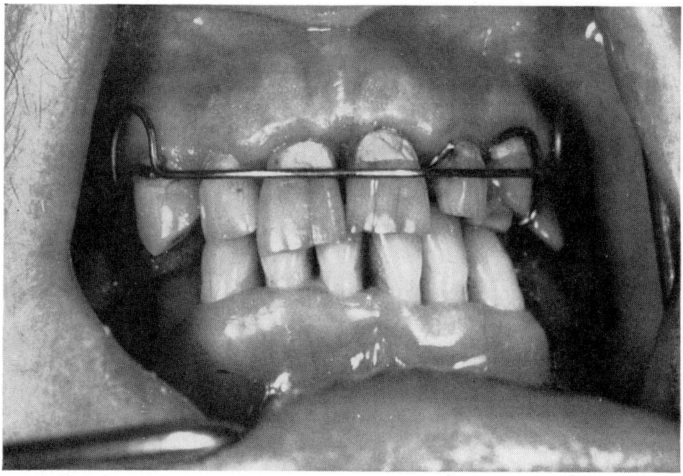

Fig. 82. Completion of orthodontic movement of dentition shown in Figs. 78 to 81; note individual movement and rotation of teeth by wires such as that seen at the gingival margin of the mesial surface of the upper left lateral incisor. Attachments for maintaining the new vertical dimension can be seen between the upper and lower bicuspids.

pliance permits these changes. The time necessary for these movements is so variable that it is worthless to give an estimate.

The patient is now ready for the final permanent steps of the occlusal rehabilitation (Fig. 82). The orthodontic appliance was used to move the upper anterior teeth into their best possible functional position, not merely to pull them in lingually. One of the spurs used to rotate and move the individual teeth in specific ways is seen at the gingival area of the mesial surface of the upper left lateral and the individual movements can be seen by comparing Fig. 82 with Fig. 78. The section of the Jackson crib appliance used to increase the vertical dimension can be seen between the bicuspids in Fig. 82. Thus the upper anterior teeth have been moved back into a good functional relationship and the anterior teeth are now in contact in centric occlusion and could maintain the vertical dimension (Fig. 83), although if allowed to do so at this point they would only be pushed out again. Articulated study casts (Figs. 84 and 85) show clearly how the teeth are in good functional position.

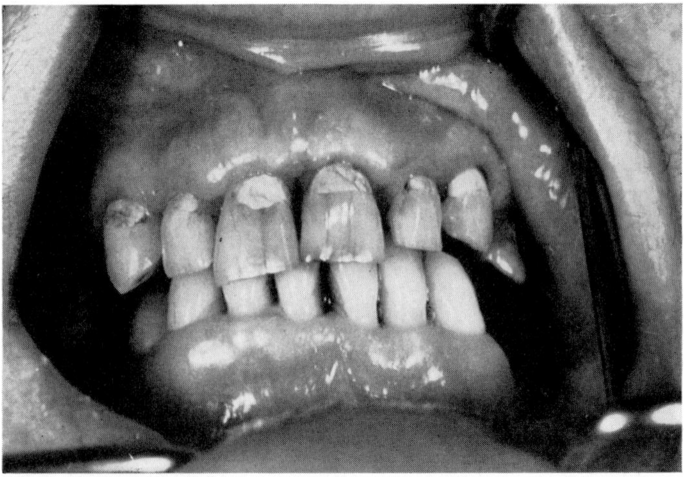

Fig. 83. The upper incisor teeth have been moved lingually so that they now contact the lower anterior teeth in a normal relationship so that the vertical dimension can be maintained for this photograph without the occlusal stops of the orthodontic appliance. Compare with Fig. 78 and note also that the upper incisors have been rotated into good position and the large diastema between the upper central incisors is closed.

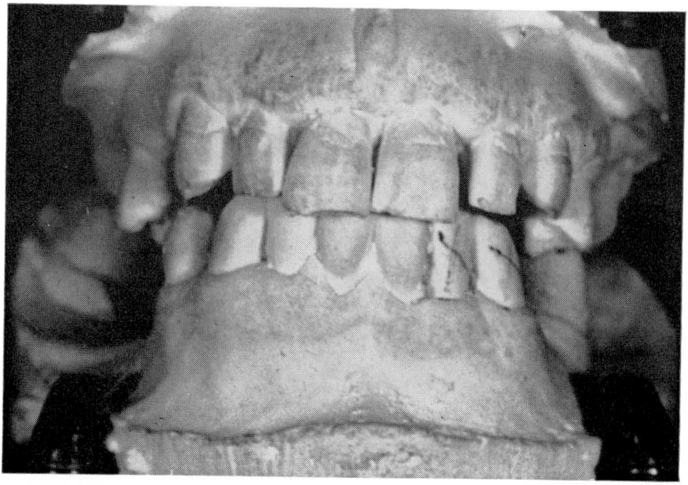

Fig. 84. Articulated study casts showing more clearly the position of the teeth in Fig. 83. Compare with Fig. 80.

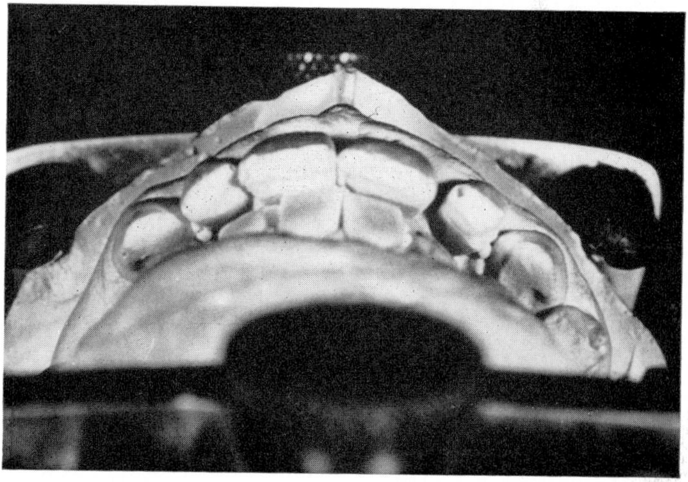

Fig. 85. Articulated study casts taken in same view as Fig. 79 to show the relationships of the incisal edges of the lower anterior teeth to the lingual surfaces of the upper anterior teeth. Compare the normal contact here with the lack of contact in Fig. 79.

The prescription for this patient called for splinting and replacement of the missing upper teeth with a fixed partial denture of acrylic resin veneer, splinting the lower right cuspid and first bicuspid in the same way, and a lower removable partial denture which for economic reasons was to be a clasp lingual bar type. The double casting technique previously described for acrylic resin veneer crowns was used, and Fig. 86 shows the gold copings in position for testing and adjusting. As discussed elsewhere, the whole mouth must be done at the same time if occlusal rehabilitation is to be successful; otherwise it is like fitting a new door into an old crooked doorframe making it necessary to shape the new door in the same crooked way.

At this point the lower nonprecious metal casting is tried in also. Wax is a thoroughly unreliable and inaccurate material for recording maxillomandibular relationships (see discussion on pages 160 to 162). Self-curing acrylic resin is the ideal material for this purpose, and Fig. 87 illustrates its use at this point to record centric relation at centric occlusion. The resin is allowed to cover only enough of the lower teeth to assure accurate seating of the casts in articulation. The upper copings are thoroughly covered, and a plaster impression is taken covering the resin and the copings. A lower impression tray is used (Fig. 88) so that

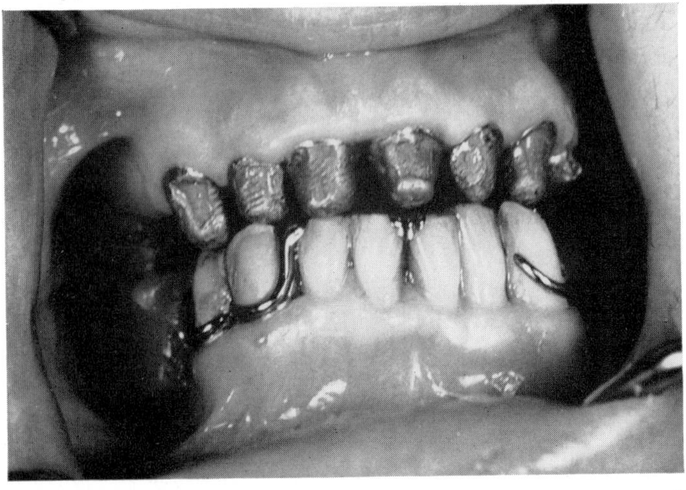

Fig. 86. The gold copings to be used in the double casting technique have been tested and adjusted. Note how they fit at the gingival margin. This is vital since this will be the permanent fit.

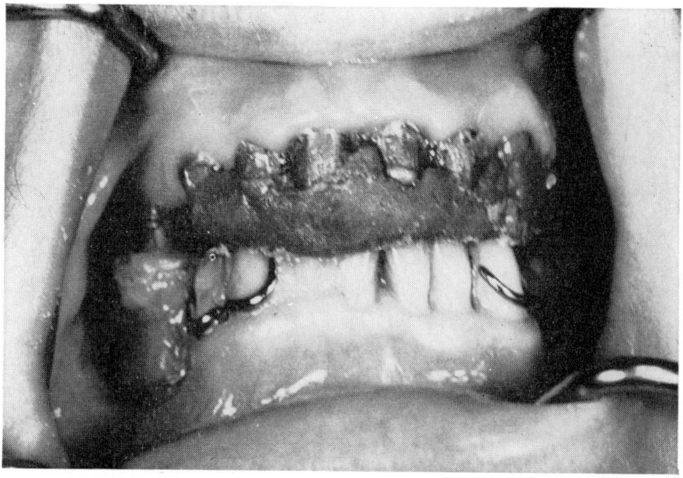

Fig. 87. Self-curing acrylic resin registering centric relation; note that the resin covers enough of the lower teeth to provide for accurate seating of the casts for articulation. Only by the use of acrylic resin is it possible to ensure the accurate articulation of the casts.

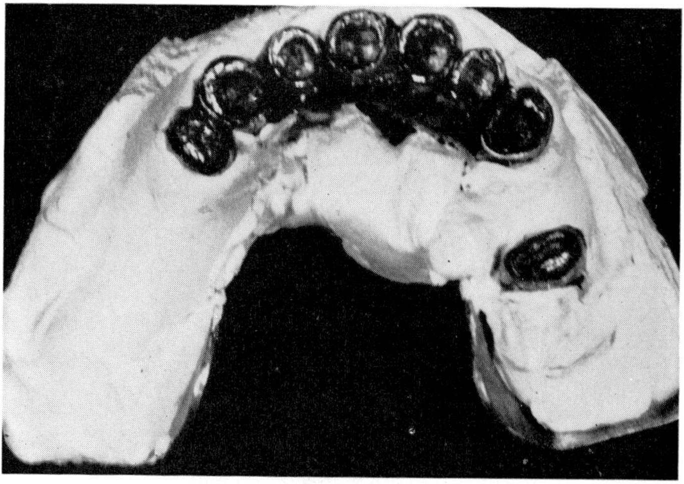

Fig. 88. Plaster impression of maxilla; a lower impression tray was used so as to limit the plaster on the palate which is of no value for fixed partial dentures. The self-curing resin used to record centric occlusion can be seen at the palatal areas of the gold copings.

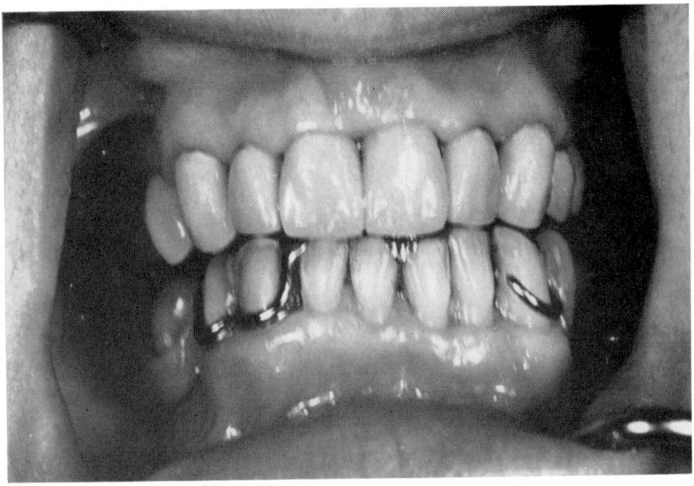

Fig. 89. The complete upper framework with the facings in white wax is tried in. It is then recarved in the mouth and the staining is prescribed. Only when the dentist himself does this can proper esthetics be obtained.

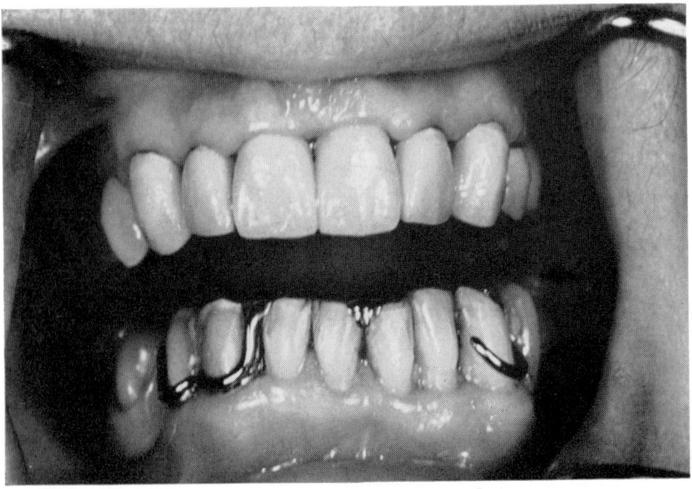

Fig. 90. The final appliances in position. Compare with Figs. 78 and 89.

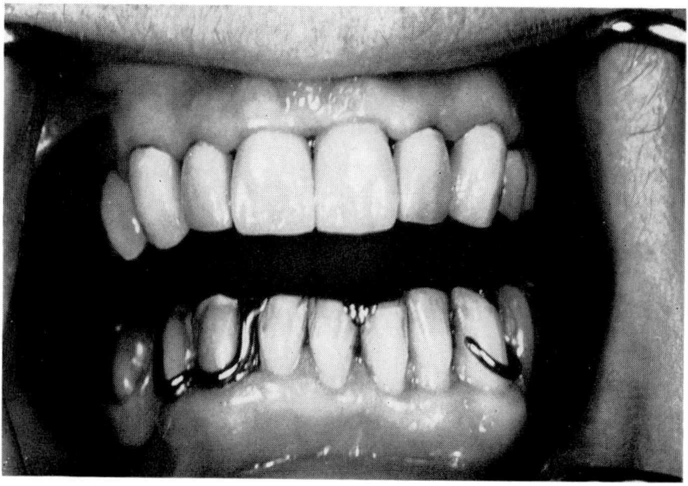

Fig. 91. Another view to show carving and staining of completed appliance. Compare with Fig. 89.

there is very little plaster on the palate to annoy the patient and to give registrations that are of no value for fixed partial dentures. The acrylic resin between the copings also prevents loss of small or thin pieces of plaster which although a small proportion of the impression can invalidate it and can necessitate another impression.

When acrylic resin veneer crowns are used for the anterior teeth, it is best to try in the appliance with white wax in place of the final resin, so that the esthetics can be checked carefully (Fig. 89). When porcelain is used, the appliance is tried in at the biscuit bake stage, the porcelain crowns are ground for esthetics, and the staining is accurately prescribed. With acrylic resin veneer crowns, the same thing is done by using a complete wax-up of the facings on the completed framework, namely, proper carving of the wax and a prescription for the staining so that sex, age, and personality of the patient are reflected in the teeth and they look, as they should, to be an integral part of the human being. Figs. 90 and 91 show two different views of the dentition after occlusal rehabilitation.

Case C. H. This case mirrored Case J. N. and is of interest because it shows more clearly the Jackson crib appliance in position (Fig. 92) with self-curing acrylic resin on the posterior teeth, which was added because the original low-fusing metal wore down so far as to affect the centric vertical dimension originally established. Occlusal rehabilitation

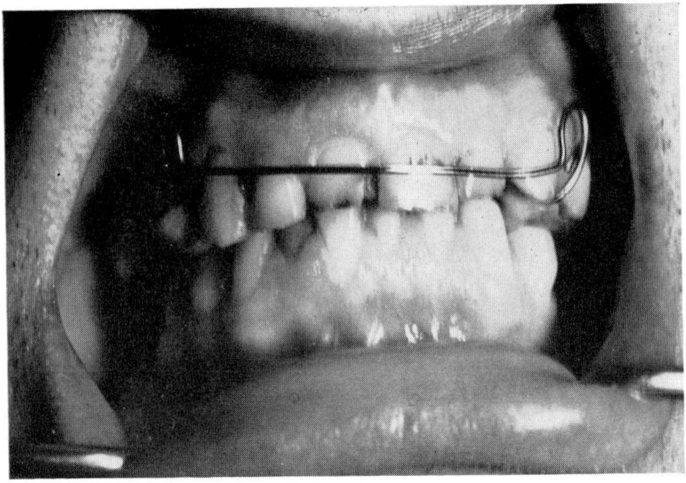

Fig. 92. Jackson crib appliance in position showing self-curing acrylic resin establishing the vertical dimension (see posterior teeth). Only at the correct vertical dimension was there sufficient space to pull the upper incisors both in and together.

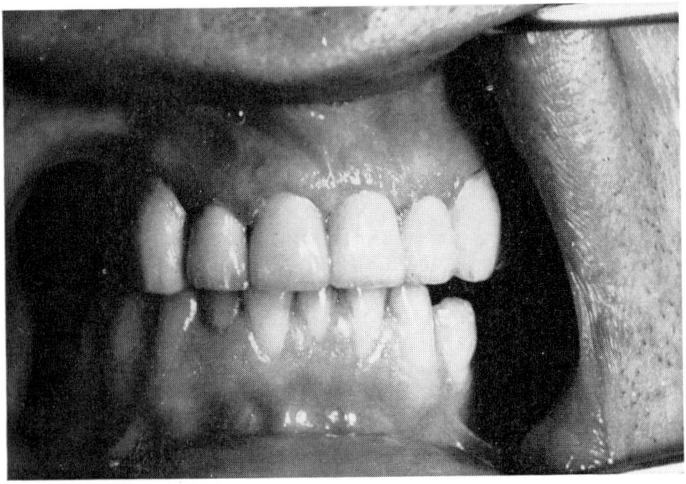

Fig. 93. Case in Fig. 92 completed by splinting upper anterior teeth with porcelain fused to iridio-platinum crowns.

Fig. 94. Willis gauge showing scale in millimeters and shortened upper fixed arm. The instrument is supplied with both arms of equal length.

was completed with porcelain fused to iridio-platinum crowns (Fig. 93). A useful instrument for measuring vertical dimension is the Willis gauge which is calibrated in millimeters with a sliding arm (Fig. 94). We modify this by grinding the stationary right-angle arm (the upper) so that it is shorter and will fit better under the nose (Fig. 95) when the moving arm is placed under the mandible. This permits the use of two hard, relatively immovable parts for measurements in millimeters. Using adhesive tape or ink on the point of the chin, the upper lip, or the nose is untrustworthy because the patient can move these tissues easily by any of many muscles involved in facial expressions, speaking, and most dangerously in mandibular closure.

Case S. R. This case is of such importance that it warrants special discussion. The patient, a woman in her middle forties (Fig. 96), presented with a history of two attempts at "bite opening" both of which ended in severe headaches and pain in the temporalis area: (1) a removable partial denture was changed and finally discarded; (2) four posterior fixed partial dentures were ground down when the pain started and resulted in the condition seen in Fig. 96. The lower incisors practically occluded with the gingival tissues lingual to the upper incisors (Fig. 97), and the upper incisors did the same with the gingival tissues labial to the lower incisors (Fig. 98). There was no contact

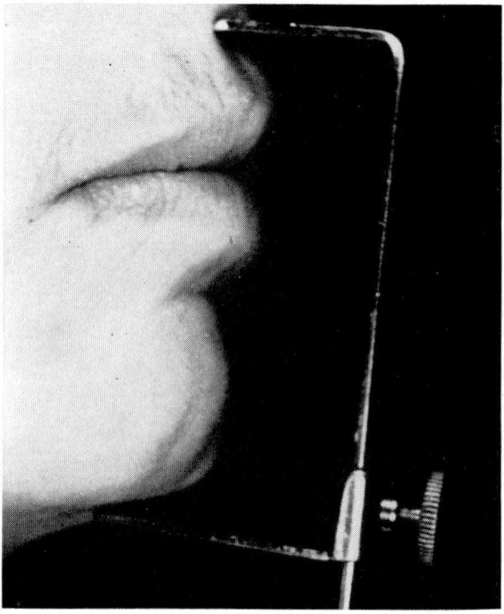

Fig. 95. Willis gauge in position showing reason for shortening upper arm and screw to permit fixing lower arm after adjustment.

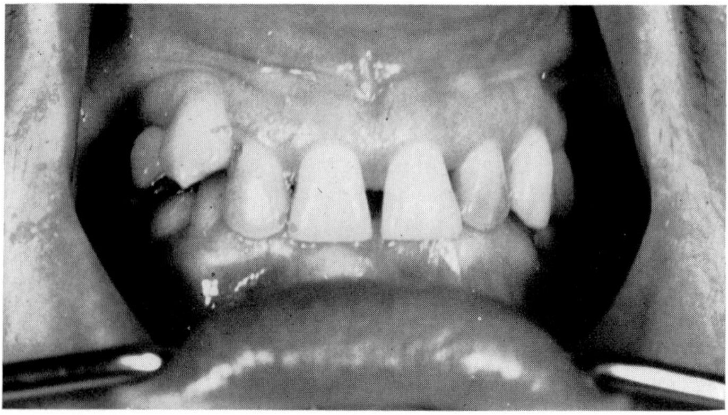

Fig. 96. Case S. R. in centric occlusion. This is an unusually extreme example of reduced vertical dimension. Strangely, the patient was in centric relation at this reduced vertical dimension, and when the correct vertical dimension was restored, the horizontal relationship of the mandible to the maxillae (centric relation) was almost completely unchanged.

between the incisors themselves in centric occlusion. Severe damage had been done to the tissues, and there was severe bone loss.

It is most important for the practitioner to learn to listen to the patient—this patient told the listening practitioner what her problem was. She said that when she was at rest, reading, or doing housework, her jaws felt as if they were far apart and it was only when she brought them together completely that she felt any strain. Various tests verified the accuracy of her description for her physiological rest position can be seen in Fig. 99. All the tests are based on functional methods, never on arbitrary measurements, because we are dealing with human beings and not with machines that can be depended on to be the same in every case. Among these tests, perhaps the most informative is having the patient swallow with a ball of equalizing wax on the height of the buccal cusps of the lower bicuspids. In swallowing, the mandible rises to centric occlusion and then drops to the physiological rest position thus giving vertical dimension at the two relations most needed for dental treatments. Another test is to have the patient make a continuous humming sound, which will be done at the physiological rest position.

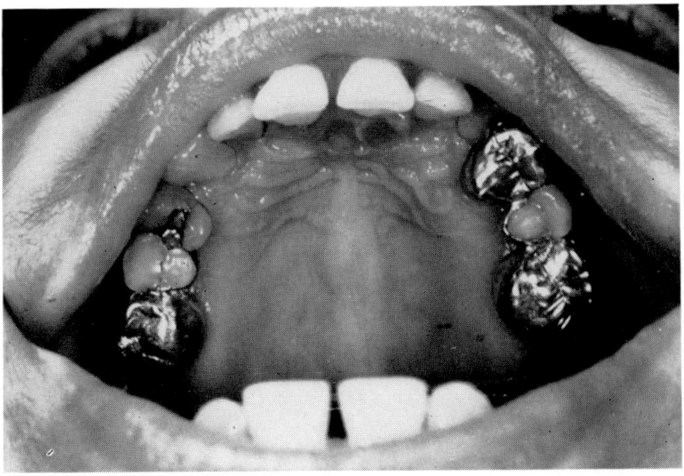

Fig. 97. Damage to lingual gingival and palatal tissues of Fig. 96 caused by impaction of lower incisors. Note how deeply the lower incisors have pressed into what is both gingival and palatal tissues at the lingual surfaces of the upper left central and have produced a lingual periodontal pocket which reached gingivally almost to the apex of the tooth.

This test has the great advantage of making it possible for the operator to look into the patient's mouth at what must be physiological rest position. The photograph in Fig. 99 was taken while the patient was making this sound. Measuring physiological rest position alone is not sufficient because normal interocclusal distance is extremely variable and dependent only on the individual patient's musculature. Any technique by which centric vertical dimension is calculated by finding physiological rest position and then using an arbitrary figure for interocclusal distance is totally erroneous and based on purely mechanical concepts that, although fine in tool and die making, have no place in the treatment of human beings with their normal and healthy variations and differences.

The patient was incapable of any lateral and protrusive movements except by opening her mouth and then closing in the desired position (Fig. 96). Furthermore, she had emotional and endocrine disturbances that made it necessary to keep dental treatments to the minimum consonant with a satisfactory functional result. The anterior teeth were to be unaltered except for necessary equilibration.

After the correct centric vertical dimension was established, a bite

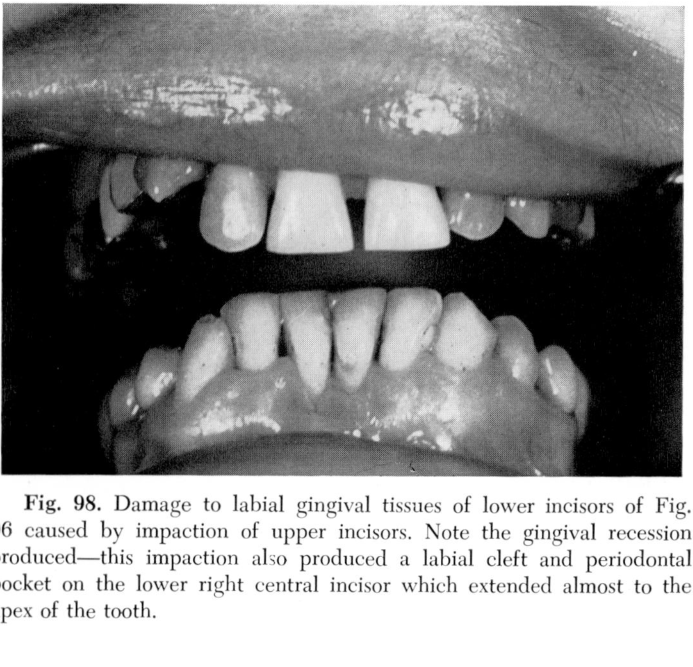

Fig. 98. Damage to labial gingival tissues of lower incisors of Fig. 96 caused by impaction of upper incisors. Note the gingival recession produced—this impaction also produced a labial cleft and periodontal pocket on the lower right central incisor which extended almost to the apex of the tooth.

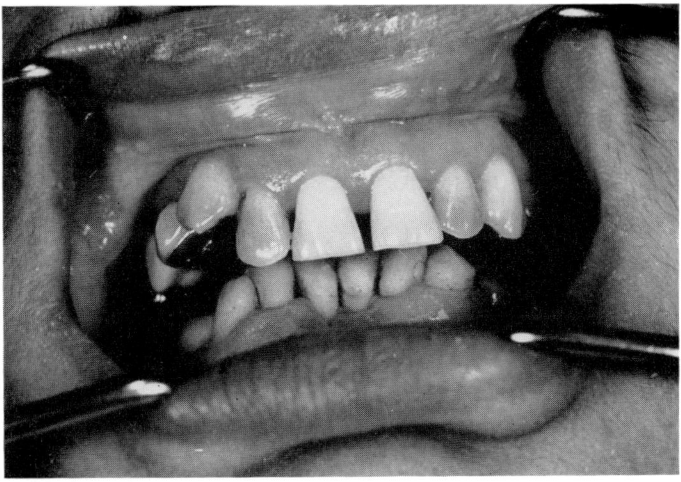

Fig. 99. This is the physiological rest position of the patient in Figs. 96 to 98. Photograph was taken while patient made humming sound, and position was confirmed by other tests as described in the text. Note gingival inflammation on the labial gingiva of the two lower central incisors produced by the impaction of the upper central incisors (see Fig. 96).

plate was made in transparent acrylic resin in the general design of a lingual bar removable partial denture (Fig. 100), covering the occlusal surfaces of all the lower posterior teeth. Note that this appliance has a flat occlusal plane with simple sluiceways to reduce pressure during mastication, is narrow buccolingually, and the total mesiodistal length was kept to a minimum; all this was aimed at reducing the occlusal table and thus minimizing the strain. When such extreme changes are necessary, and particularly when the patient has a history of damaging incorrect interference with the vertical dimension, a removable appliance of this sort to establish the centric vertical dimension is the wisest choice because removal may be necessary and must be possible. Furthermore, the extent of the operative procedures necessary introduces another element that may produce a reaction, particularly with the other problems of this patient. The extent of change can be seen in Figs. 101 and 102.

Because the change was so radical and the history so bad, four weeks were allowed before assuming that the new dimension was correct. When the change is not radical and there is no history of previous muscular difficulties, two weeks are sufficient. In this case the initial

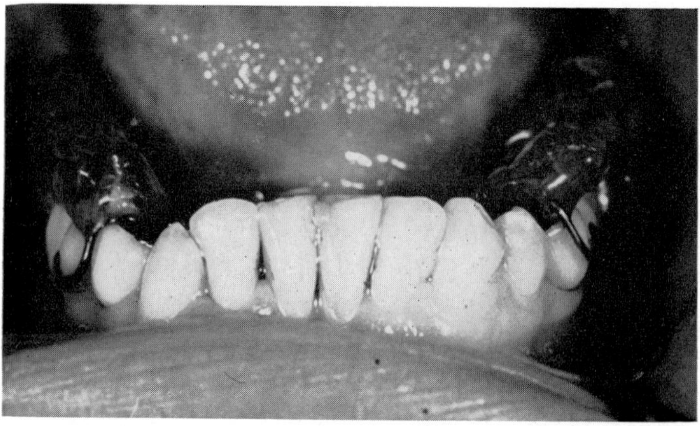

Fig. 100. Temporary transparent acrylic resin bite plate in position on lower posterior teeth; note flatness of the plane and the reduced occlusal table (see text for complete description). This restored the vertical dimension in accordance with the various tests used for reasons described in text.

centric vertical dimension was accurately determined, and the patient was comfortable for the first time in many years. In fact, shortly after the appliance was inserted the patient found herself acutely uncomfortable if she removed it for more than the time necessary for cleaning. The appliance was then split in half, the teeth on one half of the mouth were prepared, and temporary jacket crowns of acrylic resin were made to conform to the vertical dimension of the appliance remaining in the other half of the mouth. When this was completed, the teeth on the other half of the mouth were prepared and temporary acrylic resin crowns were made to conform to the established vertical dimension.

As so often happens when there is a history of muscle abuse from incorrect centric vertical dimensions being forced on the mandibular musculature, the correct centric vertical dimension was extremely critical. Even removal of the temporary crowns and recementation was enough to cause a severe reaction until the resin crowns in just one quadrant were accurately readjusted after the recementation. This produced further problems at completion. The appliance was carried through in the same manner as Case J. N. using acrylic resin veneer crowns. The final restorations were temporarily cemented with special zinc oxide and eugenol temporary cement merely rimming the crowns so that if any teeth had shifted in the short time between the impres-

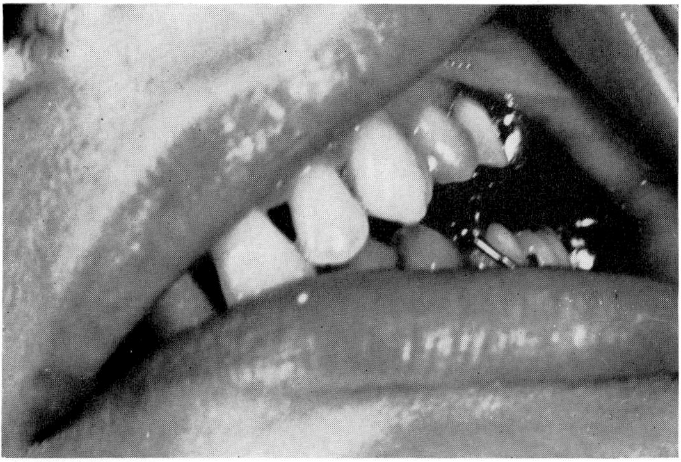

Fig. 101. Left side of patient in Fig. 100—centric occlusion with bite plate in position. Note vast change necessary to restore the physiological vertical dimension and compare with Fig. 96.

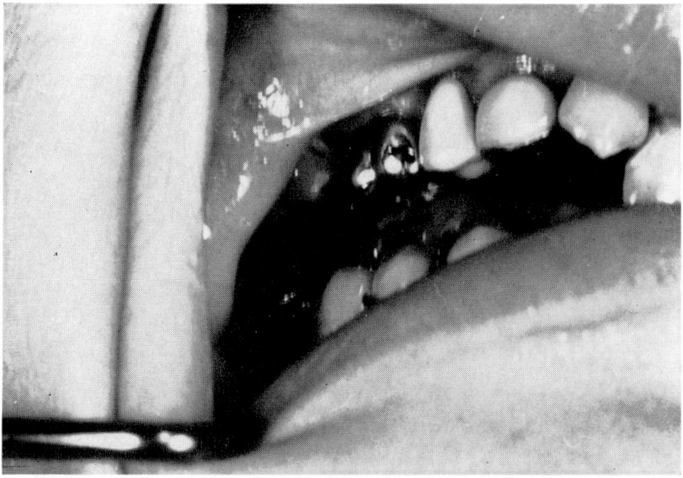

Fig. 102. Right side of patient in Fig. 100—centric occlusion with bite plate in position. Note vast change necessary to restore the physiological vertical dimension and compare with Fig. 96.

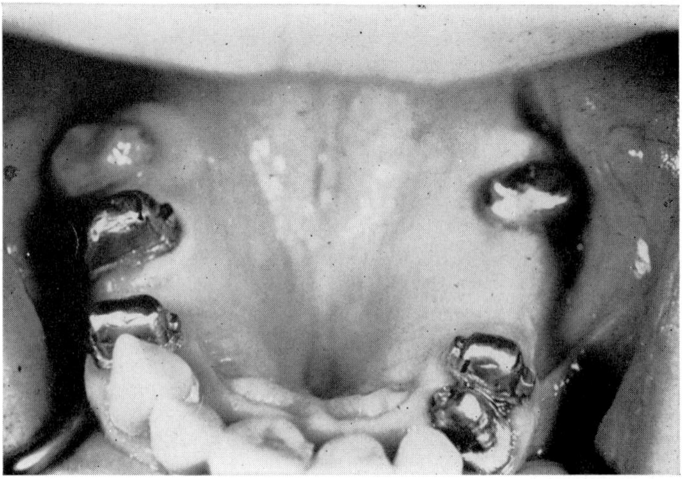

Fig. 103. Nonprecious metal transfer copings on abutment teeth. Note holes at occlusal end to check seating. The buttons on the lingual surface are for ease in removing the castings from the teeth.

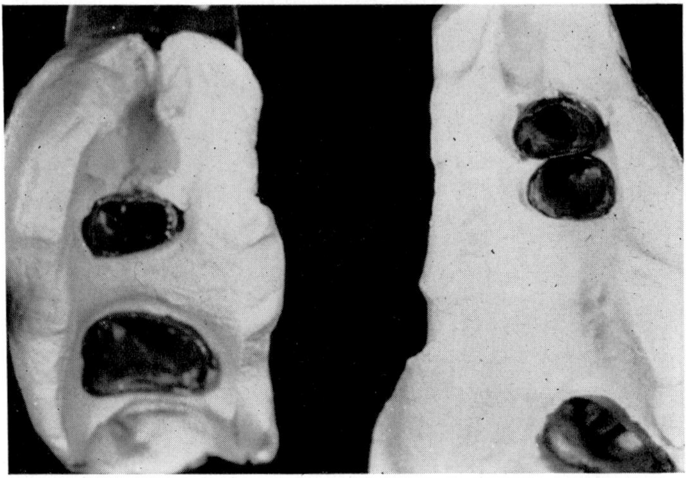

Fig. 104. Sectional plaster impressions of nonprecious metal transfer copings.

sion of the gold copings and completion of the appliance, the appliance could settle to position. One quadrant was cemented at a time, then the opposing quadrant was cemented so that the temporary crowns on the opposite side could still be used as a check for the centric vertical dimension. For such patients, a number of visits are necessary to complete the adjustments of the occlusion until it is exactly right. When the patient was completely comfortable, the anterior teeth were equilibrated, to the extent possible, to permit lateral and protrusive movements without cutting too much tooth strucure.

Case T. S. The patient, a heavy masculine man in his late forties whose profession required constant contact with the public (a dentist in fact), was for obvious reasons concerned about his appearance to the extent that porcelain fused to iridio-platinum crowns were the restorations of choice. Fixed partial dentures were required for all four posterior quadrants, and the anterior teeth required porcelain jacket crowns.

These teeth were prepared with ultra high speed instruments and individual copper band impressions with modeling composition were made, followed by temporary acrylic resin jacket crowns. On the resultant dies, nonprecious metal transfer copings were fabricated for the

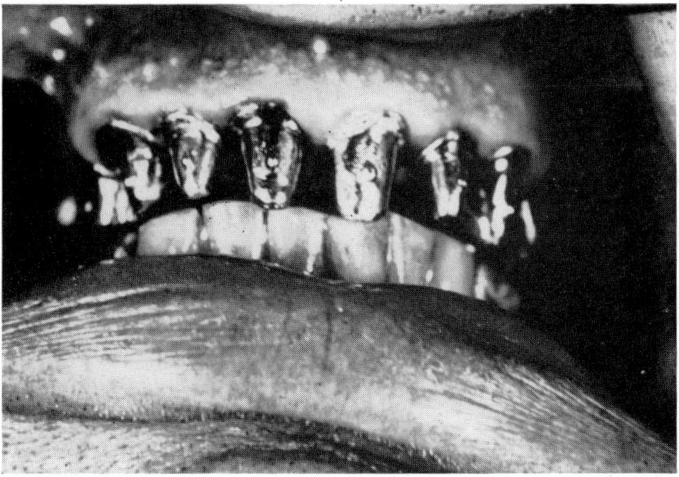

Fig. 105. Iridio-platinum castings in position; the labial buttons are merely there for ease in removing the castings from the teeth and will be cut off before adding the porcelain.

fixed partial denture abutment teeth, placed in position in the mouth, and small sectional plaster impressions were made (Figs. 103 and 104); the small openings left at the occlusal end to check the seating of the copings can be seen in these photographs. On the resultant casts iridio-platinum castings for the abutments were fabricated. In the meantime, the remaining upper anterior teeth to be covered were prepared and impressions were made in individual copper bands; the resultant dies were used to prepare the final iridio-platinum castings.

All the iridio-platinum castings were seated to place in the patient's mouth (Fig. 105), and the maxillomandibular relations were recorded after a face-bow registration had been taken. Self-curing acrylic resin is the material of choice (Fig. 106) and wax is never used. Note that one of the patient's own lower cuspids is covered to prevent possible difficulty in accurate seating of the two casts for articulation. Two plaster impressions were made at this stage: (1) the upper jaw (Fig. 107) using a lower impression tray to prevent the plaster from getting onto the soft palate and gagging the patient since no impression of

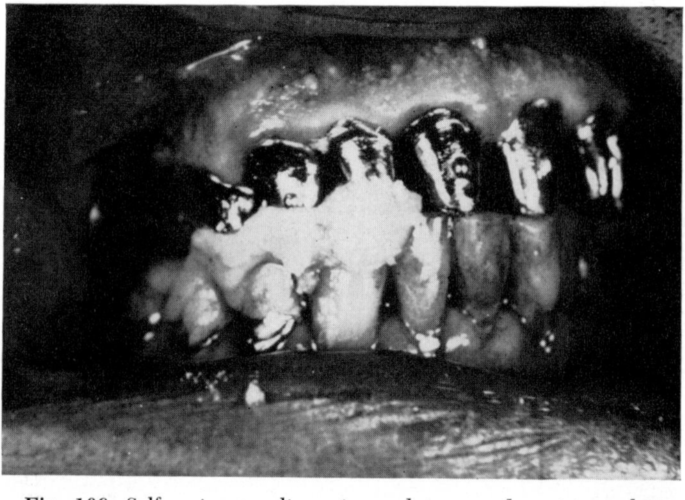

Fig. 106. Self-curing acrylic resin used to record centric occlusion; thinned out on the lower castings to show more clearly the extent of coverage. It is extended onto the patient's own cuspid because the lack of posterior teeth requires this extension to make the seating of the casts for articulation more certain on this side. Obviously, the resin must not be allowed to lock both jaws.

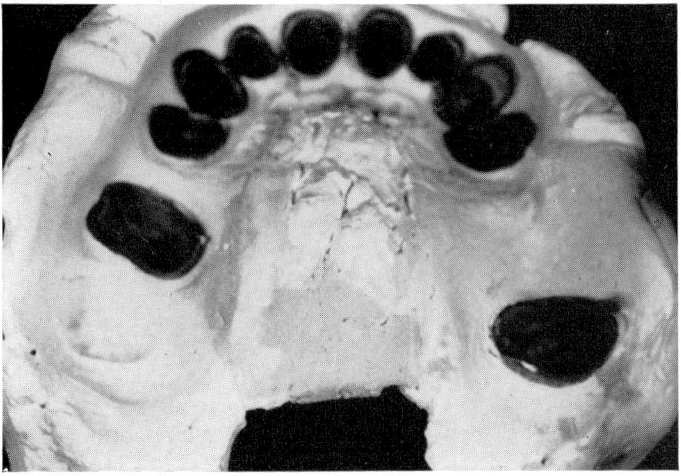

Fig. 107. Plaster impression of maxilla; use of lower impression tray limits the plaster on the palate. Note use of shoulder preparations.

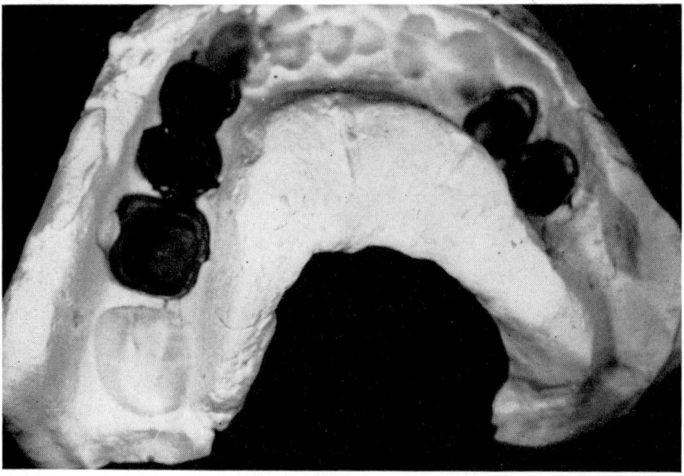

Fig. 108. Plaster impression of mandible. Note acrylic resin covering cusp of right cuspid (see Figs. 106 and 107). Again note use of shoulder preparations.

any part of either the soft or hard palate is needed for fixed partial dentures; (2) the lower jaw, with the self-curing acrylic resin in position (Fig. 108) including that on the incisal edge of the cuspid.

A simple face-bow was used to obtain the relationship of the teeth to the temporomandibular joint so that the casts could be mounted on the articulator (Figs. 109 and 110) with the same relationship. However, in the final analysis the articulator is only a machine that makes it possible for us to fabricate an appliance approximating that which should hold true for the mouth—the patient is always the final arbiter of what is correct for him, and everything must be adjusted to the patient's mouth not the mouth to the articulator.

The technician fabricates the metal framework and adds the porcelain; this should be returned to the dentist in the biscuit bake stage. One advantage of porcelain over acrylic resin veneer lies in the simplicity of adjustment when the occlusal height is low; wax is added to the correct height (Fig. 110) and the technician merely bakes on the needed amount of porcelain. This material offers the dentist an unparalleled opportunity to exercise his creative talents. The appliance should be tried in at the biscuit bake stage (Fig. 111); first the occlusion is checked carefully and adjusted to its final condition and porcelain is added where necessary. The operator should now proceed to contour and shape every individual crown to conform with the sex, age, and

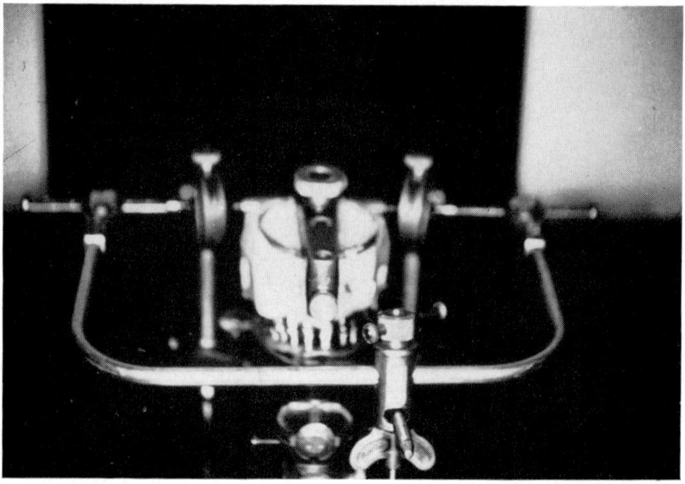

Fig. 109. Face-bow (note simple type) used to articulate casts.

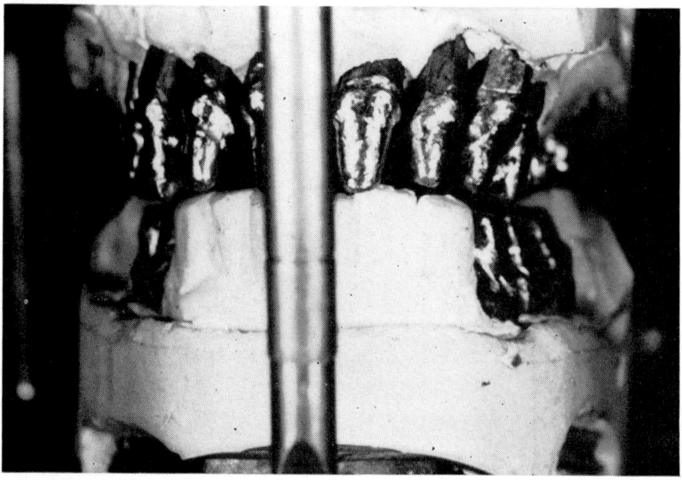

Fig. 110. Close-up of casts on articulator.

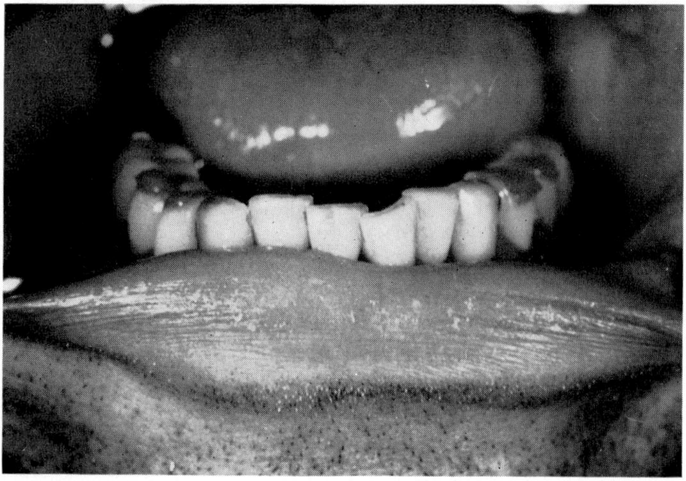

Fig. 111. Note wax added to cusps on lower bicuspids; these cusps were slightly shy. In porcelain it is a simple matter to do this, and the technician can add as much as necessary. This is simple with porcelain but introduces a major problem in acrylic resin veneer crowns.

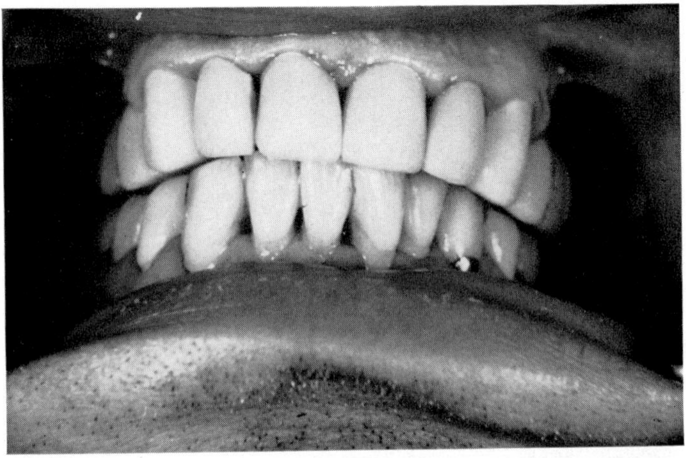

Fig. 112. Restorations tried in mouth in biscuit bake stage. This is the stage at which the operator can utilize his creative talents and can produce the excellent result possible only with porcelain restorations. Note how, even at this early stage, there is no gingival irritation despite the many teeth involved.

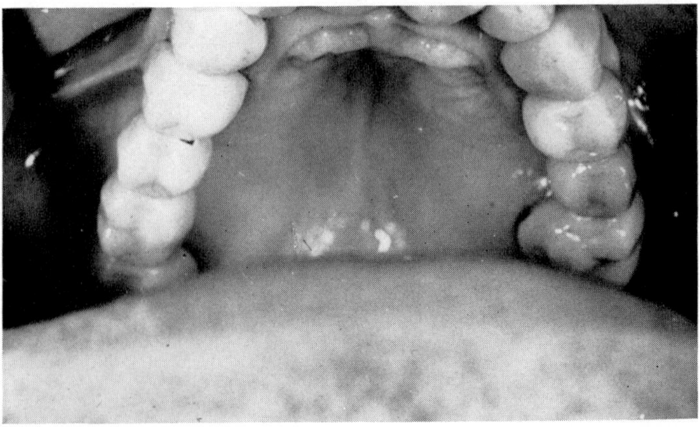

Fig. 113. Final upper posterior restorations showing staining and carving. Note how porcelain on the lingual surface is ended well short of the gingival margin to keep the bulk in the gingival sulcus to a minimum.

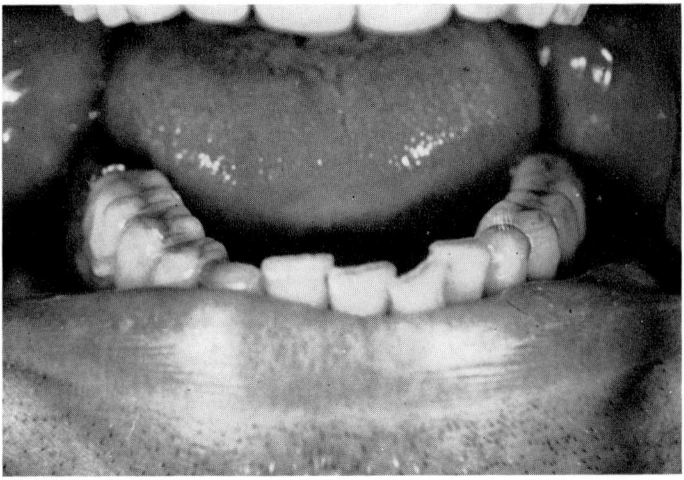

Fig. 114. Final lower posterior restorations showing staining and carving. Note buccal as well as occlusal surfaces.

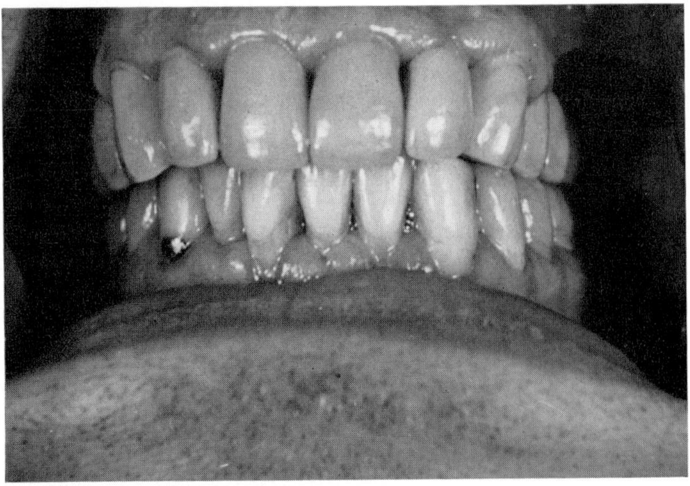

Fig. 115. Final restoration in porcelain fused to iridio-platinum crowns. Note staining and carving and compare tooth by tooth with Fig. 112.

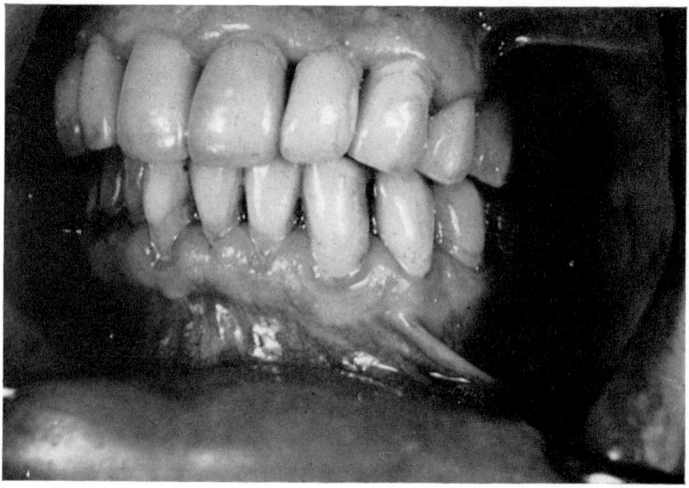

Fig. 116. Same as Fig. 115 but at different angle to show further detail in comparison with Fig. 112. This photograph was taken long after completion of the work. Note condition of the gingiva.

personality of the patient; this will require changes of the labial or buccal surface from gingival to incisal or occlusal surface, from mesial to distal surface, of the incisal edge and the occlusal surface and cusps, and the addition or change of the labial and buccal grooves and location of the root surface and cementoenamel junction. Finally, the staining must be prescribed for each individual tooth as to color, location, and intensity. This task requires time, often as much as three or four hours, but it is time well spent and the results can be seen by comparing Figs. 112 to 116 with Fig. 111.

The comfortable and secure feeling that good esthetics gives the patient is vitally important to the total temporomandibular articulation. Remember how often patients relate how they manipulate their musculature to hide unsightly teeth, and all too often grinding and clenching are due to bad esthetics. From the larger point of view, we must also recognize the effect that dental esthetics has upon the entire personality structure of the patient.

CHAPTER 14

ROENTGENOGRAPHY OF THE TEMPOROMANDIBULAR JOINT

Anatomical considerations have made the temporomandibular joint a particularly difficult area to visualize roentgenographically; as a result, many techniques have been developed to cope with this problem:

1. *Cranial-oblique view*—most commonly used and simplest
2. *Posteroanterior view*—relatively simple and second most common
3. *Arthrography*—involves injecting a contrast medium into the synovial cavities thus revealing them, otherwise of little value
4. *Tomography*—gives most comprehensive picture of the joint in its entire width
5. *Cinefluorography with image intensification*—newest technique; gives roentgen motion pictures of joint, with sound accompaniment if desired

The weakness of the roentgenographic techniques, except tomography, lies in the fact that they show the joint in profile only, so that only one plane is seen. Thus marked changes may not be seen roentgenographically. Tomography involves the synchronous movement in opposite directions of the x-ray tube and the film cassette while the exposure is being made with a mechanical focusing device (complicated equip-

A

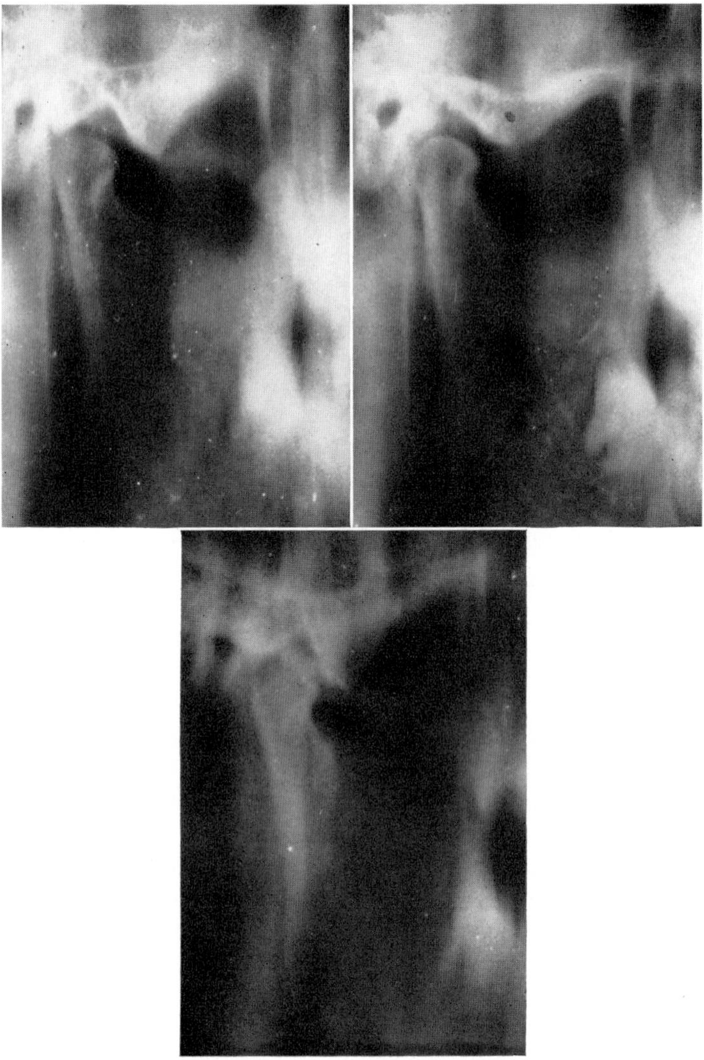

B

C

Fig. 117. A-C, For legend see opposite page.

ment not practical in the dental office). However, this technique makes it possible to obtain a roentgenographic visualization of a prescribed plane with a width of cut approximately 0.5 to 0.75 centimeter. By taking a series of exposures at successive mediolateral planes, it is possible to visualize the complete joint. Fig. 117 shows how completely tomograms can reveal any changes throughout the joint.

AN IMPROVED CRANIAL-OBLIQUE TECHNIQUE

This technique has the distinct advantage of usability in the dental office and makes it possible to obtain roentgenograms that can be duplicated for purposes of comparison. It also shows the joint in the functional relationship that most commonly obtains, namely when the patient is in an upright position with the Frankfort plane parallel to the floor. Three exposures are made of each joint: (1) with the teeth in centric occlusion, (2) with the mandible in its physiological rest position, and (3) with the mouth opened as wide as the patient comfortably can do. A block should not be used because biting on it will cause the patient to protrude the mandible.

The standard dental x-ray machine is fitted with a Fitzgerald long cone (Fig. 118); it is essential that a lead diaphragm be used to limit the rays to a three-inch radius at the mouth of the cone. If this is not done, the rays will fan out from the head of the machine and the patient will be exposed to far more radiation over a wider field than with the standard short cone, thus making the long cone a menace

Text continued on p. 224.

Fig. 117. A-C, Tomograms of mandible and temporomandibular articulation taken at various depths; approximate plane of film can be judged by degree of sharpness of focus of the teeth. **B** is a tomogram taken in the approximate plane of the third molar. The teeth are in centric occlusion for the three exposures, yet apparent relationship of the head of the mandible to the articular fossa is different in all three.

Fig. 118

Fig. 119

Fig. 118. Fitzgerald long cone attached to a standard dental x-ray machine; lead diaphragm at its attachment. (From Freese: J. Pros. Den. **8**:1044, 1958.)

Fig. 119. Interior of usual nose cone has been ground on the inside to fit accurately over the long cone. (From Freese: J. Pros. Den. **8**:1044, 1958.)

Fig. 120

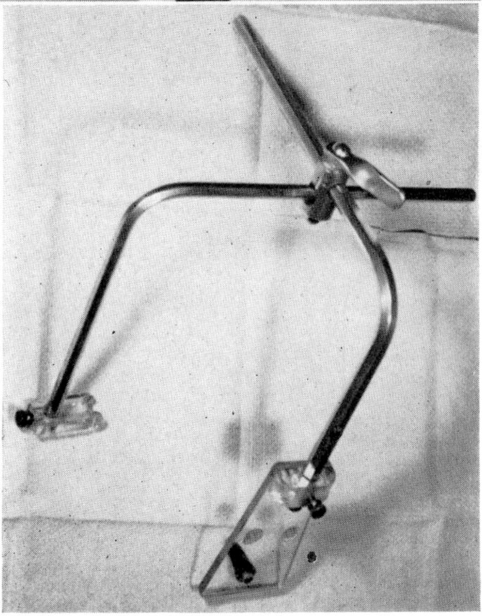

Fig. 121

Fig. 120. Device for positioning head. Note earpieces for head placement.

Fig. 121. Removable section for nosepiece and earpiece. (From Freese: J. Pros. Den. **8:**1047, 1958.)

Fig. 122

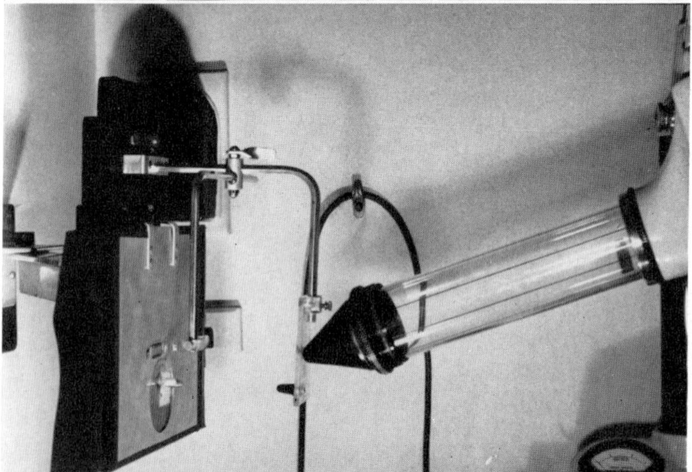

Fig. 123

Fig. 122. Device for positioning head; note three-inch circle in lead shield for cassette, letters (just above three-inch circle) to designate side of head on film, and depression for x-ray cone location. (From Freese: J. Pros. Den. **8**:1046, 1958.)

Fig. 123. X-ray machine in position with nose cone in depression on head positioner.

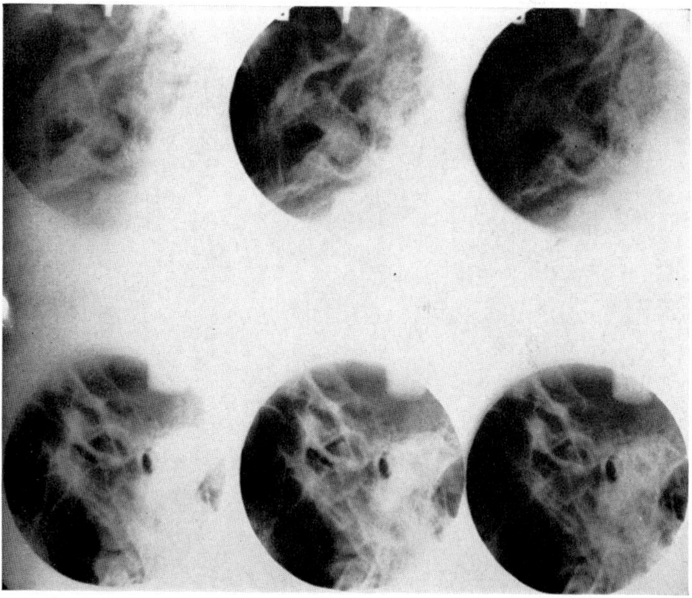

Fig. 124. Roentgenograms of temporomandibular joint made with technique described on pages 217 to 225; note that three-inch circle is not completely filled, but diagnostic quality has not been impaired.

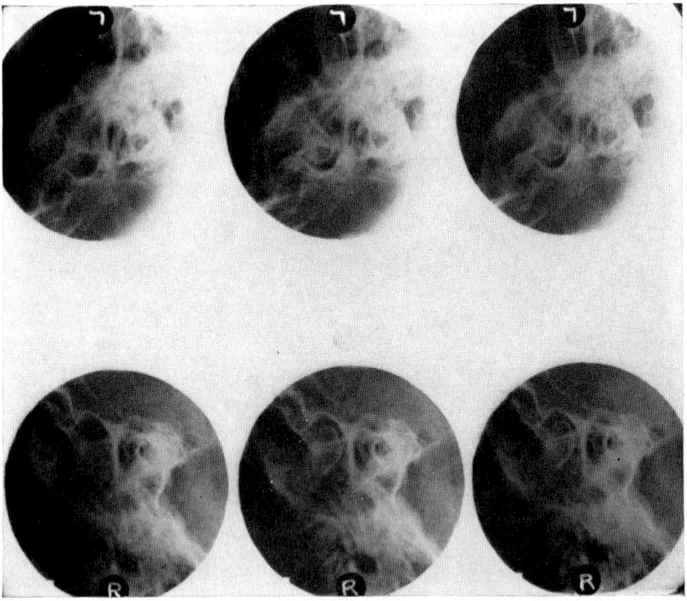

Fig. 125. Roentgenograms of temporomandibular joint using same technique; note difficulty of calibration of setup to both fill the three-inch circle and show the letters.

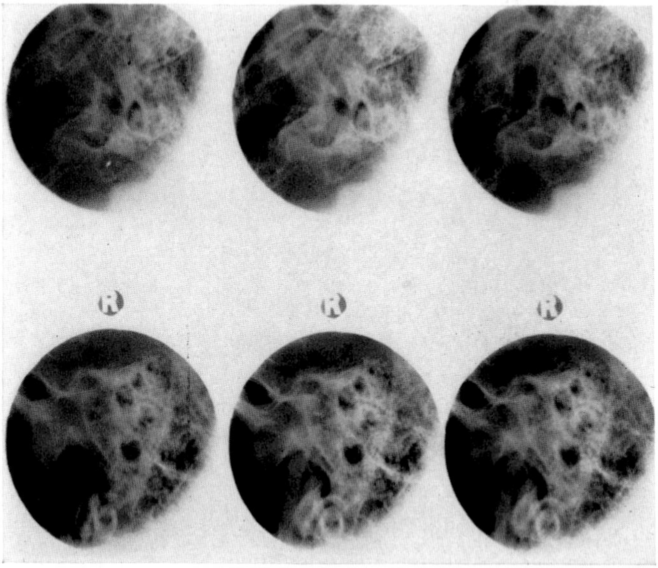

Fig. 126. Roentgenograms of temporomandibular joint showing diagnostic quality.

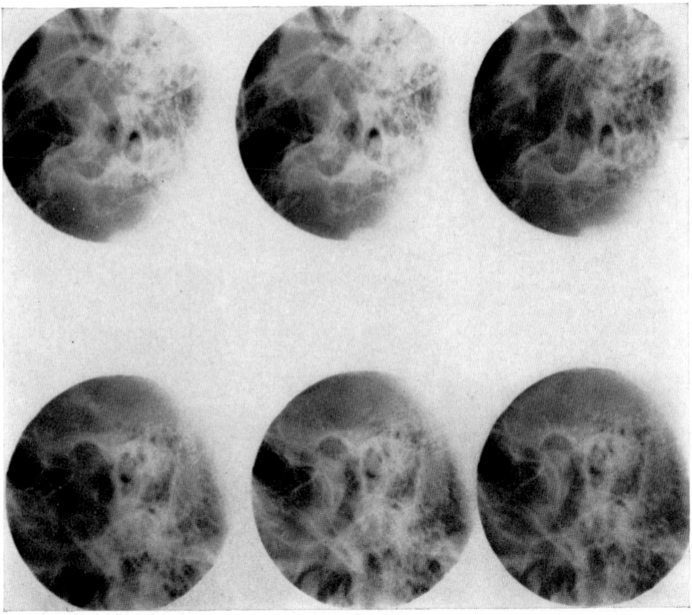

Fig. 127. Roentgenograms of temporomandibular joint showing diagnostic quality.

Text continued from p. 217.

instead of a protection. Besides reducing the amount of radiation to one fifth of what it would be with the short cone, the increased target-film distance yields roentgenograms of superior diagnostic quality. By fitting a short cone to the end of the long cone (Fig. 119), the target-film distance is increased to 22 inches plus the thickness of the subject and makes aiming the central ray and locating the machine against the necessary positioning device (Figs. 120 to 123) more accurate. Even with these precautions the three-inch circle is not always filled; nevertheless, the roentgenogram is of diagnostic quality (Fig. 124).

Six exposures are made on an 8 × 10 inch x-ray film in a cassette with a Patterson Par Speed filter using the positions of the mandible described above (Figs. 125 to 127). It is thus possible to glance along the film and see immediately the locations of the condyle in the glenoid fossa in the various jaw positions as well as the amount of movement possible.

CHAPTER 15

ELECTROMYOGRAPHY OF THE MUSCLES OF MASTICATION

Electrical activity of nerve and muscle has been known for a long time. With the development of a sensitive galvanometer by Einthoven, the electrocardiogram became a clinical instrument. In 1929 Hans Berger invented the electroencephalograph which, although it was developed for the study of brain waves, has become the basic instrument for the study of the changes in electric potential of the muscles of mastication as well as muscles in other areas.[14]

Both of these instruments measure changes in voltage that result from cellular activity. In the case of the muscles of mastication, the activity measured is the direct result of contraction of the individual muscle cells. This in turn is based upon the fact that the interior of cells has a high potassium content and a low sodium content.[1, 14] In extracellular fluid this situation is reversed, that is, the sodium content is high whereas the potassium content is low. As a result of this arrangement there is a potential difference (electrical) of approximately 80 millivolts across the membrane of a resting cell. The inside of the cell is negative with respect to the fluid in which it is bathed. An unknown energy system acts like a pump to maintain this difference. When a cell, in this case cells of the muscles of mastication, goes into an active state (contracts), ions flow across the cell membrane so that the inside of the cell becomes 30 millivolts positive with respect to the outside. This depolarization, in some unknown way, brings about the contraction of the muscle. Since the body acts like a volume conductor, that is, as if it were a large container of salt solution, these electrical events can be recorded as changes of potential on the surface of the body. The electrocardiograph records the electrical events that take place during the various stages of cardiac function. The electroencephalograph records the impulses, depolarization, and recharging of the nerves of the brain, and the electromyograph records the energy changes occurring in the musculature during function and presumably disturbances of function.

When considering electrocardiography one must be aware that material has been collected from patients with normal and abnormal hearts for more than half a century with the result that there is an excellent empirical correlation between the ECG patterns and the diagnosis of disease of the heart. As a matter of fact, it is only recently that research has illuminated the actual physical and electrical events that occur to produce these patterns. Electroencephalography has developed similarly from the stage when merely the fact of brain waves was noted to the stage of correlation of patterns observed to appear with clinical manifestations of specific disorders or diseases.

Electromyography however is in its earliest phase of investigation. The fact that an electrical record can be made by placing electrodes over the muscles of mastication is undisputed. The relation of these records and their variations to actual disease must be demonstrated. To date the essential observation has been that in the presence of occlusal abnormalities or states of muscle stress or tension, muscle hyperactivity occurs and can be seen on the electromyogram as recordings of greater energy discharge.

In 1959 Kydd[5] demonstrated that in patients under emotional stress the electromyographic records of the muscles of mastication reverted to normal when the subject's skeletal musculature was relaxed and at ease in the test environment. Apparently the electromyograph does not record phenomena that are pathognomonic of disease but rather that are a reflection of a complex of factors that have their ultimate effect upon muscle contraction. This view is consistent with the belief of many investigators in this field that, although occlusal disharmony as manifested by single or multiple premature contacts of teeth or by gross malrelation of the jaws will produce increased and disorderly action potentials on an electromyographic record, these may not be the only causes for the patterns that appear.

It may be said that electromyography has not to date indicated a diagnosis of jaw dysfunction that could not have been made by existing methods of clinical examination and analysis. This is not to say that its use as a research tool and its future reliable correlation with disease is decried. The future will establish its value as an instrument of diagnosis and prognosis.

INTERESTING ELECTROMYOGRAPHIC STUDIES

One of the earliest uses of electromyography was a study by Moyers in 1949 of temporomandibular muscle contraction patterns in Angle's class II, division I malocclusion. His further work in 1950 and 1956 on electromyographic patterns that occurred during mandibular movement and other orofacial muscle activity established the essential fact that there is evidence of the effect of gross abnormality on action potential but also established that no consistent pattern comparable to the electrocardiogram has been found.

Pruzansky in 1952 and Jarabak in 1954 developed the use of electromyography in research, and in 1956 Jarabak did an electromyographic study of the muscular and temporomandibular joint disturbances due to imbalances in occlusion. Other investigators, Shpuntoff, Perry, Hickey, Latif and more recently Ogle, have used electromyography in attempts to show the correlation between the abnormal record due in most part to occlusal interference and the postoperative record resulting from removal of these interferences. There is no question that the records obtained after the correction of occlusal interference show decreased muscle activity as evidenced by lower action potentials. However, a method of diagnosis that requires a piece of equipment that occupies most of the space in an average dental operatory and consumes so much time is certainly not intended for use by the family dentist. The value of the method lies in the future. One may hope that in the future such devices will be made available to patients at a hospital center to be used as an auxiliary tool in research and for the study of the effectiveness of attempts to restore the neuromuscular apparatus of the jaws to normal function.

REFERENCES

1. Best, C. H., and Taylor, N. B.: The physiological basis of medical practice, ed. 5, Baltimore, 1950, The Williams & Wilkins Co.
2. Hickey, J. C., et al.: Electromyography in dental research, J. Pros. Den. **8:** 351, 1958.
3. Jarabak, J. R.: The adaptability of the temporal and masseter muscles; an electromyographic study, Angle Orthodont. **24:** 193, 1954.
4. Jarabak, J. R.: Electromyographic analysis of muscular and temporomandibular joint disturbances due to imbalances in occlusion, Angle Orthodont. **24:** 170, 1956.
5. Kydd, W. L.: Psychosomatic aspects of temporomandibular joint dysfunction, J. A. D. A. **59:** 31, 1959.
6. Latif, A.: An electromyographic study of the temporalis muscle in normal persons during selected positions and movements of the mandible, Am. J. Orthodont. **43:** 577, 1957.
7. Moyers, R. E.: Temporomandibular muscle contraction patterns in Angle class II, division I malocclusions; an electromyographic analysis, Am. J. Orthodont. **35:** 837, 1949.
8. Moyers, R. E.: An electromyographic analysis of certain muscles involved in temporomandibular movement, Am. J. Orthodont. **36:** 481, 1950.
9. Moyers, R. E.: Some recent electromyographic findings in the orofacial muscles, European Orthodont. Soc. Tr. **32:** 225, 1956.

10. Ogle, M. W.: Odontogenic synalgia and electroencephalograph-recorded muscle action potentials, J. A. D. A. **62**: 687, 1961.
11. Perry, H. T.: Functional electromyography of the temporal and masseter muscles in class II, division I malocclusion and excellent occlusion, Angle Orthodont. **25**: 49, 1955.
12. Pruzansky, S.: The application of electromyography to dental research, J. A. D. A. **44**: 49, 1952.
13. Ramfjord, S. P.: Bruxism, a clinical and electromyographic study, J. A. D. A. **62**: 21, 1961.
14. Scher, A. M.: The electrocardiogram, Scient. Am. **205**: 132, 1961.
15. Shpuntoff, H., and Shpuntoff, W. A.: A study of physiologic rest position and centric position by electromyography, J. Pros. Den. **6**: 621, 1956.

INDEX